THE
PHILOSOPHICAL
FISHERMAN

Books by Harold F. Blaisdell

TRICKS THAT TAKE FISH

THE PHILOSOPHICAL FISHERMAN

THE ART OF FISHING WITH WORMS

THE PHILOSOPHICAL FISHERMAN

Reflections on Why We Fish

HAROLD F. BLAISDELL

FOREWORD BY

JERRY GIBBS

Skyhorse Publishing

Skyhorse Publishing books may be purchased in bulk at special discounts
for sales promotion, corporate gifts, fund-raising, or educational purposes.
Special editions can also be created to specifications. For details, contact
the Special Sales Department, Skyhorse Publishing, 307 West 36th Street,
11th Floor, New York, NY 10018 or info@skyhorsepublishing.com.

Skyhorse® and Skyhorse Publishing® are registered trademarks of Skyhorse
Publishing, Inc.®, a Delaware corporation.

Visit our website at www.skyhorsepublishing.com.

10 9 8 7 6 5 4 3 2 1

Library of Congress Cataloging-in-Publication Data

Blaisdell, Harold F.
    The philosophical fisherman: reflections on why we fish / Harold F.
        Blaisdell; foreword by Jerry Gibbs. – First Skyhorse Publishing
        edition. pages cm
    Originally published: Boston: Houghton Mifflin, 1969.
    ISBN 978-1-63220-279-6 (pbk.: alk. paper) – ISBN 978-1-63220-948-1
        (ebook) 1. Fishing. I. Title.
    SH441.B549 2015
    639.2–dc23
                                2015013816

Cover design by Jane Sheppard
Cover photo: Thinkstock

Printed in the United States of America

TO

all those sensible people
who think fishing
is ridiculous

Author's Note

*F*IFTEEN YEARS AGO I wrote a book entitled *Tricks That Take Fish*. As the name suggests, I hauled off and revealed how to become an expert fisherman. The book is still in print and available to those who won't be warned. As for me, I only wish that I knew as much about fishing now as I thought I knew then.

The only thing I'm certain about today is that what I *don't* know about fishing would fill a book — and it has. The chapters which follow may seem to reflect positive opinions, but they are voiced by one who does not always have the greatest faith in his convictions.

On only one score can I declare myself without reservation. I have been blest with three peerless fishing partners: my son Mike, my neighbor and perennial companion Pete Terwilliger and my close friend of many years H. G. Tapply.

Their names appear frequently in what follows. I introduce them here as those with whom I have shared a love of fishing in the most intimate way possible — by fishing many streams and lakes in their company over a long string of years. In each case this has resulted in bonds of understanding and affection much too profound for me to attempt to describe.

HAROLD F. BLAISDELL

Pittsford, Vermont

Contents

	Author's Note	vi
	Foreword	xiii
1	The Pin Is Bent	1
2	How Fishermen Fool Fish—And Vice Versa	19
3	Of Trout and Men	51
4	A Quizzical Look at Fly Fishing	77
5	The Dry Fly and the Third Dimension	109
6	Bait Fishing, A Source of Insight	133
7	Where the Grass Is Really Greener	153
8	Some Lethal Lures	183

9   Tools of the Trade   202

10 Landlocked Salmon   225

11 An Apology to Bass   254

12 Walleyes   275

13 Northern Pike   289

14 In Defense of Ice Fishing   311

15 Labrador-Ungava   329

16 The Philosophical Fisherman   356

The Philosophical

Fisherman

Foreword

Y OU CAN COUNT HAROLD Blaisdell in that brotherhood of well-loved writers of the '60s, '70s, and even early '80s—a group that includes H. G. Tapply, Frank Woolner, Corey Ford, and Ed Zern, to name a few. Typical of his contemporaries, Blaisdell was both an angler and hunter who kept setters and a bluetick hound, possessed an embarrassing number of expensive bamboo fly rods, hammered out crude fishing spoons (a few of which worked), ceaselessly experimented with techniques and tackle, was ready to camp out in the most miserable conditions if they showed promise of producing something interesting fish- or gamewise, and wrote about it all prolifically.

At the end of World War II, Blaisdell moved to Pittsford, Vermont, his home until his death in 1985. Lacking a silver spoon birthright, and with a post-war shortage of automobiles and fuel, he turned his focus to near-home venues, often with laser focus on a single body of water, parsing its characteristics to a near genomic level, and exporting his findings to a wider cast of brooks, rivers, and lakes. The result is a seemingly endless array of insights into fish and fishing that became the nexus for his extremely popular tactical books, *Tricks that Take Fish*; *The Art of Fishing With Worms*; and *Tricks that Take Trout*. These straightforward, practical texts are constructed around the premise that we'll learn more from the fish we fail to catch (most of them) than those we do, while gracefully informing us how to better the odds. The publication of *The Philosophical Fisherman* presents a surprise.

As early as 1969, when *The Philosophical Fisherman* first appeared, Blaisdell bemoans the direction of writing on outdoor subjects. The trend in popular fishing books, he says, is for "a catalog of how-to-do-it techniques, a compression of practicalities guaranteed to make an expert fisherman of a reader who can't tell a trout from a flounder." Given the titles of his practical works, one might see this as a case of the pot calling the kettle black. One would be wrong. In *The Philosophical Fisherman*, and even in his tactical books, Blaisdell's instructive advice is handled on the order of Master Po's relationship with the novice Grasshopper in the '70s TV series *Kung Fu*. Blaisdell tends to let readers find their own eureka moments, leading the way with wonderful, personal anecdotes rather than blatant preaching, which is the stuff he eschews.

Foreword

Assuring the reader that *The Philosophical Fisherman* is for those "who need nothing more than their instinctive love of fishing to be 'good' fishermen," and that he now knows less than he thought he did about the sport, one might assume Blaisdell has written a sort of romantic nostalgia bereft of what has become known as "how-to" fishing information. But no; in the midst of reflection, Blaisdell agilely slips in the kinds of why-didn't-I-think-of-that insights you can take to the bank—or in this case, brook, river, or lake—and bend to the process of turning the day into an unplanned-for success that goes well beyond numbers of caught fish, but that doesn't preclude that possibility. And he does it with humorous and wise appraisals of fishing, anglers, and humankind in general.

To compare the musings in *The Philosophical Fisherman* with those of Walton or perhaps Thoreau would not be quite accurate; in Blaisdell you'll find no hint of moralizing or pontification. Rather, he invariably punctuates introspection with a poke at himself or the foolishness of taking angling or oneself very seriously. After catching a fish from its difficult holding lie, he says: "I experienced the illusion of triumph which contained not only the impression that I had finally succeeded in outfoxing a shrewd and calculating adversary but that the trout had been made to know the humiliation of defeat. . . . This shows how silly it's possible to become." Or, "It's not my intention to belittle the traditional fallacies. . . . I lean on them heavily myself, and my pleasure is intensified by the realization that I am playing make-believe for the sheer fun of it."

He is fascinated by irrational, long-held beliefs— "I am perversely intrigued by manifestations of blind faith . . ." —and dogmatic reasoning: "The streamer fly is generally regarded as an imitation of a bait fish . . . it is fished with a twitching action. . . . The total result . . . is about as convincing as a rubber half-dollar, and the fish which hits a streamer in the belief that it is actually a small fish has most certainly taken leave of its marbles." He is never bashful with alternative explanation, however: "It is quite possible . . . to wire a hook to a beer can opener and catch a northern pike. . . . This . . . would seem to prove that northerns are mentally incompetent and totally unfit to look out for themselves . . . [but] fish strike non-imitative lures for the same reason a frog will jump for a red rag, a crow may gobble a lighted match . . . not as the result of normal impulses, but because of stimuli so strange that they provoke indiscretion."

Though Blaisdell can certainly wax lyrical—"the sound of bitterns . . . tones strangely hollow as if issuing from vocal chords strummed by the passage of bubbles . . ."—the next instant he'll be immersed in wicked enjoyment of colorful personalities such as a favorite guide whose "lined and angular face seemed to bespeak of a deep-seated cynicism toward everything and everybody, giving the impression that he was patiently waiting for the world to get the comeuppance he believed it richly deserved." Or he might explain questionable pleasure derived from enduring and then escaping brutal conditions, such as the freezing march he and perennial pal Pete made from an ice-fishing folly that conjures visions of

Shackleton's Trans-Antartica expedition. When it's over, he alludes to Melville's observation in *Moby Dick* that "warm bedcovers could be fully appreciated only if some small part of the body remained exposed to the cold."

Though he has reveled in the adventures and profusion of fish and fishing in far-flung reaches, what Blaisdell terms his "traditional point of view" centers on fishing nearby waters, where "the problems involved in taking fish that have been well educated . . . [where] the gross thrill of taking large numbers of big fish is not a paramount goal. Instead, the principal objective is to achieve modest success under circumstances sufficiently demanding to make this a reliable and gratifying reflection of angling skill. . . . Indifference to that which lies handy seems to be typical of fishermen . . . many of those who bemoan the lack of good fishing [close to home] do so without good reason and actually are victims of this strange form of blindness."

More than forty decades have passed since this, Harold Blaisdell's seminal work. His observations are as wise and as fresh today as they were then, not only in helping to lift that strange blindness of our often fallacious angling beliefs, they are also simply a heckuva lot of fun.

—Jerry Gibbs
Former Fishing Editor
Outdoor Life

The Pin Is Bent

MY FISHING CAREER nearly came to an abrupt end moments after it got started. At the age of five, and against stern parental orders to the contrary, I sneaked off and joined some older boys who were fishing in the river which ran through town. I promptly distinguished myself by falling off a high bank into deep water, where I escaped the fate I probably deserved only because one of the boys who could swim jumped in and hauled me out.

The local weekly saw fit to report the episode, and the account was read to me to make certain that I had "learned my lesson." I still remember some of the wording.

"Little Harold Blaisdell would now be singing with the angels," it declared, "had it not been for the bravery of . . ."

and it went on to describe the details of my rescue in dramatic fashion.

The paper was quite right in implying that I came mighty close to taking a trip into the beyond. But I have always thought, and many will agree, that it was unduly optimistic in predicting my destination.

As for "learning my lesson" I cannot recall that the incident dampened my burning desire to fish. I did resolve to watch my step around deep water in the future, but I had absolutely no intention of quitting. At one time or another over a period of nearly fifty years, I have fished for almost every kind of freshwater fish from minnows to Atlantic salmon. In recent years I have met younger anglers who started fishing perhaps two thirds of the way up that scale, and I have felt sorry for what they missed. In fishing, the way to gain full appreciation is to begin at the beginning.

These days, kids start with expensive spinning outfits, taking such equipment for granted as they do the sports cars which many drive to school. Change has been so rapid that it now seems almost incredible that I actually caught my first fish, a minnow, on a hook I shaped from a pin with pliers, but that's the way it was. A length of heavy-duty cotton thread served as a line, and a willow switch as a rod. With this simple outfit I spent many happy hours fishing for minnows in a tiny brook. Although I was unaware of any such circumstance, the fact that I had fashioned my own tackle from odds and ends added a satisfaction which nothing else could have supplied.

In modern fishing, all inherent difficulties — save the

wariness of the fish — have been eliminated to the limit of human ingenuity. Every effort is made to substitute gadgetry for skill and savvy. Spinning reels make casting simple, and there are even electronic devices which will locate fish. If it is true that gratification diminishes as tasks are made easier, then the sport of angling has not necessarily been served by all the modern "advances." I have become old and cranky enough to suspect that this may be the case.

To illustrate my cynicism, I don't subscribe to the popular theory that one automatically attains a status akin to sainthood by "taking a boy fishing." This is a kindness to the boy only if one has the good sense to take him fishing, but then leave him pretty much alone. Few, however, can resist the impulse to show the kid exactly how to go about it, thus cheating him of the joy of discovery.

Looking back on my youth, I feel fortunate to have fished in the absence of enlightenment other than that which I slowly stockpiled from experience. My triumphs would have been spoiled had they been achieved with outside help, and the charm of the mysteries I tried to solve would have been ruined had they been explained away. I think that I was lucky, for I began fishing when fishing had no goal but enjoyment, and when success or failure was conceded to rest in the hands of the gods. Failure evoked no guilty feelings of incompetence, and all credit for success was gratefully attributed to the kindness of fate.

Each spring the local hardware store received a shipment of cane poles, and my father would take me downtown on a Saturday night to pick out a new pair of fishing poles for the season. The poles were of varying lengths, some as long as twenty feet, and some were straighter than others. They cost a quarter.

After making careful inspection we would decide on a pair, a long one for my father and a considerably shorter and lighter one for me. Another quarter would go for a hank of green cotton line, and the same amount for new hooks and sinkers. Although the streets were crowded on Saturday nights, we'd carry the long poles home without attracting the stares which would be directed at such a rustic spectacle nowadays.

Then we'd rig the poles, a job which was fascinating to me because it bespoke so clearly the use to which we would soon put them. The too limber tips were trimmed, the lines were tied near the middle, wound in a spiral to the tip and secured with several half hitches. Finally, the lines were cut so that a length hung from each tip that was equal to the length of the pole.

The matter of securing the line near the middle of the pole was a safety measure to guard against loss should the pole splinter under the strain of a big fish. I once saw my father bust his pole on a whopping smallmouth, saving the fish with the help of the tied-back line. It thrilled me to envision the recurrence of this crisis, this time with *me* holding the pole.

My father worked in a local plywood factory and had Saturday afternoons off. During the summer these Saturday afternoons were devoted to fishing, and by Saturday noon I would have dug more worms than a dozen fishermen could have used.

I think a measure of my inborn passion for fishing was the extent to which I derived stimulation from anything even remotely connected with it. In the case of worm digging, I could feel anticipation mount with each forkful of earth turned over. It would be stretching things to say that I enjoyed the digging as much as I did the fishing, but it was a welcome substitute on a Saturday morning when it seemed that noon would never arrive.

The Connecticut River was several miles away, and we rode to the river behind a Morgan mare that was my father's pride and joy. I'd tie the cane poles in place under the seat while he hitched the Morgan to the buggy, and then we'd set out for the river with the tips of the long poles bobbing as the mare jogged along.

The river was a broad stream where we fished it, and during spring floods it often rose to awesome heights. Care was exercised to keep bridges and buildings beyond its reach, but sometimes the river rose beyond the anticipated limits and triumphantly carried these structures away. Even in summer, its brown water marched past as though in sullen warning, hinting of unpleasant secrets hidden in its dark depths. It was a river upon which a small boy gazed with soul-stirring emotions: wonder, expectation and no small amount of fear.

You didn't just walk up to a river like that and demand that it produce in accord with your wishes. You lowered a worm-baited hook into its amber water and unquestioningly accepted whatever it deigned to yield. If it chose to produce only fallfish and suckers, you received them with good grace. Perch, bullheads and rock bass were welcomed with gratitude, for they were good eating. Smallmouths — there were some busters — and walleyes were evidence that the river was in its most generous mood, and you gave thanks accordingly.

Our fishing methods were both simple and direct. When we felt a bite we "let him have it" a bit, to make sure the bait was swallowed, and then we heaved. The idea, of course, is to hook the fish and boost it high overhead in a single sweeping motion. But if the fish happens to be a three-pound river smallmouth, it will resist this scheme with tremendous strength. The resulting struggle is soon over, of course, for either fish or fisherman is the winner in a very short space of time. I might point out, however, that this was true of the Dempsey-Firpo fight, a slugfest still remembered above all others.

The river was full of fish in those days, and I'm sure that skill and the use of specialized tackle would have produced truly spectacular catches, yet the thrills of uncertainty would have disappeared had we been masters of the situation. The satisfaction of taking fish by proven techniques cannot compare with the thrill of catching fish whose capture seems a miracle. This last was my viewpoint when I was very young, and no fishing I've done since has ever been quite as exciting.

It is for this reason that I think it is a mistake to try to cram a technical knowledge of fishing down a youngster's throat. Not only may it sour him on the whole deal, but it will deny him the fun of learning through trial and error. No boy enjoys "doing as he's told," but when left to his own devices there is no limit to the effort he will expend in satisfying his curiosity.

I learned to swim, acquired a bicycle and finally, although with some reservations, was deemed sufficiently responsible to be allowed to fish where and when I pleased. At about the same time, it dawned on me that there was considerably more to fishing than blindly trusting to luck, and I began searching for better ways of making fish bite than by dangling a worm where I hoped they would see it.

I had been fishing the Connecticut for several hours one afternoon, but had nothing to show for it. There was a sandbar just upstream from where I was fishing, and a sudden commotion broke out along the edge. I looked up in time to see a terrified minnow heading straight for the sand in a series of frantic leaps; a bulge developed in its wake, and the hapless little fish suddenly disappeared in a flurry of foam. For a split second the gold and bronze bulk of an enormous smallmouth was clearly visible.

Vibrant with excitement and anticipation, I rushed to the sandbar and lobbed out my worm-baited hook. But although the big bass was most certainly in the vicinity, and obviously hungry, he showed not the slightest interest. At an earlier date I would have swallowed my disappointment and gone on fishing, but I was no longer in the mood to resign myself to defeat. If that bass wanted minnows, and nothing but minnows, I was ready to make whatever efforts were necessary to offer him what he wanted.

The nearest source of minnows was nearly two miles away, where a creamery discharged its waste into the stream which ran through town. Hordes of the tiny fish gathered to feed on this output, and I headed for this source of bait on my bicycle.

7

I found an empty tin can and then, after tying on a small hook, had no trouble catching a minnow. With the can as a bait bucket, and by pedaling madly, I managed to made it back to the Connecticut before the lone minnow expired.

I changed hooks again, impaled the minnow and lowered it where I had seen the big bass. Nothing happened for long moments, but then my line suddenly began moving off and came taut against the tip of my cane pole. This was not the nibbling type of bite that I was most accustomed to; my pole was drawn down with what seemed an inexorable force, and I promptly heaved with all my strength.

The pole bent almost double against unyielding resistance, but the standoff was of only momentary duration. It terminated suddenly when a huge bass vaulted high in the air, its glistening bulk almost too large for my startled eyes to believe. Rattling with indignation, the big smallmouth seemed to be serving notice that I had overstepped the bounds of my humble station.

This turned out to be all too true. As the bass went down he put an incredible strain on my creaking pole, and we promptly parted company. The most tragic thing about losing a big fish is the awful sense of finality that stabs one like the thrust of a knife. My ego took the full force when I saw my hookless line whip free of the water and high into the air.

Already sick at heart, I became even sicker when I examined my line. I could tell from the curl at the end that it hadn't broken; in my haste to change hooks I had done a poor job of tying, and the knot had slipped free. In one hard lesson

8

I learned the importance of attending to small details. I had always tied hook to line with a simple slipknot, but you may be sure that I promptly looked into the matter of more reliable knots. And from then until now, I don't believe I have ever trusted a knot to use before testing it.

My encounter with the smallmouth, even though I came out a loser, inspired me to try to improve my techniques, and I suppose I gradually became a better fisherman in the accepted sense of the word. Yet I doubt that this added to my happiness, and I suspect that the fisherman makes a bad mistake if he focuses on competence as his major goal.

Not but what it is gratifying to be able to cast well, to handle a big fish adroitly, to tie a fetching fly and a host of other things. But these gratifications are incidental by-products of a diversion which, for millions, fills a fundamental and deep-seated need. For all of us in whom this need resides, fishing is a therapeutic blessing, its benefits no more dependent on expertise than is a pill's curative power dependent on the deftness with which it is swallowed. In my own case, a moderate amount of competence has been the inevitable result of years of fishing and experimentation. Yet I am often saddened by my inability to recapture the purity of delight which accompanied the simple efforts of my youth.

Just up the street from where I lived was a lawn with a flowering bush in one corner. Just what kind of shrub this was I have no idea, but each spring it was watched eagerly by kids from up and down the street. All of us knew that when it burst into bloom it was time to go eel fishing.

The stream which flowed through the village joined the

Connecticut a couple of miles below town, and just upstream from the mouth it ran through a broad and level pasture. In spring it would be full to the tops of its banks, held back by the heavy flow of the Connecticut, and at that time eels appeared in the smaller stream in considerable numbers.

Passing years have erased most of my affection for eels, and I am of the opinion that there is no "good" time to catch the slimy critters. But back then we looked on eels as mysterious and exciting fish to catch, and we knew that the best time to go after them was at night.

After supper, when the time came, a dozen or so of us would converge on the spot and begin preparations. The first order of business was to collect enough driftwood to feed a large fire well into the night. This job finished, we'd go about setting our lines.

Each line was tied to a stick driven firmly into the ground. A tall, limber switch was also thrust into the ground, just ahead of the first stake, and a bit of white rag tied to the tip. Baited lines were hurled out with the aid of heavy sinkers, and secured with a loose loop to the rag-tipped switches which would signal any forthcoming bites.

During the remaining daylight the lines could be counted on to produce a few suckers and fallfish, and these we cut into chunks which would serve as a common supply of eel bait. From experience, we had learned that the eels greatly preferred hunks of fresh fish over night crawlers.

The fire was started during that exquisitely peaceful interlude when dusk turns rapidly to darkness and the lovely components of spring seem to pass in review. Peepers burst into plaintive chorus in nearby swamps, while muskrats gamboled in plain view, their shrill squeaks and disregard for our presence open indications of their amorous intent. From a greater distance came the sound of bitterns: *kerblink, kerblonk,* the tones strangely hollow as if issuing from vocal chords strummed by the passage of bubbles.

We heaped more wood on the fire as darkness closed in, and the circle of light from the leaping flames became an ostensible oasis of security. The river, now buried in darkness, became a thing of mystery, and its inhabitants creatures of an alien world. Suddenly, one of the white rags began a weird dance, and then was jerked down violently. The lucky fisherman leaped to tend his line, and all shared in the attending excitement. The creature, unseen but struggling violently, was nothing more than an eel. Yet circumstance and our emotions had contrived a framework within which the commonplace became exotic.

Quite possibly this is the key to fishing: the ability to see glamor in whatever species one may fish for. Regarded objectively, a fish becomes a prize worth seeking only when we endow it with romantic qualities which are the products of emotion.

The fond memories of the fishing I did when very young are undoubtedly due to the exalted status I accorded wholesale to any and all fish that would bite my hook. I was aware of adult prejudice — the alleged inferiority of certain species, and the high desirability of others — but these were opinions which I neither shared nor understood. I could hardly wait for suckers to run in the spring, for yellow perch to move toward the shorelines and for bullheads to start biting. I fished for minnows as seriously as I fished for all else, and all fishing was equally wonderful. Then, at last, I fell victim to prejudice. I had caught plenty of sizable fish, including smallmouths that all but broke my cane pole, yet I got what was perhaps my greatest thrill from catching a fish barely six inches long. The fish was a brook trout.

Although the region in which I grew up afforded good fishing for other species, the trout fishing was limited and hard to reach. An uncle took me brook fishing when I was hardly six years old, and the experience was so demoralizing that I had little interest in trout fishing for a long time thereafter. My trouble was that I couldn't make head or tail of stream trout fishing. The stream didn't seem deep enough to hold fish, and watching my uncle catch several trout from what seemed to me to be the most unlikely places only added to my frustration. I never got a bite and came home bitterly disillusioned.

But I listened to local talk of trout and trout fishing, and as I became a bit older I was impressed by the near reverence in which trout obviously were held. And gradually the urge to catch a trout became overwhelming.

The nearest trout brook, a tiny stream, was several miles from town at its nearest point, and it was necessary to tramp several additional miles upstream to reach the best fishing. There came a day when my desire to catch a trout forced me to take the necessary five-mile hike.

After putting what I judged to be the required distance behind me, I cut an alder for a pole and rigged it with line, hook and sinker. Then I began fishing, with only the foggiest notion of where to fish or how. I waded through spots which seemed to hold no promise, only to watch in dismay as trout streaked away in fright. In what seemed to me to be more likely places I couldn't draw a nibble.

Finally, I came to the remains of an ancient wooden dam, its center long since destroyed by floods, and only the sections near shore still standing. I climbed up on one of these wings and surveyed the pool in the middle of the stream. Then I happened to glance downward, and through the wide cracks in the weather-beaten planking I could see clear, deep water directly beneath me. I baited with a fresh worm and lowered my hook through one of the cracks.

To obtain a better view, I lay flat on the planking and put my face close to the crack. I could see my dangling worm, and as my eyes adjusted to the gloom I could make out several slender fish. Mottled backs and white-striped pectoral fins identified them as brook trout, and I could feel my pulse begin to hammer.

I lowered my bait to within inches of the bottom, and when nothing happened I jigged it a bit. One of the little fish immediately darted in and grabbed the worm, and a moment later I hauled my first trout up through the crack.

Odd as it may seem, all previous fishing triumphs faded to nothing with the capture of this tiny fish. I examined it minutely, almost as though fearing that the rich coloration would somehow prove to be other than genuine. The realization of any burning ambition always seems too good to be true, and this case was no exception. I could hardly believe that at long last I had caught a trout.

The reason for this reaction has never failed to puzzle me. Was I born with some special affinity for trout, as a setter pup inherits a passionate interest in game birds? I'm sure I don't know. But I do know that I hold trout (and salmon) in an esteem which I find impossible to accord other species of fish.

Since I hold all fish in relatively high esteem, this preference for trout is only a matter of degree. Out of curiosity I have just made a quick tally, and can account for at least thirty-five species of freshwater fish which I have caught at one time or another. With but few exceptions, I had rather fish for any and all than to count money. But the fact remains that from the day I caught that tiny brookie, I have embraced trout fishing as the ultimate in all freshwater angling.

If I learned general fishing the hard way, I learned trout fishing by an even harder route. Nowadays, a beginner can watch skillful trout fishermen along almost any trout stream, and can deduce the generalities of trout fishing by observation alone. Excellent tackle is readily available, and directions for its use rehashed in the outdoor magazines.

Youngsters of my era enjoyed no such advantages. In my locale, at least, accomplished trout fishermen were rare, secretive of habit and reluctant to disclose their secrets. In small, rural communities such as mine, general stores were the only source of equipment, and their proprietors, usually nonfishermen, catered only to the fisherman's most basic needs.

Because of these circumstances, learning the approach to trout was a matter of pioneering with crude equipment. I didn't look on this as a hardship then, nor do I now. What truths I learned, I learned directly from the trout. Although I fished with an alder pole, and later with a telescopic steel rod, I gradually came to know something of the trout for which I fished. My curiosity concerning their affairs was boundless; I examined the contents of their stomachs, watched them rise to mayflies and saw them scrounge nymphs from the bottom. Most important, I came to appreciate their highly developed sensitivities, and to realize that my crude methods and tackle were no match for their remarkable powers of discrimination. Eventually, I found myself in the rather strange position of knowing full well how trout could be taken, but lacking the means of carrying out my ideas.

In later years I have run into fishermen in just the opposite predicament. They have all the necessary tackle which I lacked, but they are without the empathy which I possessed at an early age. To my way of thinking, the latter is of far greater importance.

Years ago, when I was teaching school in northeastern Vermont, a friend and I hiked through miles of woods to reach a remote stream. When we arrived at the stream, I was dismayed to find that my reel had worked loose from my rod, and was hopelessly lost somewhere back along the trail. All I could do was tie a nine-foot tapered leader to the top guide and make the best of it. The wilderness stream was well populated with hungry brook trout, however, and with a wet fly at the end of my leader I managed to fill my limit.

Thanks to the abundance of wild trout, this required no great angling skill, but despite the number of fish present, my companion creeled only a fraction of the legal limit. He knew very little about trout and their habits, and this lack was a much more serious handicap to him than the lack of line and reel was to me.

I learned to bait cast before ever seeing another fisherman fish by this method. My rod was the telescoping kind, shucked together to provide stiffness; the reel, a cheap device designed for no purpose but to hold surplus line. On free spool it shimmied like the front end of an old Model-T Ford on a bumpy road, and almost every cast terminated in a backlash. But I managed to catch bass and pickerel on this outfit, and the wretched deficiencies of my tackle made each triumph all the sweeter. Also, thanks to those early experiences, I can better appreciate the efficiency of the tackle with which I fish nowadays.

I did my first fly fishing with the very same outfit, for the simple reason that I had no other. Nobody told me that I needed a heavier line for fly casting, and I nearly broke my arm trying to cast flies on a bait casting line before finally figuring this out for myself.

I have just checked my stock of fly lines and find that I have more than twenty, of varying weights and tapers. All are wonderfully supple and glossy, designed to pour through the guides of a rod as smoothly as cream from pitcher. There were no lines like that around when I began fly fishing.

What they did have in local stores were horrors designated as "enameled" lines. These came coiled on pieces of cardboard, and their chief characteristic was that of retaining this coiled state under any and all circumstances. The small arbor of my casting reel created much tighter coils, with the result that line stripped off preparatory to casting behaved like a handful of broken clock springs.

About the time I shifted to an enameled line I learned about dry flies from a Weber catalog. I dug up enough money to order all of a half dozen, plus a couple of tapered gut leaders. Both were items I had never before laid eyes on.

The first time out I spent an afternoon doing what I believed to be dry fly fishing, but never raised a trout. But I kept stubbornly at it, and at dusk a heavy hatch developed. In a short time I was surrounded by rising trout.

At long last, my fly — a Pale Evening Dun, and thus a pattern to be remembered with affection — came over a trout foolish enough to tolerate the dragging effect of my kinky line. The fly disappeared in the center of a swirl, and I was fast to a rainbow well over a foot long. I felt the hook sock home, and when the rainbow shot high above the water I knew the thrill of a long-awaited miracle coming to pass.

There have been few fishing thrills to match it since, yet in a certain sense it was a thrill that has never ceased to echo. I still relive a small part of it with every trout I take on a dry fly, for neither time nor repetition has destroyed the illusion that the rise of a trout to a dry fly is properly regarded in the light of a miracle.

Today there are hundreds of fishing books that would have spared me much experimentation had I had access to them in my youth. Yet I doubt that I would have enjoyed following the directions of experts as I enjoyed those successes which came after much fruitless trial and error.

There is more to it than that. Instruction in those things that are "right" does not necessarily lead to an understanding of *why* they are right. Such understanding is best gained by the gradual process of eliminating those things which are "wrong," and the depth of a fisherman's knowledge is therefore more the product of past mistakes than the absorption of advice passed on by others.

This is perhaps no way for a fellow to talk who is setting out to write a book about fishing. Hard and fast tradition has it that such a book should be a no-nonsense catalog of how-to-do-it techniques, a compression of practicalities guaranteed to make an expert fisherman of a reader who can't tell a trout from a flounder.

So pronounced has this trend become that some fishing books are actually bound in waterproof covers so that they may be safely carried in the tackle box. This implies that the novice, armed with such a book, has very little to worry about; to know what to do in any given situation he need only consult his text.

When fishermen adopt the habit of studying a book between casts, fishing will have come to a pretty pass indeed. There is little danger of this eventuality, however, for no book can serve as a substitute for experience. This is a blessing, for were such a book possible, it would take much of the fun out of the game.

The chapters which follow will not be aimed at any such unrealistic and undesirable goal. They will consist largely of speculations voiced by a fisherman who realizes that he knows considerably less about fish and fishing than he thought he knew twenty-five years ago. They will be directed to the many nice people who need nothing more than their instinctive love of fishing to be "good" fishermen.

2

How Fishermen Fool Fish—
And Vice Versa

A NUMBER OF YEARS AGO I wrote a magazine article
about the inconsistencies of state fishing regulations. I sent a
questionnaire to the fish and game department of each state,
and the total response was interesting and edifying.

Fish and game officials of most states hold positions of po-
litical vulnerability, so some replies were understandably
guarded and noncommittal. Others were surprisingly frank,
and the consensus of these forthright responses was that most
fishing regulations, particularly those which applied to warm-
water species, were unnecessarily restrictive, to say nothing of
being much too complicated.

Although the results of the project are not pertinent to this
chapter in general, one common observation is worthy of
mention. It was the opinion, openly expressed by a number of

officials, that hook and line fishing is far too inefficient to pose a serious threat to fish populations. In Ohio, where all fishing regulations had been scrapped, it was reported that fishing had actually improved as a consequence. The number of *small* fish was reduced — a dubious tribute to angling skill — and this had resulted in increased numbers of larger fish. Some of these must have been caught for the trend to have been noticed, but others probably eventually died of old age.

Far too often, we fishermen make the common mistake of underestimating the strength of the opposition. With misplaced faith in what we regard as our skills, we believe that when we take no fish this is conclusive evidence that no fish are present. We may even jump to the same conclusion when we *see* no fish in waters in which it appears to us that no fish of significance could possibly hide.

The fallacy in such thinking is delightfully identified in *The Life Story of the Fish,* an altogether fascinating book written by Brian Curtis.

The clincher is drawn from the author's personal experience and has to do with a thirty-foot section of stream which had been blocked off at both ends for experimental purposes. The section was only eight feet wide and two feet deep, and because of what seemed optimum visibility, the author "knew" that a total of three trout had been trapped between the barriers. He succeeded in catching two of these by angling and freed them in open water. When the last of the trio resisted his best efforts, he finally set a trap in the stretch. The next morning the trap contained six ten-inch trout, of which never more than one had been visible at any given time in

surroundings which provided little more means of concealment than the glass tank of an aquarium.

This illustrates the important truth that fish have mastered
the art of concealment to a degree which we, deluded by our
human limitations, find it difficult to appreciate. We are also
blind to the extent to which fish are protected from our best
angling efforts by their inborn sense of caution. Their inherent ability to deduce the presence of danger, no matter how
cleverly disguised, is every bit as magical as their ability to
hide where to do so seems an impossibility.

We tend to conclude that because we see a few fish we
therefore see them all, and we also assume that the deception
which put a few fish in our creels is sufficiently refined to fool
all fish in general. A little reflection will reveal the glaring
error in this line of thought. The fish that takes our bait or
lure has to be the exception. Otherwise, with fishing pressure
such as it is, there soon would be no fish left in our lakes and
streams.

Unlike wild game, fish cannot roam over extensive areas,
and compared to game are therefore much more vulnerable.
The relatively small areas to which they are restricted are
well known to fishermen, of course, and their exploitation is
thus simplified. On the more popular stream, hardly a day
passes during the fishing season in which they fail to see one
or more lures or bait offerings, and their survival in the face of
this constant temptation is an eloquent tribute to their highly
developed senses of restraint and caution.

In Vermont, one is able to fish streams in which trout still
reproduce naturally, and where sometimes, although by no

means frequently, fishermen are lucky enough to catch wild trout which weigh several pounds. This represents a triumph which is fully appreciated only when measured against the vast number of times such a trout has resisted capture.

It seems safe to assume that a two-pound trout will have been large enough to be caught on hook and line during at least three fishing seasons. In the Battenkill, for instance, such a trout may well have been fished over an average of four times a day. Basing calculations on a five-month fishing season, as many as 1800 unsuccessful attempts may have been made on the trout's life before it was caught in its final moment of weakness. The number of tries is a guess, of course, but certainly not a wild one. Even with generous allowance for possible exaggeration, the feat of taking such a trout is a triumph achieved in the face of staggering odds.

Despite every possible expenditure of human ingenuity, fishing remains a game in which the fisherman comes out second best ninety-nine times out of a hundred. Fortunately for our pride, most of our defeats go unnoticed; it would probably be completely demoralizing if we ever knew exactly how many trout refuse our offerings in any given mile of stream. In spite of all that we would like to believe we are actually no match for the fish, and it is only when one accepts the humility of this circumstance that he begins to appreciate the challenge of angling.

An old coon hunter once told me of his first coon hunt, and how, when the dog brought a big coon to bay on the ground, he attempted to dispatch it by hauling off and kicking it. The coon dodged and quickly retaliated by tearing a big chunk from one of the hunter's brand-new rubber boots. "I could see right off," the old hunter told me, "that that wa'n't no way to go about it."

There is undoubtedly a best way to go about killing a coon, but there may not be any best way to go about catching a fish. The most popular and natural, perhaps, is to concentrate on the fish we are fortunate enough to catch, and then attempt to identify the method by which their indiscretion was provoked. I believe, however, that more enlightenment will result from considering the far greater number of fish that we *fail* to catch and search for the reasons of our failure.

By way of illustration I can draw on an incident in which my son Mike figured when he was eight years old. Before going into the details I should explain that Mike is now in his mid-twenties, and that we have shared many fishing experiences in the intervening years. I expect to allude to these frequently, probably with little regard for their chronology. As a result, Mike will shuttle back and forth as far as age is concerned, but from early childhood to the present he has fished with an interest and enthusiasm which have undergone little change.

People often observe that Mike resembles me, but this does him an injustice. He is some three inches taller than I am, for one thing, but if we were exactly the same height and age it would be easy to tell us apart. The fellow wearing a perpetual scowl would be me, and the one with the smile would be Mike.

A sunny disposition has been one of Mike's outstanding characteristics since infancy. Although his appearances in these pages will be in alternating role of child and adult, one description applies throughout: a born fisherman who has always fished hard, and for the money, ever since he was old enough to hold a rod, and always with a happiness that has kept him smiling.

In the particular instance to which I now return, my wife Edna, Mike and I were spending a summer vacation at a camp on Lake Champlain. One day, after lunch, Mike and I were setting out to go fishing, and I was in the process of untying the boat when I happened to spot a huge sheepshead, or freshwater drum, finning lazily in the shadow of the dock. These fish are common in Lake Champlain and usually run between one and three pounds. Some grow much larger, however, and the one lurking along the edge of our dock was at least a ten-pounder.

Without mentioning the fish to Mike, who was intent on other matters, I baited one of our rods with a worm and told him to lower it over the edge of the dock. Puzzled, Mike did as directed, and the worm dropped down to the level of the big sheepshead. Mike, however, could not see the fish, for he was standing nearly the length of the rod from the edge of the dock. The sheepshead immediately spotted the worm and finned up to within inches of it for a close inspection. He continued to study it closely, but refused to gobble it.

"Jig your line a little," I ordered.

The action perked up the sheepshead's interest. He circled the bait, approached from a new angle and then came to a halt as before, his nose within a foot of the worm.

"Let it right down to the bottom," I told Mike.

Mike dropped the tip of his rod, and the worm settled to the bottom and remained motionless. The big sheepshead studied the worm in its new situation only briefly. Then, with unhurried confidence, he stood on his head, calmly sucked in the bait and moved majestically toward deeper water.

Mike's rod took on a strain so slowly that he was equally slow in realizing that he had a bite. When he finally felt the ponderous weight of the fish, he let out a yell and set the hook. The next instant he was slinging his reel hand around to dispel the pain of knuckles smartly rapped by the spinning handle of the reel. But he clung to the rod, and after a long and noisy struggle that brought neighboring campers out on their porches, finally brought the fish in to where I could net it. Mike was accorded a loud round of applause from the sizable gallery and wound up being quite the hero.

Now, as fish go, a sheepshead is thought of as being on the stupid side, yet even this admittedly dull-witted one had a built-in sense of caution which had to be indulged and reconciled before he could be persuaded to gobble a worm which he very obviously wanted. The relevant question is whether it is more important to note the simple trick by which the fish was conned into biting, or to investigate the reasons why he refused to bite until this measure was applied. In my opinion, the latter is of much greater importance for an understanding of the unavoidable inefficiency of hook and line fishing.

The situation was basic, and typical of the most common of angling endeavors: to attempt to play on a fish's hunger by offering either a genuine item of food or its imitation. In this case the real thing was used, eliminating the possibility of rejection because of unconvincing imitation. This fish knew full well that he was looking at a genuine worm, and his eventual response proved that he was hungry for it. What made him hold off? Were his suspicions aroused by the combined presence of hook, line and sinker?

Although this seems likely, it is easily refuted by the fact that the fish immediately ignored all three when the worm settled to the bottom. This points up the thing which a fisherman always has going for him: no fish is smart enough to deduce the significance of the tackle used against him. To a fish, the purposeful design of a barbed hook in no way suggests its cruel intent, nor does a line or leader reveal its inherent threat. Fish see such things merely as inanimate objects, by themselves, cause for neither interest nor concern.

So now we come to the real reason why the sheepshead refused the worm, a reason which is simply stated but which has enormous significance. He refused it simply because it didn't behave naturally. Under normal circumstances a worm settles to the bottom. This one sank only partway, then hung in one position in open defiance of gravity. Unlike humans, fish are not moved to curiosity by such mysterious phenomona, and they are not tempted, as are humans, to meddle with things which behave strangely. On the contrary, they are governed by strong instincts which order them to leave such things strictly alone.

We still have uncovered only part of that which is significant. The bait was only a worm, and what has a ten-pound sheepshead to fear from a mere worm, even from one which exhibits eccentricities of behavior?

To answer this question is to explain why fish are so very

hard to catch. Nature has compensated for the vulnerability imposed by the restriction of habitat by seeing to it that fish react with suspicion and fear to all deviations, even though they be manifested by the most innocent and trivial items. Although land creatures are much more intelligent, it is interesting to note that this instinct is not as highly developed in them. Perhaps it existed in the dim past, but it has been largely supplanted by evolved powers of reason. For the most part, although with certain exceptions, land creatures tend to fear only those things which by reason and experience they know to be capable of doing them bodily harm. Lacking similar powers of discrimination, fish simply play it safe by carefully avoiding anything and everything which seems the least bit strange — at least in the case of those common items of food, and their imitations, with which we are presently concerned. It is this unreasoning sensitivity which explains why fish can be both stupid and extremely hard to fool.

Getting back to the sheepshead, his fear and suspicion were the direct result of the unnatural behavior he observed in the worm. That this, in turn, was the result of the line's influence upon the bait was in no way apparent to him, but it is important to us to recognize this factor as the real heart of the problem.

Since the connection between hook and line cannot be avoided and is bound to have an undesirable effect upon the bait's behavior, the curse of this interrelation affects every bait fisherman. More than any other single factor, it is responsible for the moderation of his success, and the great frequency with which he fails.

It is tempting to refute this claim by pointing out that it is perfectly possible to catch fish by dangling a worm from a bobber, and that trout will sometimes rise to a dry fly that is guilty of serious drag. But this is not contrary to my argument, which was prefaced by the claim that the fish we catch are the exceptions, while those that resist our efforts are the rule. Most will continue to resist and refuse, in spite of all we can do; try as we may, we can catch only the few. Paradoxically, the greatest share of these will be caught by those fishermen who most fully appreciate how few are to be expected.

In this type of fishing, where the intent is to persuade fish to snap up items of food or their imitations, success depends in large measure upon recognition of the inevitable effect which the line has on the bait, and upon appreciation of the undesirable consequences. Only when the importance of this factor is realized does the need to minimize its effect become apparent. Minimize is the proper word, for the possibility of eliminating it completely is extremely remote.

Panfish are relatively unwary, and comparatively easy to catch. Yet, in clear water, I have watched yellow perch, sunfish and other plentiful species do nothing more than study my bait for as long as it was held motionless. When the bait was raised a foot or so, then allowed to sink back on a slack line, one of the watching fish would usually move in and grab it. Suspicion was dispelled by a momentary manifestation of normal behavior.

This illustrates another thing the fisherman has in his favor. Fish live almost entirely in the present, and their evaluation of a situation is seldom influenced by past impressions, even those of the immediately preceding moments. Thus a bait or lure which has previously aroused suspicion by its unnatural behavior can suddenly become acceptable when the fisherman contrives a momentary appearance of innocence in its behalf.

This distinction, the difference between natural and unnatural behavior, is never equally manifest to both fish and fisherman. The sensitivity and perception of the fish are far keener than those of the fisherman, with the result that the fisherman is often penalized for violations of natural behavior which are too subtle for him to recognize. All too often he discounts the possibility of imperfection in what seems flawless presentation, while at the other end of the line a fish is made suspicious by what, to his eyes, is a glaring anomaly.

There is a long, broad pool in Vermont's Otter Creek where in bygone years big rainbows used to cruise at dusk, tipping up to suck in mayflies so gently that their rises barely dimpled the surface. Sad to relate, all but a few of the rainbows have disappeared, but during evenings of the past my fishing partner and neighbor Pete Terwilliger and I used to stalk these feeding fish by canoe, trying to drop our dry flies ahead of them as they cruised the pool.

Before continuing it is appropriate to introduce Pete, for, like Mike, he will appear often in the chapters to follow.

Shortly after the end of World War II, Pete's father fled the frantic pace of a New Jersey existence and bought an inn in Pittsford. I happened to live next door to the inn at the time, and a common love of fishing and hunting soon brought us together. Pete was then thirteen years old, but an inborn affinity for the outdoors won him a full partnership in enterprises which included trout fishing, bird hunting, fox hunting, deer hunting and enough related activities to fill the calendar.

Then, while in his prime, Pete's dad was fatally stricken with cancer. Pete, still in his teens, was forced to give up college and take over the role of family breadwinner. Now in his early thirties, he is the owner of a thriving garage and filling station business, the father of five children, chairman of the local school board — and still my next-door neighbor.

In the meantime our outdoor association has continued, although our respective roles have changed. There was once a time when I could show Pete how to cast, how to tie flies and a host of other things. Needless to say, he needs no such help from me now. Instead, it is I who benefit from Pete's willingness to pick up the decoys, tote the heavier load and indulge my creaky joints in a dozen other ways.

I could describe Pete as blond, trim, and at the risk of his wrath, even handsome. But more manifest is a coordination which is apparent in his every move. He has only to pick up a paddle or hand tail a salmon to give the impression that he can measure up to any situation which happens to arise. After nearly twenty years of close companionship, I know this to lie very close to the literal truth.

Getting back to the pool in Otter Creek, the water was completely flat, with very few visible crosscurrents, and our flies always *seemed* to float without the slightest drag. Yet we knew from long experience that most of those seemingly perfect floats would be ignored by the feeding fish; it was a common experience to have one pick off naturals all around the fly, while ignoring the fly for reasons which we could not detect.

Yet we came to notice a very peculiar thing about the

whole business. Usually the fly would alight and start its float without drawing comment from us. We would watch it drift over the fish in silence, and in almost all such cases it would be ignored. Then the fly would come down in a fashion that could scarcely be called different, yet with some intangible quality of perfection about it that would immediately draw excited exclamations from both of us. "Oh, oh!" we'd say in unison. "Get ready!" And when this happened the trout would almost always tip up for the fly without the slightest reservation, this in spite of the fact that he had previously scorned repeated offerings of the same fly.

The quality of perfection in the float that took the fish was so subtle that we could barely sense it, but to the fish it was much more strongly evident. Magnified by his powers of perception, the slight misbehaviors of previous floats had loomed as glaring danger signals, but he remained ready and willing to gulp the same fly the instant it ceased to display cause for suspicion.

Unfortunately, the fisherman can never expect to see things the way fish see them. But if he fools around with them long enough, he will develop an empathy which will help him to predict and anticipate their responses with something approaching accuracy.

Just how far a fellow can go in establishing sensory rapport with fish is a matter open to question. But George MacArthur, of Grand Lake Stream, Maine, once told me of a fisherman who apparently believed he had achieved the ultimate in this subtle art. We were trolling streamers for landlocked salmon in Grand Lake, and George, who was my guide, was keeping me royally entertained between strikes with a steady succession of yarns.

"I used to guide an old fellow who liked to fish for togue," he said. "We'd drag bottom in fifty and sixty feet of water, and the old man would watch the tip of his rod like a hawk. Every once in a while he'd suddenly lean forward and get ready to set the hook in a fish. He'd sit coiled up like that for a minute or so, then finally he'd lean back and relax. '*I almost had a strike*,' he'd whisper, and darned if I don't think he *believed* it!

"Then there was this other fellow . . ." and George was off on another yarn. But I wasn't paying strict attention, for I was wondering if the old fellow actually did possess some power of detection by which he could read the intent of fish some fifty feet beneath him. I have seen fishermen so gifted that such a feat would not seem beyond them.

About that time, and while George was yarning on, I suddenly saw a big swirl develop behind my streamer. When no strike resulted, I interrupted George's story.

"I think I almost had a strike," I told him.

George paused just long enough to grin, then resumed his story.

Seconds later, the water behind my fly boiled again.

"I think I almost had another strike," I said.

George grinned again, but with no real appreciation. Like all good storytellers, and George MacArthur is a master, he had little patience for frivolous interruptions.

Another few seconds, and the water erupted again, and this time the rod plunged and the reel sang. The salmon had dogged my fly a hundred feet or more before working up enough courage to zoom in and nail it.

"Now, maybe you'll believe me," I told George, as the hooked salmon climbed into the air.

Whether one can become so attuned to fish that he can sense their unseen presence is a possibility that I can neither affirm nor deny, but even I can tell that a strike is imminent when swirls start showing behind my lure.

An admirable book on trout fishing, Ray Bergman's *Trout,* is devoted almost exclusively to the faithful recording of the author's varied experiences. It is a splendid work, its stature as a classic quite beyond the reach of my humble praise. Instead of presuming to resolve the problems of trout fishing with stock answers, the author devotes many pages to proving, even if inadvertently, that no such cut and dried solutions exist. His many triumphs were achieved by exactly the improvisations I have mentioned, and no common denominator is to be found among them, other than a deep understanding of trout and their habits.

I have just opened my copy of this book at random, and the first line to strike my eye states that the fisherman can never afford to overlook any possibility. In the face of the present passion for by-the-numbers instruction, such loose advice may seem rather wishy-washy. But I have far more respect for this realistic observation, and for the man who wrote it, than I have for more modern "experts" who purport to provide all that needs to be known about fishing with a few swift strokes of revelation.

It is possible, of course, to fish a dry fly "by the numbers" and actually take trout. Cast upstream, strip in slack and try to avoid drag, just as the books say. But the fisherman who, from long study and association, fully appreciates the critical sensitivities of the trout he fishes for will take many more. He will strive for refinements of presentation which seem unnecessary to the mechanical fisherman, recognizing, if not always achieving, the subtle modifications dictated by the ever-shifting pattern of the situations he encounters.

I live in a region where it is common practice to call in a "dowser" when one wants to dig a well. The dowser walks around holding a forked branch, and the branch will allegedly dip downward over any spot where one can dig and strike a supply of water. There are those who do not hesitate to dismiss water dowsing as a fake, but I cannot bring myself to do it in good conscience. I have known fishermen whose ability to catch fish seemed equally mystical and inexplicable. None has ever written a word about fishing.

The talents of these highly gifted fishermen are always broadly manifest. Whether it's jigging smelt through the ice, drifting minnows for bass or taking trout on dry flies, these fellows who "have the touch" make the rest of us look like beginners. It is quite possible, even probable, that they do the right thing at the right time instinctively and couldn't account for their success if they tried. It is equally likely that their art is such that others couldn't duplicate it, even with the benefit of direction. Consciously, or unconsciously, these fishermen fool fish by presenting their bait, or imitation thereof, in a manner as free from the damaging influence of line and leader as their intuition and ingenuity can contrive.

Since the effect need be only slight and momentary, the subtle touches by which it may be achieved are almost infinite in variety. Maximum exploitation thus stems only from maximum experience, but a start can be made by those of meager experience in simple and basic situations.

Let's say you are worm fishing. Your boat is anchored in still water and you may be fishing for pond brookies, small-mouths or maybe panfish. In this situation, many fishermen clamp on a sinker and lower their bait until it dangles a foot or so above the bottom. There is no denying the fact that this approach will take fish, but it is possible to take more with the advantage of more convincing presentation.

Try this: Tie a tapered leader to your line, and to this tie as small a hook as it's practical to use. Hang a worm on the hook by jabbing it only once near the middle, and lob it out with no sinker to hurry its descent. The unweighted worm will settle slowly, the thin, flexible leader will exert minimal influence, and the result is a close approximation of a natural food item that is free of all restraint.

If you were a fish, with virtually no power of reason, but with an overpowering instinct to shun everything that deviates from the norm, which would you be inclined to grab? Would you go for the worm mysteriously held in a fixed position, or for the one slowly settling toward the bottom in the conventional manner of all sinking objects.

If you were a yellow perch, you would recognize the distinction and prefer the sinking bait, but you might also grab the stationary worm. If you were a bass, with a more highly developed sense of caution, you would be less inclined to do the latter. And if you were a trout, and thus a bundle of constant fear and apprehension, the chances are good that only the freely sinking worm would put you in the creel.

There is a manmade pond not far from my home, into which the fish and game department causes hatchery trout to be dumped at regular intervals. This is a well-meant attempt to compensate for our steadily shrinking trout fishing. Many flock to the spot, and to numerous counterparts, the aspect of artificiality obscured by the exalted presence of trout. Most heave out worms, often dangling from bobbers, usually with high expectations, and especially so if the hatchery truck has just driven off. Yet many, if not most, come away disappointed. The fish, although hand reared and hand fed, are still trout, and retain a trout's instinctive sense of caution to sufficient degree to see cause for alarm in such crude efforts.

I know a crackerjack fisherman who is just mean enough to elbow his way through the crowd and proceed to catch his legal limit of these fish, basking in the envious stares and remarks of those who can hardly get a nibble. He fishes in the manner I have described, using a tapered leader and tiny hook, and allowing his bait to settle without any help from a sinker. As a final, deadly touch, he uses shucked-out stick caddis larvae as bait, and while hatchery trout exercise a certain amount of discrimination, they are no match for this fetching presentation.

The "tricks" that fool fish often seem to be unrelated, but I believe that they are usually subservient to a single ruling principle. In this type of fishing the principle can be stated as a need: the need to disguise the line's influence on bait or lure to a degree compatible with the sensitivities of the fish. The ways in which this can be attempted are almost infinite in variety, but their virtue stems from their allegiance to this basic concept.

Now we come to what I believe to be a distinctly different form of angling, although not all will share my viewpoint to its extreme limits. This division of angling is that which includes the use of spoons, wobblers, spinners, plugs, popping bug, streamers — and even wet flies when they are retrieved against the current or agitated in still water.

It seems reasonable to regard such fishing as a distinct category, for it is set apart by a very obvious distinction. This difference centers around the fact that the lures used are such that they have little or no fish appeal unless activated by the fisherman. Discounting exceptions, a motionless spoon, spinner or streamer will draw no strikes. And while bass and pike may hit a resting surface plug or bug, the strike is inspired by action which preceded the moment of rest.

This being the case, the situation is just the reverse of the one with which, to this point, we have been concerned. Instead of fishing so as to minimize and counteract the influence of line and leader, both are now employed deliberately to impart motion and action to lures which otherwise would hold no attraction for the fish. It is in assessing the reasons why fish are attracted to lures of this type that I take leave of popular concepts.

It is traditional to attribute the effectiveness of many of these lures — spoons, for example — to their "minnowlike" appearance and action. Manufacturers claim these as built-in characteristics, fishermen have come to accept the claim as axiomatic, and it is quite generally taken for granted that fish hit a spoon or wobbler with the idea that it is some sort of bait fish. Speaking as an observer who has come to hold the perceptive powers of fish in great respect, such a viewpoint seems almost criminally degrading. By standards of common sense, it seems utterly ridiculous.

In terms of sweeping efficiency, the Dardevle spoon is probably the most deadly lure of its kind ever invented. When used in appropriate sizes it will account for almost every species of game fish and panfish, and the savage manner in which it usually is attacked bespeaks the unique fascination which it holds for its victims.

If I had a dollar for every mile of water through which I have cranked red-and-white Dardevles it would amount to a sizable fortune. In all that time, however, I have never seen the slightest resemblance between a fluttering red-and-white Dardevle and any form of bait fish (or any other form of life) that I have ever observed. Basing my opinion on the belief that I would be much easier to fool than the fish in such matters, I have never been able to swallow the theory that a northern pike latches onto a Dardevle with the notion that it is a forage fish. In the first place, the northern can *see* that it isn't a fish, exactly as I can see it isn't. Also, in striking, the northern usually launches his long length in pursuit of the spoon like a living torpedo — and this, contrary to popular belief, is not the way members of the pike family go about catching food.

Many fishermen think it is, but only because that is the way pike and pickerel *attack artificial lures.* The truth is that they expend no comparable amount of energy capturing the fish they feed upon, nor do they go about it in any such savage and spectacular way.

I once scooped up a tiny pickerel, brought it home alive in my minnow bucket and kept it throughout an entire summer in a fishbowl. It refused all food other than tiny live minnows, and I was forced to keep a supply of these on hand for its sustenance. Each day I placed several of these in the pickerel's bowl and watched what followed with never-failing fascination.

In the first place the minnow fry were completely oblivious of their danger, this in spite of the fact that the bowl provided no concealment and the little pickerel was at all times in plain view. Instead of becoming frantic, as one would expect, the minnows swam about complacently, their passive indifference to the pickerel's presence posing as dramatic evidence of the special dispensation which nature accords the predator.

The pickerel's behavior was equally surprising, for although possessed of an appetite which he eventually demonstrated, he never once chased after the minnows. Although he could have caught and gobbled the lot of them in a matter of seconds, he always chose to remain in one position as though transfixed.

Eventually, one of the unsuspecting minnows would stray to within an inch or so of the pickerel's malevolent snout. The pickerel would then close the small gap with a movement almost too fast for the eye to follow, and the hapless minnow would disappear as though by magic. The deadly waiting would be resumed, with identical results, and soon the last minnow would be gone. But in the whole process, the little pickerel never moved more than an inch or two from his chosen position in the center of the bowl.

I believe this example to be typical of pike behavior, rather than the dashing pursuit with which they are generally believed to capture their prey. This is an observation based not merely on my observations of one tiny pickerel, but on long experience fishing for pickerel and northern pike.

Third Lake Machias, a favorite bass lake among the many fishermen who come to Grand Lake Stream, Maine, also supports a pickerel population of great concentration, at least in the upper section of the lake. The shorelines are alive with them, and a popping bug dropped along the edge of the dry-ki often brings two or more pickerel charging out from their hiding places. Not only do they make the water boil violently when they hit the bug, but they usually create a clearly visible wake as they streak toward it. It makes for exciting fishing, largely because of the attending commotion.

But in spite of the fact that the popping bug stirs up a succession of ructions, one can look up and down the shoreline and see not the slightest sign of disturbance elsewhere. In all probability, thousands of pickerel are going about the business of stuffing their gullets as the need and opportunities arise. Yet in so doing they appear almost never to create any visible disturbance.

Within a mile of my home is a creek where I often fish for northern pike. There are days when these northerns will go for big popping bugs, and the violence with which a ten-pounder assails a bug is something to behold. There are many pike in the creek, or were the last I knew, and I have caught hundreds of them. The big ones usually explode under a bug with a blast that throws water high in the air, and if a spoon is running near the surface the commotion attending strikes is always visible. But although I have fished this creek for more than twenty years, I have seen less than a half-dozen pike create any comparable disturbance in the normal course of capturing their prey.

So I don't believe that pike and pickerel go chasing after bait fish at all, but it is their habit to lie hidden until the bait comes to them. If this is true, then the fact that they *do* chase after a spoon tends to refute the belief that they take it for a minnow. In addition, they do not *attack* the fish they feed on in a fit of anger; they simply gobble them as calmly as a horse crops grass.

It seems silly to assume that they are aroused to anger by the everyday process of taking on food, yet their belligerence is unmistakable when they rip into a spoon. This would seem to indicate that their motive in attacking the spoon is of emotional, rather than gastronomical, origin — that they have been aroused to a high state of excitement not to be inspired by the commonplace stimulus of hunger.

In the village of Chester, Vermont, there is a bridge which crosses a stream that flows through the town. At one time, and it still may be true, the stream was posted in the vicinity of the bridge, and underneath the bridge lived many large rainbow trout, plus a few truly tremendous browns. Tourists came to know of the trout, and it was a common sight to see families on the bridge, scattering the remains of picnic lunches on the water below.

The results were very upsetting for a trout fisherman to watch. Seeing a three-pound rainbow rise to a chunk of doughnut dropped by an eight-year-old was hard enough to take, but watching a brown of twice that size lumber up for a quarter of a ham sandwich made the cruel irony of life seem almost unbearable. But what makes the circumstance worthy of mention here is that hundreds of healthy minnows swarmed to compete for the handouts, and to these the big trout paid not the slightest heed.

If you have ever fished for trout, you certainly know what would have happened had someone, in defiance of the law, cast a small spoon in the midst of those swirling trout and twitched it enticingly. I, for one, would stake my all that the spoon would have taken a hard belt from one of those trout before it had gone more than a few feet. Because it looked like a minnow? Let's not be silly!

Trout feed on minnows when they happen to feel like it, but like pike and pickerel they go about the business quietly and unobtrusively. I'd hate to spend as much time in jail as I've spent on trout streams, but in all that time I have seen few, if indeed any, trout hotly chasing after minnows. I've caught plenty of trout on minnows, as far as that goes, and the grabbing of the bait has seldom been marked by any special violence.

I have also caught many trout on spoons and wobblers, and here the exact opposite has been the rule. Trout tend to go at a metal lure in a way which suggests a gamecock's attack upon its adversary. They rise to a state of belligerence quite out of keeping with their general nature, and this belligerence is as evident as it is in the case of lure striking pike and pickerel. And it is just as clearly the product of a stimulus much more exotic than hunger.

In the preceding chapter I wrote of watching a smallmouth chase a minnow almost onto dry land, and I must admit that I have seen this happen many times. I have also seen walleyes chase schools of minnows to the surface and am aware that these two species sometimes do pursue their prey. But even in their cases, I cannot believe that they strike spoons with any idea that they are minnows. Fish simply aren't that unobserving and naive.

The invention of the metal spoon is said to have taken place on Lake Bomoseen, a nearby Vermont lake which I have fished many times. The spoon's invention is alleged to have been inspired when a fisherman dropped a teaspoon overboard, and a lake trout, a species long gone from the lake, made excited passes at it as it fluttered into the depths.

The story sounds credible, for a lake trout, particularly an unsophisticated laker of the past, would have been aroused by the spoon's gyrations. As a youngster, long before spinning lures came on the scene, I discovered that twinkling bits of shale dropped into deep holes would bring trout zooming from hiding, exactly as the teaspoon of legend could have attracted the laker.

For all anybody knows, the inventor may have attributed the lake trout's interest to a conviction on the part of the trout that the teaspoon was a small fish. He may have fashioned the first trolling spoon with the idea of imitating a minnow, and if so, this concept goes back unbroken to the moment of the lure's conception.

Yet I am brash enough to believe that the concept is false. What I do believe is that the inventor of the metal spoon inadvertantly hit upon a device capable of triggering irrational responses in fish, responses which can be provoked only by resorting to unconventional stimuli. Such a thing is not unheard of, and examples can be cited of the strange and unaccountable ways in which creatures sometimes react to stimuli quite outside their normal range of experience.

One is the strange fascination which a gamboling fox or dog has for wild ducks. Foxes have been credited with worrying a stick on a beach in a deliberate effort to entice rafted ducks to within reach. Normally the most cautious of creatures, ducks are reported to be mysteriously attracted by the cavorting fox, and to draw ever closer until the fox is finally able to grab one with a quick dash.

Hunters have seized upon this strange circumstance by using tolling dogs trained to romp directly in front of a duck blind, a ruse which reportedly brings curious ducks to within range of the guns. Why the sight of an alien creature at play should have this extraordinary effect is a complete mystery, but the fact that it does is in no way refuted by the lack of explanation.

I once knew an old lady unfortunate enough to come into possession of a young crow, and foolish enough to make a pet of it. This was an indiscretion which she and her neighbors came to have good cause to regret, for there is no more diabolical nuisance than a tame crow. This one eventually made life so unbearable for all around that the old lady stroked it over the head with a length of stove wood, putting sudden end to what had become an epidemic of mischief.

I was a youngster at the time and a friend of the old lady's grandson who was about the same age. We were seated on his back steps one morning when the crow came around the corner of the house, strutting with measured deliberation, his eye cocked at every step, lest some opportunity for devilment escape him. He came to a halt directly in front of us, studying us with glittering, reptilian eyes which bespoke a keen curiosity in what he obviously regarded as a lower form of life.

"You wanna see something?" the grandson asked.

He drew a wooden match from his pocket, scratched it and held out the flame for the crow's inspection. The crow cocked his head, shuffled his feet around nervously, and then, as though under a spell, sidled up to the burning match. Finally, with compulsive suddenness, he grabbed the flame in his beak. The immediate result was a feathery convulsion, punctuated by a loud and steady stream of crow profanity.

"Does it every time," the grandson said.

Now a crow is about as smart as anything that wears feathers, and it was clear that grabbing the match resulted in excruciating pain. Normally, crows can be depended upon to avoid all painful situations, both by instinct and the exercise of reason, and in the unlikely event of a mistake it is usually doubly certain that it won't be repeated. Yet here was a crow incapable of resisting an impulse of whose painful consequence he was fully aware. For him, and for all crows in general as far as I know, the flame of a match automatically triggered a response that was completely irrational.

Finally, and perhaps closest to the point, there is the example of a frog leaping to snatch at a bit of red rag. When I was young I didn't hesitate to catch frogs on a rag-baited hook, but a keener sense of compassion now prompts me to recommend experimentation with the rag tied only to a line. If one has never done it it is worth doing, for it will illustrate the compulsive effect I'm attempting to identify and will shed light on the secret by which nonimitative lures achieve results.

Frogs are neither very bright nor hard to capture. They do make every effort to stay alive, however, and the effect of human approach is to erase concern for all else but their safety. Thus, when one approaches a frog, the creature is poised to leap, and all other matters have been thrust out of mind.

Alerted to danger, the frog is immune from all conventional temptations. Yet if a red rag is dangled in front of his nose, his apprehension will disappear almost immediately. He'll shift around a bit to gain better traction, and then he'll make a leap for the rag. Once he has it he'll rid himself of it promptly, using a front foot to disengage it from his mouth if necessary. Yet he'll jump for it again and again, indulging pointless emotions which the rag has in some strange way inspired.

It is my belief that, in most cases, fish strike nonimitative lures for the same reason that a frog will jump for a red rag, a crow may gobble a lighted match or ducks invite disaster by gravitating toward a stick-tossing fox or dog. They do so, not as the result of normal impulses, but because of stimuli so strange that they provoke indiscretion.

It can be argued that it is more important to know what lures fish are likely to hit than to understand why they hit them. Certainly, it is to a fisherman's advantage to be familiar with effective lures, but I think it is of even greater importance to understand the true reason for their effectiveness. Fishermen who use lures with the idea of provoking and arousing fish to the point of recklessness will employ shadings and touches of manipulation different from those used by fishermen trying to imitate bait fish with the same lures. And I feel certain that fishermen in the first category will take more fish.

Here again, success depends to a great extent upon an understanding of the fish sought. There is a very fine dividing line between the lure action which provokes maximum excitement and excesses which result only in fright. The challenge is that of working as close to this line as possible without overstepping it. And in this matter an appreciation of fish sensitivity is the only guide.

What I have said about spoons and wobblers I believe to be true in large part with respect to plugs, bugs, spinners, streamers and wet flies that are worked or agitated. Although the success of all these lures is quite generally attributed to their imitative qualities, this claim seems extremely farfetched. Superficial inspection and observation will reveal that they resemble nothing else under the sun in appearance, and the lifelike action which they allegedly manifest is not even an approximation of the real thing. Their success, I believe, rests in their unique ability to excite fish to a state of belligerence quite beyond the control of their normal powers of discretion.

Some will undoubtedly argue that certain lures in this category are both lifelike and imitative. Landlocked salmon fishermen may insist that the Nine Three is a convincing imitation of a smelt, and when trolled behind a canoe it behaves like a smelt. All I can say is that I have never seen a Nine Three that looked anything like a smelt to *me*, nor have I ever seen a smelt swim in a straight line along the surface of a lake. If landlocked salmon are hoodwinked into thinking a Nine Three is a smelt, then they aren't the fish I've always taken them to be.

The Chittenden Reservoir lies only a few miles from my home in Pittsford, and this body of water is stocked regularly with rainbow trout, and to a lesser extent with browns. Most that are caught fall in the ten-to-twelve-inch bracket, but a few survive to reach lunker size. Each year one or two fish are taken which tip the scales at nearly the ten-pound mark, and once in a while Mike and I take our boat to the reservoir for an off-chance shot at one of these whoppers. We dredge bottom with metal lines, but we still have to catch our first real buster.

At the start of one such jaunt last summer, I snapped on a big red-and-white Flatfish that I ordinarily use for pike.

"A trout hits that thing, he's gonna be at least a five-pounder," I told Mike.

I was still paying out line when I felt a nudge which I took to be contact with the bottom. This surprised me, for I knew the approximate depth at that point and figured the lure to be riding well above the bottom. Nevertheless, I cranked in some line to gain clearance — and felt another light bump. I reeled in to see what the devil was going on, and discovered a

48

skinny little nine-inch rainbow pitifully entangled in the
lure's array of treble hooks. Subsequent trolling resulted in
more slight bumps and the multiple impalement of several
more infant trout.

It would be ridiculous to insist that those small trout piled
into that big Flatfish with any intention of *eating* it. They
couldn't possibly swallow a bait fish almost as large as they
were, and they certainly wouldn't have been attracted by the
imitation of a bait fish so completely beyond their capacity.
Instead, the lure had aroused them to a state of truculence
quite out of keeping with their small size, a striking manifestation of the peculiar powers by which this lure has gained
widespread popularity.

It is a circumstance of no small significance that effective
lures of this type bring frequent strikes from fish hardly larger
than the lures. Even six-inch fallfish, themselves minnows
and almost innocent of cannibalism, will often hang themselves on lures scarcely smaller than they are — if the lures
have the power to excite them sufficiently. As further evidence, minnows much smaller than these lures will tag them
throughout a retrieve, demonstrating the consistency with
which all fish seem to inherit this mysterious vulnerability.

In this chapter I have tried to identify two distinct angling
categories which I believe to be set apart by basic differences.
I have done so because of the conviction that each is best implemented by those who best understand its underlying principle.

A knowledge of these principles will suggest ways of putting them to use, and this puts the show on the road. Coming

at it from the opposite direction — learning the tricks without first learning the trade — is, as with the case of the old hunter kicking the coon, no way to go about it.

One of the nice things about writing this chapter is that the consequences will not be earthshaking if my convictions are all wrong and my ideas all cockeyed. Fishing is one field in which fact and fancy mingle graciously, and it doesn't really matter whether one adds a bit more of one or a dab more of the other.

3

Of Trout and Men

SOME MEN COMPLAIN that their wives don't understand them, but my wife understands me all too well. She has me so well doped out that she usually knows what I'm going to do before I know it myself. To her, I'm not merely an open book; I'm an open *primer*.

The only thing about me she can't figure out is my love of fishing, and particularly my passion for trout fishing. She accepts my affinity for trout and wishes me well in my fishing. But she does so in much the same spirit as that in which one indulges a child's whim.

She is not alone in her inability to account for the strange fascination some men find in trout. In spite of all that is proclaimed for bass, pike, walleyes and other game fish, trout are accorded a romantic distinction which, to fishermen, sets them apart from all other species of freshwater fish. Whether trout actually merit this distinction is a question of little real significance. Worthy or not, the trout is the sentimental favorite, its position so firmly established that it is quite beyond serious challenge.

To try to explain my own sentimental leaning toward trout, I can offer nothing more substantial than that they seem to me to be the "wildest" of all the fish in our lakes and streams. They are the quickest to sense danger and take flight. No other freshwater fish can match them in flashing speed and fluid grace. They are the least tolerant of the effects of civilization. Finally, they are of a distinctive appearance which suggests their quality of wildness.

This is not as much suggested by coloration or body shape as by the distinctive appearance of the head. The distinction is not lost on artists who paint pictures of fish, for their paintings of trout and salmon invariably capture that fierce and haughty mien that is seen in the heads of the hawk and the eagle. Paintings and drawings of other fish lack this quality. The vacancy of expression in the smallmouth bass, for instance, is in sharp contrast to the aristocratic hauteur which is implicit in the appearance of trout and salmon.

Trout are different from other game fish when classified more objectively. On the evolutionary scale they rate as "primitive" fish, while such species as perch and bass are regarded as "advanced" forms of fish life. This superiority is accorded because of anatomical specializations not manifest in trout: sharp spines in the fins, a more protective scale covering and a more efficient fin arrangement.

52

These differences constitute biological advantages, and it is clearly evident that fish in possession of these specializations are able to survive where trout perish. But to the fisherman these evolutionary advances have an aspect of coarseness which he instinctively deplores. He finds it hard to recognize exotic qualities in fish for which the problem of survival has been so successfully resolved. He is drawn to trout, again instinctively, by the very deficiencies which make their continued existence uncertain.

At any rate, men fish for trout for reasons which can only be defined in terms of romanticism. This being the case, it is not surprising that the methods of trout fishing incorporate both practical measures and those designed to be ritually symbolic of the proper degree of devoutness. This often tends to dismay the beginner, for as intended, it conveys the impression that trout fishing is extremely complex and difficult. Since the beginner cannot distinguish between necessity and affectation, he may be overwhelmed by their sum total.

Trout are quite unaware of their exalted status. All the romance of trout fishing exists in the minds of the angler and is in no way shared by the fish. It is not a game in which the opponents agree upon certain rules and then engage in a contest in which such rules are binding. Nevertheless, the trout fisherman likes to think that such a circumstance exists. It pleases him to believe that trout are aware of his efforts to outsmart them and are equally determined to outsmart him. As in checkers, where a piece must be jumped when proffered, he comes to feel that trout are under much the same sort of obligation to rise to his fly whenever he presents it properly.

This is at least true in my case, for I indulge in just this sort of whimsy when I fish for trout.

One evening recently I worked my way upstream on nearby Furnace Brook (a stream about which I shall have more to say later) to a run that to me had become an enigma. A leaning tree afforded abundant shade at the head of the run, and a deeply undercut bank along one side virtually assured the presence of trout. Yet during one evening after another, I had failed to raise a trout in this extremely likely stretch.

I was absolutely certain that there were trout there, and the conviction that they were deliberately and consciously resisting my best efforts deepened with each unsuccessful attempt to take them.

A thick screen of long grass drooped from the undercut bank and trailed in the water. I drifted my fly within inches of this canopy as usual, and as usual it was ignored. Finally, I overshot my cast a bit, and the fly disappeared behind the curtain of trailing grass. I was on the verge of yanking the fly back before the leader snagged on the grass, when I noticed that the pliant tips allowed the leader to pass beneath them. I let the hidden fly continue on its way, and suddenly heard a resounding *blurp* from behind the grassy screen. I set the hook, and a dandy brown trout came rocketing out of his hiding place and jumped all over the run as certain rare browns have a habit of doing.

My elation at taking that particular fish was quite beyond rational justification. I experienced an illusion of triumph which contained not only the impression that I had finally succeeded in outfoxing a shrewd and calculating adversary, but that the trout had been made to know the humiliation of defeat.

This shows how silly it's possible to become. Trout do not play games; they have no concept of conquest or defeat, and unlike fishermen, they have no sense of pride to be guarded against puncture. Trout simply exist, possessed of sufficient natural shyness and prudence to avoid both obvious and subtle dangers, but vulnerable enough to fall for ruses which camouflage the danger signals. No trout has brains enough to realize that he is being "fished for," but the trout fisherman enhances his sport by picturing them as fully aware of this circumstance.

By way of example, consider the thoughts which usually accompany the choice of a fly. Let's say that no insects are hatching, no fish showing and the angler is forced to make an arbitrary choice. After considerable deliberation, usually pointless, he settles on a No. 14 Quill Gordon as his selection.

What is he thinking? That perhaps the trout in the stream have made a conscious resolution somewhat as follows: "Today we will scorn all patterns of artificial flies with the exception of the Quill Gordon. We will make things even tougher by ruling out everything but No. 14 Quill Gordons. Fishermen who fail to guess our preference will be out of luck. But if a fellow *does* tie on a No. 14 Quill Gordon we will all rise to it, for we are jolly good sports and always play by the rules."

For obvious reasons, fishermen do not admit, even to themselves, that they entertain any such naive and childish notions.

But if they refuse to dignify these notions by admission, they subconsciously nurture nebulous and unexpressed versions of these and other absurdities. For while the trout fisherman's efforts are ostensibly aimed at taking trout, his preoccupation is concerned with preserving the illusion that his elaborate methodology is at all times justified. He satisfies himself on this score by refusing to see trout for what they actually are, but as creatures endowed with imaginary characteristics which serve to create the desired image.

I have mentioned the nearby Chittenden Reservoir, and that on rare occasion it yields a huge trout. Since this does happen — although the chances against it are probably more than a thousand to one — those who fish the lake invariably have the possibility in mind and hair-raising tales of lunkers hooked and lost are extremely common. When you have heard one such yarn you have heard them all, for the teller invariably asserts in essence: "He was so big I just couldn't do a thing with him!"

This declaration is made in all seriousness, despite the fact that the fisherman had more than a hundred yards of stout spinning line on his reel and an open lake in which to play the fish. By declaring that he "couldn't do a thing with him," he means he couldn't do what he idiotically elected to try: to horse the big fish ashore by brute strength, moments after it was hooked.

But the tendency toward romanticism is so strong among fishermen that these tales are accepted at face value. The obvious truth — that the fisherman had only himself to blame — is rejected in order to preserve the titillating legend that

56

the Chittenden Reservoir is the home of awesome monsters possessed of inexorable brute strength.

A fisherman leaves a stream with an empty creel and declares to one and all that he "tried everything he had but couldn't find the fly they wanted." This clearly implies the notion that trout always "want" a fly of a particular pattern and substantiates my observation that trout fishermen tend to regard trout fishing as a game in which the trout consciously participate.

The defeated fishermen never lacks a sympathetic audience, for listeners share his quaint belief that all that stood between him and success was the trouts' jealously guarded secret. They have often found themselves in the same boat and are fully aware of the limits to which trout will go in order to fool fishermen. Here again, the possibility of failure because of commonplace reasons is instinctively dismissed. The unique ardor of the trout fisherman is best complimented by blaming failure, not on his own ineptness, but on the devastating cunning of his wily antagonist.

Such flights of fancy are not to be denounced, for it is by their indulgence that trout fishing becomes most keenly enjoyable. If we delude ourselves, as indeed we must, our harmless pretense serves a worthy cause. But although we may gain greater pleasure, this does not gainsay the fact that we have taken liberties with reality in order to do so.

Large brown trout are usually very hard fish to catch, and this has won them a reputation for intelligence and cunning which I strongly suspect is undeserved. Once a brown reaches trophy size he becomes more and more a night feeder and is hard to take during hours of daylight largely because he spends much of the day in a state of suspended animation, almost completely indifferent to food carried by the current and thus indifferent to any imitations offered by fishermen. Fishermen like to believe that big browns survive because they are wise enough to resist temptation, but I am inclined to believe that their survival is accomplished largely by settling into a daily stupor which places them beyond the reach of temptation.

The true test of a brown's sagacity comes when he is on the feed at night, or when he has been roused from his daytime lethargy by some unusual circumstance such as a hatch of exceptionally large flies or a sudden rise of water. Then, when he is on the alert and actively seeking food, he is likely to demonstrate no greater wisdom than do trout of other species.

Years ago I was worm fishing a stream on a hot day and had almost nothing to show for it. The water was low and clear, and although I drifted my bait into shaded pockets and under windfalls, I had caught only a pair of very small trout.

Finally I came to a favorite pool and worked it carefully and thoroughly. Time and again I guided my bait through the deepest part, but no trout grabbed it.

In the meantime, a heavy thunderstorm was in progress upstream from where I was fishing. Lightning zigzagged against a backdrop of purple clouds, the heavens rumbled ominously and I was prepared to make a run for my car at any moment. But it proved to be one of those storms which are violent but soon over. Before it could reach me the thunder died down and the dark clouds dispersed. I counted myself lucky to escape a soaking and then forgot about it.

A short time later, while I was still stubbornly fishing the same pool, I became conscious of a swelling sound in the upstream direction. I looked up and saw a minor flood of brown water rushing toward me. Bare rocks disappeared beneath the roily water, and soon the heavy flow swept into the pool.

I clamped on a heavier sinker, and put my biggest night crawler on the hook. Then I flipped the bait into the now brawling current at the head of the pool. The crawler was grabbed almost instantly, and I set the hook in a three-pound brown trout.

This fish had undoubtedly seen my bait each time it drifted through the pool, but the theory that he refused it because he was too smart can hardly be defended in the face of what happened eventually. Until the flood came along, the brown was in a characteristic daytime trance which gave me nothing to work on. Once his interest in food was awakened by the sudden rise in water, he became a pushover for a tumbling night crawler.

With prolonged experience, most trout fishermen reach the point where the taking of trout on bait becomes relatively unattractive. This dim view of bait fishing supposedly arises because of the conviction that it is unsportsmanlike, but I doubt very much that this is the true reason. It is suspect if for no other reason than it implies a nobility and gentility to which few trout fishermen, I least of all, can lay honest claim.

In my own case, I think the reason I am reluctant to use bait on trout is that it simplifies the process. When I take a trout on a worm I am keenly aware of the prosaic nature of the operation and no longer able to see trout in the romantic perspective essential to maximum enjoyment. Fly fishing permits and encourages this sentimental distortion of view, for its complexities are sufficient to disguise a certain amount of romantic liberty. A trout is a trout, whether taken on a worm or on a tiny dry fly, yet my concept of a trout while I am bait fishing is considerably less glamorous than the concept I have of the same fish while I am fly fishing. I am sure that my preference for fly fishing is due, in part, to this purely selfish consideration, and not at all in deference to the dictates of "sportsmanship."

No two people have the same sense of values, and I'm sure there are many fishermen who enjoy taking trout on bait fully as much as I enjoy taking them on flies. The same holds true for spinning enthusiasts, and for those whose persuasions lie at various points along this scale of preference.

Remember the old calendar pictures in which a lavishly equipped fly fisherman was caught in the act of furtively slipping a kid a five-spot for a lunker trout the kid had caught on his alder pole? These pictures have disappeared from the scene, and in all probability their ponderous humor was an exaggeration. Yet they contained the seeds of certain truths which are worthy of study.

Along the banks of trout streams will be forked sticks at the edges of deep pools, left by bait fishermen who propped their rods in the forks. Like the kid in the calendar picture, they lob out heavily weighted baits and then do nothing but sit and wait. This technique is looked down on by more sophisticated trout fishermen, but during the course of a season these bank fishermen usually haul more big trout from a given stream than do all the other fishermen combined.

In the first place, they use tempting bait — usually one or more night crawlers. In the second place, they unconsciously conceal the unnatural influence of the line on the bait, the biggest bugaboo in hook and line fishing.

They heave out their baits with complete disregard for the splash made by the heavy sinker and the fact that it probably alarms every trout in the pool. They do not expect early returns, however; they look on that single cast as a long-term investment. Once it is made, they intend only to sit tight.

The night crawler plunges to the bottom and lies there. The pool is deep and slow moving, so this is exactly what trout expect any night crawler to do. If the slow current acts on the line to any extent, its slight influence is absorbed by the heavy sinker. The drag factor is thus completely eliminated.

Absolute quiet prevails. Trout that may have been alarmed by the disturbance of that one cast gradually relax and once more go about their business. And the normal business of large trout, whenever they are interested in food, includes making periodic inspections of their domain, which consists of a slow and deliberate tour of their respective pools, with the intent of discovering something substantial in the form of food.

I have sat and watched enough quiet pools to learn that this is standard behavior among large trout, although it is a characteristic which escapes general attention. I suspect that while smaller trout can depend on stream currents to bring sufficient food past a single location, large trout find the same amount of food inadequate. To satisfy their greater needs they are forced to seek out food over a wide area.

These cruising fish usually show little interest in the surface, focusing their attention almost exclusively on the bottom. They dip down to make close inspection of any item which attracts their interest and gobble it if it proves edible.

The bank fisherman, in all likelihood, is quite unaware of this habit. He sips through one can of beer and goes to work on a second. He is pleasantly relaxed and places his trust entirely in what he imagines to be luck. To recast, move to another spot or otherwise attempt to engineer his own success is contrary to his philosophy. Success, as far as he's concerned, rests in the hands of fate, and he is content to let it lie there.

No conscious technique could be more deadly, for a lunker trout has set out to make the rounds of the pool. He probes here and there, a circumstance of which the fisherman remains blissfully unaware. Eventually the big trout comes over the night crawler, turns quickly and scoops it up without the least hesitation. And why not? There is absolutely nothing in the night crawler's presence or appearance to arouse suspicion.

The fisherman comes awake in a hurry when his rod takes on a slow bend as the trout, the night crawler already swallowed, resumes his cruise. The fisherman gives a mighty heave, and for the next few moments all is commotion. Finally, more thanks to stout tackle than angling finesse, the trout is hauled ashore. The elated fisherman admires his prize and cheerfully attributes his success to a remarkable stroke of luck.

It is ironic that the trout fishing method held in the lowest esteem embodies all that is required to take trout, even the largest: inducement that is innocent of visible (to the trout) cause for suspicion and caution. It is equally ironic that the majority of those who employ it are ignorant of the reason for its deadly potential and fish with the impression that they are merely taking potluck.

Although bottom fishing will account for large trout that are not easily fooled by other methods, few fishermen care to fish that passively and patiently. As soon as they fish more aggressively, natural presentation must be achieved by manipulation. Otherwise, drag will have the same adverse effect that it has in dry fly fishing.

Unsuccessful bait fishermen are usually those who fail to appreciate the significance of drag, while those who consistently make good catches do everything possible to eliminate it. They use light leaders (in the interest of flexibility), as little sinker weight as possible (none at all whenever conditions permit) and fish with hooks of the smallest practical size. And in most cases these drag-conscious fishermen prefer to fish upstream for the same reason that dry fly fishermen do so: to allow the bait to drift with the current with the least possible restraint.

Another thing which distinguishes the accomplished bait fisherman is his realization that worms are not the most fetching bait he can use on trout. More trout are caught on worms than on all other natural baits combined, but only because worms are the bait most commonly used.

Actually, trout have little opportunity to feed on earthworms, other than on those that are draped on hooks. Under normal conditions, streams contain virtually no earthworms, and in spite of popular belief, I doubt that any substantial number is washed into streams by even the heaviest rains. Proof of scarcity becomes evident with the examination of stomach contents. Worms are found in few trout gullets, including those of trout caught in high, roily water. That trout look on worms as highly desirable food is beyond question, but the fact remains that earthworms are not common to their experience, and this element of strangeness can reasonably be assumed to constitute a negative factor.

On the other hand, every stream supports many forms of life which trout regard as equally delectable, if not even more desirable. And it stands to reason that an advantage is gained by using bait that is fully as attractive as a worm and, at the same time, reassuringly familiar.

It is for this reason that some of the most successful fishermen I have known spend considerable time along streams with a dip net, turning over rocks in the riffles and scooping up a variety of organisms which they use on trout with deadly effect. It is because of the attraction that these forms of life hold for trout, and other fish, that they are forced to hide under rocks in order to survive. Consequently, any that can be hung on a hook usually make superlative trout bait.

Among such baits are hellgrammites, small crayfish, salamanders, sculpins and any nymphs or larvae large enough to thread on a tiny hook. Most common of all are the stick caddis larvae which cling to the upper sides of rocks at the bottom of the stream. That they can survive in plain view is proof that trout do not relish them to any extent when protected by their tough covering, but when this is removed, and the larva lightly impaled on a No. 12 hook, they will take trout where the juiciest worm may go begging.

In addition to these items, others will turn up which may defy classification but which may produce spectacular results when used as bait.

One fisherman told me of finding gelatinous masses (possibly salamander eggs) on the undersides of rocks at the mouth of a tiny feeder stream. Out of curiosity he tried hanging small gobs on his hook, and discovered that they were tough enough to stay put if handled gently. He also discovered that the trout couldn't seem to leave this unconventional bait alone. Unfortunately, he declared sadly, his supply was soon exhausted and no amount of searching could produce more.

The same fisherman also showed me a sample of some large larvae he had discovered in another small stream. They were dark, fat and rubberlike in appearance. They were outside my experience, and the best I could do was hazard a guess that they were larvae of the crane fly. I suspect, however, that this was incorrect.

Whatever they were, according to my fisherman friend, trout went for them as eagerly as they had gone for the egg masses. Again, his supply was small and irreplaceable — but he murdered the trout while it lasted.

There was a time when I found fascination in just such experimental bait fishing, but it has lost most of its appeal because of a personal eccentricity which I have already mentioned. But I learned much about trout during this period, as will others who explore the same possibilities.

When spinning first became popular in this country, immediately after the end of World War II, I turned to it with enthusiasm. But this enthusiasm has also waned. Nowadays I resort to bait fishing and spinning for trout only when conditions make these moves imperative. Only within the contexts of fly fishing can I picture trout as I wish to perceive them. I am not ashamed to indulge my whims in the interest of pleasure, but I feel better about it for doing so knowingly.

Most bewildering of all to the beginner, perhaps, is the matter of fly patterns. What he reads and hears creates the impression that the secret of success is in selecting precisely the proper fly at any given time. He infers that trout of the moment will rise to one particular pattern, and that one only. Therefore, by some mysterious means, he must select that single pattern from among a staggering number of possibilities. He also comes to believe that if by some miracle he hits on the right choice, the battle is virtually won.

The probable truth is that he would do just as well to make a blind choice. Many fishermen have written at great length about such things as matching the hatch, favorite patterns, imitative equivalents and much, much more. Put all of these observations together, and there emerges a hodgepodge of confusing nonsense.

In *The Fisherman's Handbook of Trout Flies,* written by Donald Du Bois, there is a listing that contains no less than 5939 different trout fly patterns. The text is fascinating, and I enjoyed it thoroughly. Most intriguing are the author's calculations by which he identifies the astronomical number of patterns that is theoretically possible. Since each fly is supposedly tied to meet a particular need, this presupposes a day, an hour or a minute, during which each of the 5939 will be preferred by the trout over the remaining 5938. Experience will prove that trout can be discriminating and selective to an exasperating degree. But as common sense would lead one to suspect, their selectivity is not such that 5939 alternatives are required to assure its satisfaction.

While selectivity is supposedly a critical factor in all fly fishing, I am inclined to believe that it is of relatively minor importance in most phases and of major significance only in dry fly fishing. Even in this area, trout do not regularly exhibit the narrowly defined preferences with which they are generally credited. Periods of maximum selectivity are relatively rare, and at the other extreme are interludes when they will rise to almost anything. In between lies a middle ground, marked by a willingness to respond to well-presented flies which vary considerably in pattern and size. Happily, this circumstance prevails much of the time.

When my son Mike was very young, he pestered me to take him fly fishing. There is a deep hole in Furnace Brook which local youngsters use as a swimming hole, but it is heavily populated with trout which seem undisturbed by the swimming, and which rise all over the pool most evenings after the last swimmer has left. They would give Mike something to cast to, I knew, so we approached the pool one evening at dusk.

I had rigged Mike's line with the stub of a tapered leader, discounting that he would hook a trout in any event, but figuring that he would snag plenty of brush in his flailing. And in the same vein, I took along a box of bedraggled dry flies which I had discarded as having no value, save for the hooks.

Small trout were in evidence everywhere, and Mike had at them excitedly. Just as I expected, I was busy freeing his fly from the brush behind him much of the time, but between hang-ups he was happily doing what he imagined to be dry fly fishing for rising trout.

I was sharing his enjoyment when a lunker of a brown trout suddenly rose majestically in the center of the pool. His rise was that slow head-and-tail roll which large trout make, so deliberate that I could make out the big red spots against the rich golden color of his exposed side. He moved upstream a bit and came up again, cruised toward the side of the pool and showed himself once more.

I grabbed the rod away from Mike and made a frantic search of my sorry collection of flies for something that might bring him up when tied to the stubby leader. The best bet seemed a heavily palmered No. 8, a big powderpuff of a fly that I had tied for some long-forgotten reason. I put it on as quickly as possible, and then waited. When the big brown came up again, I dropped the bushy fly a bit upstream from him and quickly handed the rod to Mike.

The gob of hackle drifted over the fish, and he rolled up and took it without the slightest show of either haste or hesitation. Mike, who had never hooked a fish on a dry fly in his life, simply stood transfixed. I let out a yell that may have been heard all over town, and Mike heaved on the rod. But it was too late; the brown had already found feathers not to his liking and had spat them out.

68

The irony of the situation was almost too painful to bear, and I shall not dwell on it. Suffice it to say that the brown's willingness to rise to that particular fly illustrates the fact that the fisherman usually enjoys much more latitude in the matter of pattern selection than is generally acknowledged.

For here was a huge brown trout, supposedly the most selective of all trout, rising to mayflies. This was clearly apparent, for a brisk hatch of mayflies was in progress and they were all of one type and size. By all the sacred rules of fly fishing, the only way to have taken that trout on a dry fly was to select a pattern and size which matched the appearance of the living insects. Yet this "necessity" was rudely refuted by what transpired. Instead of "matching the hatch," a ritual supposedly of sacramental importance, I tied on a fly that bore not the slightest resemblance to the hatching insects. And in spite of this act of heresy, the trout promptly rose and took it.

There is a catechism of trout fishing which is rich in contrived complexities, and which the inexperienced tend to accept without question and hold in reverence. Actually, fly fishing for trout is considerably less complicated than the romantic notions which it tends to inspire. It has its profundities, but these are encountered in a context that is relatively simple. True, trout are so difficult to fool that far more resist the fisherman's best efforts than are taken in by them. Yet the fisherman has usually done his best, and can do no more, when he has observed principles that are relatively few in number and fundamental in nature.

Most important by far, in my opinion, is the matter of presentation. Unfortunately, this often receives too little attention because of the prior belief that the "right" fly is the panacea, and that a "wrong" choice of pattern dooms one to failure. As for me I have long since resigned myself to fishing the wrong fly, for the simple reason that I doubt very much that there is ever a right fly. Even if there were, I'd much rather fish the wrong fly right than to fish the right fly wrong. I have strong faith in *any* dry fly that is fished without drag, and very little faith in any pattern that is allowed to drag.

In dry fly fishing, the prevention of drag is the big problem — and there is no stock solution. It is not nearly as much a matter of leader length, tippet diameter or even casting skill, as that of correctly appraising the water in advance and deducing the probable effect of its various currents on line and leader. This is a knack that comes only with experience, but once it is acquired the fisherman sizes up each new situation in this light as a matter of course.

He will strive for perfect presentation, but this is usually an impossibility. The course over which a dry fly drifts is almost always marked by various means of judging the degree to which the fly responds to the influence of the current: bubbles, flecks of foam and the flow of the water itself. Close observation will invariably disclose a discrepancy between the pace of the fly and that of the water. A fleck of foam, for instance, will either pass the drifting fly, or the fly will pull ahead of the foam. Almost never do the two maintain the constant positional relationship that would be proof of a drag-free float.

Even if perfection is beyond attainment, success can be won by a sufficiently close approach to perfection. The secret of closing this gap so that it falls within the limits of trout tolerance is largely a matter of realizing what must be done. In other words, the fisherman who recognizes the imperative nature of this requirement will shift his position or modify his cast to avoid the drag. And he will fool trout by virtue of this single circumstance.

Of less importance than presentation, but considerably more important than the choice of pattern, is the matter of size. During much of the time that trout are feeding at the surface they will rise to a No. 12 or No. 14 dry fly which gives them no cause for alarm. There are other times, however, when they will only rise to flies that are much smaller. This tendency increases as the fishing season advances, probably because the mayflies which hatch late in the season are usually much smaller than those of May and June.

Trout must be hard put to derive sustenance from these tiny insects, and it seems logical to assume that they would welcome the appearance of more substantial items. The mysteries of trout fishing often defy logic, however, as they do in this case. For trout feeding on midges will usually ignore a No. 12 or a No. 14 dry fly, and although the reason may lie beyond human understanding, it is a fact which the fisherman must honor if he is to take the trout in question. Instinctively he welcomes the need to use tiny flies, as they provide him with romantic pride in any subsequent success. As a result, he tends to exaggerate the frequency with which the need for tiny flies arises, and he also tends to exaggerate the success he achieves by their employment.

Nonfishing friends sometime drop in when I'm tying flies, and I bask in the amazement they express when I show them the smallest flies I have in stock.

"Yes, indeed," I say grandly when they ask me if it is really possible to catch trout on such tiny hooks. Then I exploit their gullibility by a dissertation which implies that while ordinary fishermen could scarcely hope to, I, by virtue of great skill, land many whoppers without difficulty.

It is now late August. Streams have held at good levels, thanks to a wet summer, and the hatches of larger flies have continued longer than usual. It has been only in the past couple of weeks that I have had to use really small flies, and I estimate the result of my "great skill" about as follows:

Of the trout I have raised to midges I have hooked less than half. Of the half that I have raised, I have popped the leader against one out of every five, and nearly half of those safely hooked have come off before I could land them. As for the "whoppers," the biggest of those taken has been all of thirteen inches long.

Those whose knowledge of dry fly fishing consists largely of what they read, often entertain the belief that the demand of late-season, low-water fishing can be met at no cost to production. The fisherman simply ties tippets of 6X or 7X to his leader, bends on a No. 20 fly and goes on taking as many trout as before. In actual practice, it doesn't work out that way.

Late summer action usually begins at dusk, a time when it is almost impossible to see a No. 18, or smaller, dry fly on the water. The fisherman is seldom certain of his fly's location, so the rise of a taking fish usually comes at an unanticipated spot. This causes a split second of delay in setting the hook, for which the angler attempts to compensate with a harder than usual yank. Providing the fish is hooked at all, this is often more than his wispy tippet can take.

In any event, the hooks are so tiny they fail to grab a good share of the time. When they do, their bite is so superficial that they often pull out or work free in spite of every effort to be gentle. Fishing with extremely small dry flies is a fascinating facet of trout fishing, but its reputation of efficiency is due largely to the fisherman's tendency to forget the many fish that are missed, broken off and otherwise lost, and to remember only those (relatively few) that he manages to land. The fishermen who can reconcile themselves to this high incidence of loss are few in number. Thus, while many acclaim this phase of fly fishing in the abstract, those who actually practice it are but a small fraction of those who sing its praises.

In spite of all testimony to the contrary, the least important consideration in fly fishing is the choice of pattern. In this respect, the term "pattern" should not be construed to include sharp departures from conventional design, for unique differences do sometimes result in deadly effectiveness. The term "pattern" is used here to designate variations of color, materials, and the like among standard fly forms: streamers, bucktails, dry flies and wet flies.

To suggest that pattern is of relatively small importance is to flout one of trout fishing's oldest and most sacred beliefs. It has long been accepted as gospel, for instance, that brook trout, particularly wilderness brookies, are especially fond of gaudy wet flies such as the Parmachene Belle, Silver Doctor, Montreal, Royal Coachman and the like. The Gray Ghost streamer supposedly casts a spell over landlocked salmon, and the Quill Gordon is often described as the "most killing" of all dry fly patterns. Yet I suspect that there is little in fact to substantiate such notions, and that if the truth were known it would indicate that the choice of pattern matters far less than fishermen are pleased to believe.

Visiting fishermen sometimes ask me what patterns I recommend for particular Vermont streams, and they are visibly shocked when I tell them that I don't think it makes much difference what patterns they use. Of course, mine is just one opinion against many, and quite possibly wrong. But I have sufficient faith in my skepticism to test it from time to time. Results to date have tended to solidify my conviction that the belief that for each day, or hour, there is a single pattern of ultimate appeal is nothing more than a myth.

Because of this conviction I have always intended to tie a supply of scarlet dry flies, or purple or orange; wings, hackles, tails and bodies all the same outrageous color, and fish with nothing else for a spell. I've never got around to it, but only because I'm too lazy. I may be wrong, but I have a strong suspicion that these flies would account for fully as many trout as would the most painstaking selection from among standard patterns.

What I *have* done many times is to switch from a pattern that is producing to one that is markedly different. If the trout are coming well to an Adams, for instance, and I break it off in a fish or in the brush, I replace it with a fanwing Royal Coachman to see what will happen. And what invariably happens is that I take trout as readily on the fanwing as I had been doing on the completely different Adams.

Few fishermen get to see this side of the picture, for fishing time for most is too precious to waste on experimentation. When they run into a streak of luck they wouldn't change to

74

another pattern for love or money, for they are hooked on the conviction that the pattern they are using is responsible for their success. They come away with a good catch, and the ingrained belief that with no other pattern could they have done as well.

The next time out they tie on the same pattern, and perhaps fail to raise a fish. They try others with the same result. Do they sensibly conclude that the fish simply aren't feeding? Very seldom. Instead, they entertain the belief that the trout have transferred their preference to some other pattern which would work wonders if only they, the fishermen, could come up with it.

In much the same vein, I have often ignored the advice of guides and tied on a streamer pattern other than the one land-locked salmon allegedly were "taking." As nearly as I can judge, this deliberate contrariness has paid off about as well as has compliance with popular preference. If a guide tells me that salmon are hitting a Goldenhead, I am happy to believe him. For then I feel pretty sure that they will also hit just about any streamer I choose to tie on.

Here again, the supposedly supereffectiveness of a particular pattern is seldom put to the test. Few fishermen are brash enough to tie on anything but the local favorite at what they imagine to be the unnecessary risk of failure. Thus, while a particular streamer pattern may account for virtually all the salmon taken on a lake during a spell of hot fishing, this circumstance is robbed of significance by the failure to give other patterns a try. Unless I miss my guess, dozen of others would have produced as well.

Trout fishing has little justification other than the enjoyment one derives from it, and it is probably true that many trout fishermen gain maximum enjoyment by entertaining beliefs that are little other than romantic. It is not my intention to belittle the traditional fallacies which add to the fascination of trout fishing. I lean on them heavily myself, and my pleasure is intensified by the realization that I am playing make-believe for the sheer fun of it.

What this amounts to is that in the actual business of taking trout I am guided by the relatively few basic principles upon which I believe success depends. These principles do, indeed, make exacting demands upon the fisherman, but they are nothing more than common sense concessions to the powers of discrimination which trout possess and manifest. At the same time, I *picture* trout as much shrewder, far more wary and ever so much more capricious than they really are. Although I take trout by ordinary means, I delude myself by pretending to believe that there is an element of magic in my methods, and by regarding trout as fish which can be fooled only by occult maneuvers.

4

A Quizzical Look
at Fly Fishing

THE TERM "fly fishing" seems to apply explicitly to the taking of fish on lures designed to imitate flying insects. Actually, only a small part of that which is accepted as fly fishing has anything to do with real flies or their imitations. While some phases of fly fishing require a high order of skill, others demand only moderate proficiency — and some call for virtually no skill at all.

As an example, take the matter of trolling streamers and bucktails for landlocked salmon during those weeks of early spring when landlocks frequent the surface. All that's required is to pay out perhaps fifty feet of line behind the canoe and then hold the rod until a fish strikes. Anybody who can sit in a canoe is likely to do as well as the most experienced salmon fisherman.

The trolled streamer supposedly imitates a smelt or other bait fish. Despite this, and the lack of skill involved, the process comes under the heading of fly fishing by popular assent, and the fisherman who takes salmon on a trolled streamer thereby is entitled to a distinction which he could not claim had he taken salmon on a trolled wobbler or laced-on smelt.

My saltwater fishing experience is very limited, a fact which I continually deplore. But I remember a night of fast fishing for school stripers in a New Hampshire tidal river. My companions and I had anchored our skiff in a strong current and used fly rods to twitch sand eels against the outgoing tide. The slender little bait fish put almost no strain on our rods, and, fished without sinkers, rode just under the surface.

Soon we could hear fish breaking and moving upstream. Shortly thereafter they began hitting our sand eels. They hooked themselves on the strike and fought like demons in the fast current. For the fellow who likes to feel strong fish on a fly rod, it was wonderful fishing.

I told a fly fishing friend about it later, and he obviously regarded our use of natural bait as an unfortunate circumstance.

"Too bad you didn't try a streamer," he said. "They probably would have hit it."

"But they hit the sand eels almost as fast as we let them out," I declared.

"Yeah, but you could have taken 'em on *streamers.*"

To my friend, this would have made a great difference — the difference between fly fishing, a sacred institution, and bait fishing, a lowly pursuit. As for me, when the distinction becomes that small it loses all significance. For others it is of great importance, every inch of the way to the very vanishing point.

My earliest concept of a fly was the standard wet fly. This was because it was the only type of fly used by the fishermen I knew during my early youth, and I gullibly accepted the theory that even the most gaudy patterns somehow imitated the natural flies upon which trout fed. The fact that I had spent many hours on streams without once spotting any insects which they remotely resembled never prompted me to question this belief. I watched fishermen skitter their wet flies along the surface, and I saw trout come up and smack them. This, too, I took for granted, confident that these fishermen of adult wisdom were tempting trout by imitating the natural behavior and appearance of their regular source of food.

That I should have done so seems incredible. Streams were my regular beat. I had overturned rocks in riffles, studied pools by the hour and bait fished for trout with a burning passion. And never, in all those hours, had I observed anything that looked the least like a "Professor," "Montreal" or "Silver Doctor." Furthermore, I had never seen insects of any description skitter upstream along the surface of strong currents, let alone see trout rise to any such oddly behaving items.

There are thousands of wet fly patterns, but while they differ with respect to color and materials from which they are made, these standard patterns conform to a single, traditional design: flat "wings" that lie along the top of the hook, a "tail," a tapered body and hackle fibers which project downward from under the base of the wings and which supposedly are an imitation of legs. Generations of anglers have fished with these patterns, and all evidence seems to indicate that they have done so in the belief that an imitative quality is inherent in the design.

The truth is, of course, that the conventional wet fly bears not the slightest resemblance to any living insect, and when it is twitched along the surface, or barely beneath, its behavior is as anomalous as its appearance. That it will take fish is a proven fact, but that fish mistake it for an insect, belittles their powers of perception.

The term "fly fishing" has come to have a far broader meaning than its literal interpretation suggests. It has been stretched to include taking bass on imitation frogs made of deer hair, catching tarpon and other saltwater species on six-inch streamers, provoking pike to attack jumbo popping bugs and fooling Atlantic salmon with feather creations of great beauty and artistry, but which have no counterparts in the insect world. Since a certain prestige accrues to the taking of fish "on flies," it goes without saying that the concept of what constitutes a "fly" will be most generously elastic.

If the exalted connotations associated with fly fishing are in many cases mythical, does it have real virtues worthy of preservation? In my opinion it does.

One of the most significant is the type of rod employed. Actually, the fly rod is the deadliest of all rods for it gives hooked fish the least chance of escape. Yet while in the process of playing fish, the fisherman enjoys the feeling that the battle is touch and go from start to finish — and so it is, though not because of the rod. This feeling leads to the satisfying illusion that each good fish landed is a triumph executed in the face of highly unfavorable odds and evidence of a high order of skill.

Another important consideration is that "fly" casting requires coordination and timing greatly in excess of the demands of other forms of casting. No great skill is required to sling out lures with spinning and bait casting outfits, and with practice one reaches the point where he can extract nearly the full potential from each. In fly fishing, just the opposite holds true.

Although I would never do so with a spinning or bait casting rod, I sometimes rig up a fly rod and strive for distance on my back lawn. Fortunately, I am well screened from view, and my well-established reputation for idiosyncrasy is spared further amplification.

I work out maybe thirty feet of line and marvel at the ease with which I can keep it in the air; the merest flick of the rod seems to suffice, and the effortless process seems open to almost limitless extenuation. I strip additional footage from the reel and release the loose coils on the next forward cast. The stripped line shoots through the guides so forcefully that the reel turns against the click as the extended line tugs at it. This seems to be further evidence of almost unlimited possibility.

I continue to strip more line, and results remain constant. By putting a bit more zing into the forward cast I can "shoot" each addition of slack. And since I haven't even extended myself, the prospect of working out the entire thirty-five yards of fly line poses as an attainable goal.

But each addition to the "shoot" forces me to add a bit to

my backcast, and with exasperating suddenness I lose the rhythm and timing which, until now, have made the process seem so simple. One moment I can bite into the backcast at precisely the proper moment to gain the required leverage. The next, with only a few more feet of line in the air, I can't find the inertia against which the rod must work. I shorten up a bit, and all is fine again. Heartened and inspired, I strip a little more line — and am promptly reduced to ineffectual flailing as before.

I resort to my version of the double haul, but this doesn't help much. It would, if I could master the technique, but I have never been able to. Sometimes I can pull it off, gaining speed and resistance which result in a gratifying gain of distance. On the next cast, alas, I'm likely to come up with a rodful of nothing. It is all very maddening.

I have discussed this source of frustration many times with my long-time friend, H. G. Tapply. Tap, well known to millions of sportsmen for his "Sportman's Notebook" which appears monthly in *Field & Stream,* is a splendid fly caster. He is a picture of fluid grace to watch, the narrow loop of his backcast snaking behind him to be caught and driven forward at precisely the moment of maximum leverage. He shows no signs of effort or strain, and the observer is given the impression that the limit of Tap's casting range is determined only by the amount of line he chooses to strip from his reel. But this is true only up to a point; then comes the futile flailing I have mentioned. Why should it be so easy up to the cutoff, then so impossible? Tap and I have shoved this question around many times, but we've never come up with an answer.

We have arrived at no answer of our own, but Tap was once offered a bit of advice by an onlooker. Tap was fishing a large stream at the time and had spotted a fish rising far out in the river. The trout was rising steadily, and ripe for plucking, but the range was too great and Tap's strongest bids fell yards short of the target. Finally he waded ashore in defeat and remarked to the bystander that the fish was beyond reach of the likes of him. His observer, as so often happens, was at no loss for a solution. "Why don't you tie on a longer leader?" he asked in all seriousness.

I'd feel better about my fly casting limitations if I could believe that my rods were partly to blame. But to learn the sad truth that the blame lies entirely within me I need only drop in at the Orvis Company in Manchester, Vermont, and get Wes Jordan to demonstrate one of the rods he designs. Wes, who for years has designed the superb rods for which Orvis is famous, is widely recognized as one of the great, if not the greatest, rodmakers in the history of angling. Less generally known is the fact that Wes can exercise in his fly rods a very large portion of the guts he builds into them.

What makes this so remarkable is that Wes Jordan is over seventy years old and is just a little guy. I'd guess his weight at no more than a hundred and thirty pounds, and that may be on the heavy side. I'm nearly twenty years younger, at least fifty pounds heavier and half a foot taller. I've worked at fly casting since in my teens and certainly should be able to out-cast a frail-looking little man of over seventy. Hah!

Wes invites me to try the selected rod first. It has the feel of latent power typical of all Orvis rods, and I dip into this reserve as deeply as I can. I put everything I have into a final heave, then turn the rod over to Wes.

What follows is utterly demoralizing. I thought I was making the rod work? As nearly as I can judge, Wes takes up at about the point where I left off. Backcasts whistle behind him at almost bullet speed, and at exactly the proper instant the forward casts lever against the extended line with explosive energy. More line goes out, and Wes gains even more speed and drive by double hauling. Soon I've seen a hundred feet of line laid out by a little bantam of a man who looks incapable of the feat, but who goes to work with a rod as though he were hung together with coil springs and rubber bands.

I drive home muttering vows that I'll learn to push out as much line or break my arm trying. It turns out, of course, that I do neither. I can't get the line out, for unlike Wes Jordan, I'm not a bundle of coiled springs and catlike reflexes — and it's impossible to break an arm flailing against nothing.

Perhaps I've overemphasized this aspect of fly fishing, but I feel that it is a major factor in the sport's unique appeal. Among a dozen bait casters or spin fishermen there will be very little difference in casting ability, unless some are the rankest of beginners. But among the same number of fly fishermen there is likely to be a wide range of casting skill, and at each level each fisherman will be doing his darndest to improve his technique. There is never a more worthy antagonist than oneself, and fly casting is a proper arena for this private conflict.

Of course, the ability to make extremely long casts is seldom of high importance in fly fishing. Accuracy and delicacy of presentation count for much more, but all belong in the same context. They combine to make fly casting a much more interesting challenge than the casting involved in any other method of angling.

Thus, while the greater thrills of fly fishing are often attributed to the dramatics of the "rise," I suspect that this is only a partial accounting. Of equal importance are the triumph of presentation by means of an art that requires great coordination and timing, plus the illusion of bucking heavy odds created by the fly rod's deceptive appearance of frailty.

I am sometimes visited by fishermen of great enthusiasm, but small experience. Almost invariably, these individuals have read everything about fishing they can get their hands on, and their heads are stuffed with a conglomeration of technical specifics which puts me to shame. Because I have written about fishing, these visitors assume that I have resolved the whole business in terms of leader calibrations, rod actions, line weights, pattern specifications and all the rest — matters about which they are academically astute, and which they are ever eager to discuss. My predicament immediately becomes embarrassing, for I can only mumble vague and evasive answers when I'm obviously expected to make crisp pronouncements about technicalities which, in truth, I'm too much of a slob to worry about.

But whenever I take these visitors to a stream, it is usually apparent that they have no overall concept of how to go about the job.

In fishing it is highly important to understand the general

pattern of the most appropriate approach, for only then can one converge on the problem with those technical measures which are relevant. As an example, take the matter of "fly" fishing for smallmouth bass. The most effective method consists of casting to the shoreline with popping bugs, streamers and large wet flies. The idea is to drop the lure near a likely hangout, then cause it to stir up a commotion by means of a jerky retrieve. Pauses, slight tremors and sudden "pops" combine to pose a tantalizing challenge which often results in savage attack.

Since the lures used in this fishing are relatively large, and thus meet with considerable air resistance, the fisherman who tries to cast them on a long leader which tapers to a fine point immediately meets with difficulty. He realizes that a shorter and stiffer leader will make his casting much easier, but if he has acquired a categorical faith in long, finely tapered leaders, he is plagued by a dilemma. Won't a short, stiff leader cut down his chances?

To both his relief and surprise, he eventually discovers that apparently the smallmouths couldn't care less. They come to his bug or streamer as readily as before. It took me a long time to accept this as a fact, for the theory that a long, fine leader is a help in all situations seems too logical to question. But I am at last convinced that the short, heavy leader which facilitates casting will not cut down the number of strikes in the least.

Does this mean that smallmouths can be taken on short, coarse leaders under all circumstances? It most certainly does not. It is a far different story when bass are rising to a hatch of mayflies. I shall have more to say about this in a later chapter, so let it suffice here to declare that when rising to mayflies, smallmouths often make demands that put trout to shame. They tend to ignore any dry fly that shows the slightest sign of drag, and a long leader, tapered to a fine point, becomes an absolute necessity.

This is a circumstance worthy of study, for it illustrates the important truth that the same fish may behave quite differently in different situations. As long as a smallmouth lies along the shore, he is likely to pounce on a popping bug that has landed in his vicinity, even though the bug may be tied to a heavy leader only a few feet long. Let the same bass begin rising to mayflies, and he will tolerate only a nearly perfect presentation.

Much of the significance is missed if one concludes that this is a peculiarity confined to smallmouth bass. Instead, this duality on the part of smallmouths illustrates an eccentricity of behavior which virtually all fish manifest and points up the difference between two distinct patterns of fly fishing. In one, the matter of leader length and diameter matters little to the fish; in the other, it is of vital importance. To me, it is of far more value to recognize this basic distinction than to know the exact calibrations for leaders of various lengths and weights.

Armed with this general knowledge, a fisherman is not going to make his casting unnecessarily difficult by using long, light leaders where they serve no practical purpose. On the other hand, he will immediately fish long and fine whenever the situation calls for him to do so. His leaders may not conform exactly to the specifications recommended by experts, but they will tend to satisfy those requirements which are of concern to the fish.

In addition to serving as a connection between line and lure, a leader serves one or the other of two completely different purposes. One is to impart movement to the lure in an effort to excite and arouse fish to the point of striking. The other is aimed at precisely the opposite effect: to eliminate any pressure upon the lure so that it may manifest the unaffected drift of a natural item of food.

Cautious, difficult fish are often described as "gut shy," but I'm sure you could toss unattached leaders into a stream by the gross without disconcerting such fish in the slightest. Their interest is focused on the lure alone, and the leader is important only in the way by which the lure reacts to its influence or demonstrates its freedom therefrom. In one case, provocative action is required to draw strikes; in the other, any abnormal movement will result in alarm and suspicion. In neither case are the fish conscious of the leader itself, but only of its effect upon the lure.

The line of demarcation between provocative and imitative fly fishing is as clear-cut with respect to trout as it is with respect to bass. There is a long, deep pool on my favorite stretch of Furnace Brook, and a few evenings ago I reached this pool toward the tag end of dusk. There had been no previous hatch of any consequence, but as I approached the pool it suddenly became alive with rising fish. Enough light remained so that I could distinguish the emerging flies against the sky, and I saw that they were very tiny.

I had been using a No. 12 dry fly, but was reluctant to change. Always lazy, I tried the easy way first and put the No. 12 over the feeding fish. That it was studiously ignored came as no surprise.

With no relish for the job, I found a seat on a log and tied on a 6X tippet by the light of my flashlight. Then I tied on a No. 18 fly which I could hardly see in my hand, let alone hope to follow on the water.

The trout went for the tiny fly eagerly. Fishing more or less blindly, I missed many, struck at others that came for naturals rather than my fly, hooked some which promptly came off and actually managed to land several rainbows and browns that were around a foot in length. All in all, it was a fine flurry of action.

When it became almost completely dark, a much larger fish began rising at the base of the undercut bank directly across stream from me. I switched my full attention to him, of course, with high confidence that I could get him to take the small fly by repeated casting. Unfortunately, my confidence was misplaced. Dozens of casts later the trout was still blurping away in the same location, his indifference to my offering so convincingly demonstrated that I was forced to concede defeat.

I withdrew only long enough to switch to the stubby remnants of a worn-down tapered leader and to tie on a scraggly hair bug which I had tied on a No. 8 long shank hook for just such situations. I dropped the bug above him and gave it a couple of quick twitches when I judged it to be opposite his station. He promptly nailed it with a savage attack that threw water high in the air and which made a glorious *kertowse*.

The trout tore up and down the pool in grand style, but it was a vain effort on his part. With a No. 8 hook in his jaw, and fighting a leader that probably tested at least ten pounds, he didn't really stand a chance. I soon had him in the net, guessed his length at fifteen inches and turned him loose — a brown trout that was nothing to crow about as browns go, but one that I felt very smug about taking.

The circumstance of the taking makes this particular fish worthy of mention here, for he is conveniently illustrative of the distinction with which we are concerned. This brown obviously detected flaws in my presentation during the period while I was attempting to fool him with an imitation of the insects he was feeding on steadily. I had been unable to effect a single drift sufficiently free of unnatural influence, for you may be sure he would have risen to my fly during any float in which he saw no cause for suspicion. Unable to attain the necessary perfection, I had been stymied.

The solution, the hair bug, represented temptation in quite another form. Here was no mere approximation of the commonplace, a crude imitation to be coolly disdained among an abundance of the real things. Instead, this appeared as a mysterious "something," in isolation and without known standards by which the normalcy of its behavior could be judged. It posed a stirring challenge which the trout, emboldened by darkness, simply couldn't resist. Since the bug's erratic action would have been the same, regardless of the leader's length and diameter, these factors were of virtually no importance in that particular situation.

A Quizzical Look at Fly Fishing

The important thing for the fisherman to realize is that in all imitative fly fishing he is bucking a shrewd, objective evaluation of his lure's behavioral conformity, while in provocative fly fishing he is deliberately turning to anomaly to create those intense emotions which result in indiscretion.

By way of further illustration, I'll draw on a habit which wins me a fair bonus of fish during the course of a season, and which is absurdly simple. Each time I move upstream to a new position, I make a long downstream cast with my dry fly and let it trail as I work my way against the current. Since I'm likely to forget about it if the going is difficult, I have learned to leave the line free against the reel to avoid a popped tippet in case of a strike on the tight line.

Strikes do result, with enough frequency to make the simple trick worthwhile; the reel lets out a sudden screech, usually while I'm fumbling for solid footing, and I'm fast to a fish that I did very little to earn. The important thing, however, is that these strikes come after I have finished putting the same fly over the same water with all the naturalness at my command. In this guise, the fly has been deemed unacceptable, but when presented in quite another manner, the same fly has been judged by standards that obviously are altogether different.

In the first instance, I am sure the fly was avoided because of the leader's influence, this in spite of its long length and very fine and flexible tippet. When the effort to achieve a natural float was abandoned, and the fly deliberately dragged upstream, the result was a provocative action (which triggered a sudden strike) and no longer the subtle deviations which created no excitement and served only as a warning to the unaroused fish.

Snelled flies are such an abomination that they have all but disappeared from the scene, but their general use in the past will serve as another case in point. The snells were invariably stiff and of large diameter, and most certainly counteracted any advantages of a fine leader. Yet this did not seem to deter the trout; fishermen twitched their wet flies against the current, a purely provocative measure, and fish came up and smacked them. I have never tried fishing a heavily snelled dry fly, but I'm pretty certain that the snells that had no adverse effect in wet fly fishing would virtually kill the dry fly fisherman's chances.

As I have attempted to illustrate, fly fishing is a field of considerable breadth, and the principles which apply in one area may be unreliable in others. It is therefore imperative that one have a general understanding of what he is trying to do, for only then is he in a position to apply appropriate and various refinements.

I have said the matter of pattern selection is generally accorded undeserved importance because of the hope of discovering a fly of such great appeal that success becomes little more than the matter of its employment. There is no such fly. Of the thousands designed, not one is sufficiently effective to compensate for faulty presentation. Yet no one can fly fish to any extent without acquiring personal preferences. I have an instinctive "faith" in certain favorite patterns, but their superiority exists more in my imagination than in fact. I suspect that the fisherman's preference is often inspired by niceties of fly construction which are lost upon the fish. I doubt very much, for example, that the body of the conventional, high-riding dry fly is of the slightest importance.

For years I have gone to the considerable bother of winding on stripped peacock quills to achieve the appearance of seg-mentation that is characteristic of mayfly bodies. Viewed by human eyes, the effect is an artistic triumph. But since the body of a dry fly rides above the surface, there seems good reason to doubt that fish see it clearly enough to appreciate its imitative qualities, or to take exception to any lack thereof.

Last winter I found the courage to dispense with bodies on the dry flies I tied. I simply wound the working thread along the shank and gave it a coat of varnish. I have used these flies through more than half a season, and they seem to be fully as effective as the more elaborate flies I tied in the past. To tie a Quill Gordon without a quill body seems almost an act of heresy, for it offends traditional convictions. But while trout fishermen may look on the omission as shocking, the trout don't seem to be able to tell the difference.

How does blind faith in particular patterns come about? Probably by attributing outstanding success to the pattern employed at a time when fish were so eager to hit that they would have taken almost anything. This belief prompts con-tinued use of the same pattern, during which periods of good fishing are more or less inevitable. Each such interlude wins the fly increasing admiration, until its reputation as a "killer" is eventually firmly established in the mind of the user. If he sings its praises eloquently enough, the fly can become a re-gional favorite.

Several years ago, Pete Terwilliger and I spent several days taking a canoe trip on Maine's Moose River. The cruise is known in the Jackman region as the "Bow Trip," due to the fact that the river describes a huge loop. Although the trip covers many miles of river, the finish is only two or three miles from the starting point.

Our guide had implicit faith in a single streamer pattern, the Gray Ghost. Before we set out, he inquired if we had a supply and implied that success was largely a matter of using this particular pattern. Like a fool, I replied that we were well stocked without taking the trouble to check, an indiscretion that I was soon to regret.

It turned out that the river was very high, so neither Pete nor I were surprised when the fishing proved meager. But it also turned out that among our dozens of streamers there was not even a single Gray Ghost. Our guide, knowing that he had me over a barrel, insisted that the poor fishing was due to this lack, and in no way due to the high water. He wouldn't think of setting out without any Gray Ghosts. He had asked me, hadn't he? I had said I had 'em, hadn't I? So what could I expect?

This went on for so long that "Gray Ghost" became a dirty name as far as I was concerned. Even to this day, I am inclined to tie on any other streamer pattern in preference to a Gray Ghost.

The water dropped quite rapidly, and the fishing improved. Trout and landlocked salmon began hitting our supposedly ineffective streamer patterns, and toward the end of the trip the fishing became excellent. This cut no ice with our guide.

According to him, we could have had equally good fishing throughout the entire trip if only we'd had some Gray Ghosts.

While such confidence in a single fly is misplaced, it is a hard thing to avoid. Exceptional fishing results in a glow of benevolence which causes a man to see everything in the best possible light, and particularly the fly he happens to be using.

A few years ago I tied up a few Dark Cotys, largely because I had tried to dye a neck a dun color and it had turned out more blue than dun. The body of the Dark Coty consists of blue-gray fur mixed with a "mite of scarlet wool," and I took pains to include the trace of scarlet in the muskrat fur dubbing — an embellishment that is certainly pure nonsense.

The next time out I tied on one of the flies — and promptly ran into a concentration of hungry brook trout. I wound up with one of the best catches of brookies I have ever made on close-to-home waters, plus the feeling that the Dark Cotys had much to do with the happy outcome. Common sense tells me otherwise; brook trout were rising all around me, and when brookies are feeding heavily they tend to be anything but fussy. Yet I still think of the Dark Coty as a particularly deadly pattern, and its subsequent failure to live up to this designation to any marked degree has not completely destroyed this illusion.

Of course, the advantage of fishing with a fly in which one has great confidence is not to be discounted. Lacking confidence, efforts tend to become halfhearted, and results suffer as a natural consequence. If a fisherman believes that a fanwing Royal Coachman casts a magic spell over trout, he is probably better off fishing this pattern than one which may match the hatch but lack his confidence.

This sort of pinpointed devotion exacts a compromise and for that reason is to be avoided as much as possible. One should fish with confidence, but justifiable confidence is far more valuable than that which is inspired by prejudice. In this respect, I believe a general confidence in all patterns to be both desirable and justified. Once you accept the premise that all flies will take fish if you merely fish them properly, you are on solid ground. And you enjoy the advantage that comes with facing any problem squarely and honestly.

There are always those instances when triumph appears to be the product of the slight and arbitrary distinctions which I have belittled. Fish may ignore one pattern after another, then suddenly hit like mad when yet another pattern is offered. This has all the appearance of cause and effect, but more likely than not it is an illusion. In other words, the shifting moods to which fish are forever subject are at work while the fisherman experiments with various patterns, and it is easy for him to credit a particular fly with results that are entirely due to temperamental changes in the fish.

My faith in broad understanding, rather than technical specifics, extends to all areas of fly fishing. Examine the contents of a few trout stomachs, for example, and certain general truths of much value become evident. Incidentally, the most revealing way to examine such a mass is to put it in a bottle of clear water and shake until the various items have become separated and recognizable.

Results will reveal that trout feed on a wide variety of insect life, often during a single period of feeding. There are likely to be winged insects, obviously taken at the surface, and at the same time, various nymphs and larvae gathered from the bottom. The dozens of items of a well-stuffed stomach attest to the fact that feeding goes on almost constantly, and at all depths. This is significant to the fisherman, for it denotes a constant interest in food which makes fish, at least in theory, constantly vulnerable.

Of perhaps even greater significance is the fact that trout subsist largely on forms of life that are incapable of "swimming" to any appreciable extent. Nymphs and larvae survive by hiding under rocks and burrowing into mud and silt. Whenever they emerge or are dislodged, they are almost completely at the mercy of the current, and remain so until they achieve adult form and take flight. Thus, flight and pursuit seldom play parts in a trout's feeding routine. The trout simply stations himself where he can inspect food-bearing currents and picks off items which have no means of escape, almost at leisure.

Since he is accustomed to living food which diplays almost complete helplessness, the trout's suspicion is usually aroused by any item which shows the ability to move in opposition to the current. This, then, is the effect to be avoided as much as possible when fishing dry flies, artificial nymphs or free-drifting wet flies.

Here again, as much depends on an understanding of underlying reasons as on the mechanics of execution. The cards are stacked against a stereotyped approach, and for the good reason that many subtle factors are involved. Consider the

97

feeding trout that refuses to take in spite of a series of seemingly perfect floats over his position. The fisherman has dropped down to the finest practical tippet diameter, his fly matches the hatch in size and appearance and his casts are sufficiently "quartering" so that only the fly and terminal end of the leader comes over the fish. What's wrong?

In the face of such negative results, the fisherman has reason to suspect that the fish has inadvertently taken a station where contrary and conflicting currents make a dragless float impossible, and that further efforts will prove futile.

Yet the fisherman who admits defeat at this point has overlooked one important consideration completely. He has concentrated on the trout's position, about which he can do nothing, and has disregarded his own position, which he can change very easily. Simply by moving a couple of steps the interplay of forces governing the fly's drift can be changed substantially, and from the new position the trout's lie may no longer be prohibitive. An acceptable drift may now be a possibility, in which case the seemingly difficult fish promptly winds up in the net.

Due to the multiplicity of variables ever present, the problem of achieving dragless drifts and floats lies beyond the reach of hard and fast rules. A decent rod, tapered line and a well-tied fly are essential, and it is fairly obvious that a natural float is best attempted by casting either upstream or quartering the current in the upstream direction. But to offer specific advice beyond a certain point is to be of no service, chiefly because of the ever-shifting nature of the problem.

When I spot a rising fish, for instance, I do not consciously ask myself how to go about taking him. Nevertheless, by some informal process, I arrive at a decision. At least, I proceed without hesitation, and with an inner confidence, often misplaced, that I am somehow doing the proper thing.

I have tried to determine the basis for this feeling of confidence, and for what it may be worth, here it is: I note the rising fish with customary elation, but also, seemingly at almost the same instant, I "know" the exact spot where I want my fly to alight. This doesn't mean that my fly always lands where I want it to, nor that I have necessarily selected the spot where it *should* land.

The important thing is that there is usually one particular landing place for the fly which will assure the best drift, and I am instinctively aware of this circumstance. I suspect that the degree to which this spot can be deduced from a rising fish's position is an accurate measure of a fly fishermans' skill, and a major determinant of his success. The process by which the deduction is made defies analysis, for it is a matter of unconsciously evaluating a composite of factors which is never twice the same. These factors are meaningful only when surveyed in their totality and lead to no conclusion when considered individually.

Wingshooters, and would-be wingshooters, will appreciate this distinction. The charge of shot must be aimed at a particular spot to intercept a flying grouse, and this spot is determined by the speed of the bird, the angle of its flight, the speed of the shot, the speed of the swing and the speed of the shooter's reflex action. Yet the art of wingshooting is not to be mastered by the conscious consideration of these individual factors when a bird gets up. Instead, the competent wingshot is one who has acquired the ability to react reflexively to the sum total of the involved variables, and without conscious concern for their individual significance. To hit the flying bird it is obvious that the dictates of each of these variables must be satisfied, and the expert shot reacts in a manner which takes all into account. But he does so without deliberate calculation, and if you ask him how he manages he is almost certain to answer that he hasn't the slightest idea.

Picking the proper landing spot for a fly must be done in much the same way. Conflicting currents, obstructions, depth and other important details do not register as factors of individual significance. Yet, with experience, they convey an overall impression of where the fly should drop, and the avenue by which it should approach the fish.

A situation that will serve as an example is the one in which a trout is rising near the tip of a projecting ledge. One current sweeps by the tip of the ledge unaffected; another hits the ledge, slows and then flows around the tip. In effect, the two currents represent two separate sources of food. Since the trout is in a position to survey both, it is logical to believe that it will gather in food brought by either of the two currents. Oddly enough, a trout in such a position often will disregard items carried by the unbroken current.

More often than not, the trout's attention will be focused exclusively on the slowed flow which comes curling around the tip of the projection. To take him on a dry fly, it is therefore necessary to drop the fly where it will be carried against the ledge, pause in the cushion of slowed water and then finally sweep around the point. The drag problem becomes very difficult in such a situation, but there is often no alternative but to cope with it.

A fisherman with only superficial knowledge of trout nature will fail to appreciate the requirements of the situation. It does not occur to him that a trout can be so perverse as to concentrate on only one of two equally convenient sources of food.

The trout fisherman who has acquired sufficient empathy will be well aware of this possibility, and his empathy will tell him that the trout, as is true in most such cases, is concerned only with items which are carried around the ledge and oblivious of those which are swept past it. This fisherman "forgets" the rising trout and concentrates on dropping his fly where the desired line of drift will result.

In broad pools, and in lakes, surface feeding trout may cruise about, and the problem then becomes that of anticipating their movements and dropping a fly ahead of them. This is the exception, however; in most cases the trout's attention is concentrated on a very small area, and the problem consists of drifting the fly to within these narrow limits.

The totality of a trout's commitment to one tiny area of preoccupation is not generally appreciated, for by human standards it fails to make sense. It is a confounding phenomenon, prompted by some strange edict of trout nature, but one which the trout fisherman must learn to accept and take into account.

Quite often, for instance, a trout will set himself up in business at the base of a steep bank, and his rises will come so close to the bank that it seems that his nose must almost bump against it with each slurp. To the fisherman of meager experience it seems safe to assume that a fly which drifts within a *foot* of the bank will certainly win this trout's attention. Unfortunately, this is a wrong assumption. In almost every such instance, a trout will have eyes for only those items which literally brush against the bank in their passage, and to draw a rise the fisherman's dry fly must dribble along the bank in precisely this manner.

The principle remains much the same when one is fishing a drifting fly in the absences of visible rises. The fisherman should *assume* the presence of a fish in each likely spot, then cast so as to effect a drift or float compatible with the lie of a fish that is imaginary until proven otherwise.

The problem of deducing the most telling line of drift is as vital to the nymph (or sunken wet fly) fisherman as to the dry fly fisherman. The mention of nymph fishing invites inspection of a form of fly fishing which is often described as deadly, and as frequently purported in print and conversation accounts for large numbers of trout. I suspect, however, that much more is written and said about nymph fishing than is ever actually done about it.

In theory, nymph fishing should be the deadliest of all fly fishing methods. Nymphs and larvae make up the bulk of a trout's diet, and while surface feeding takes place only intermittently, bottom feeding goes on practically all of the time. But although nymph fishing has the superficial appearance of a telling means of exploitation, it is extremely difficult. A most convincing case for nymph fishing can be set down on paper, but the problem of execution is enormously more difficult. As a result, true expertise in the technique is much rarer than is testimony of its efficacy.

I have taken a fair number of trout on nymphs and sunken wet flies, but always with the frustrating feeling that the job was beyond me, and that I was only half doing it. A trout should be a pushover for a tumbling nymph which shows no sign of drag — but how in the world does one contrive a dragless drift? And to compound the difficulty, how does one get a nymph down to the bottom where it should be fished?

The big trouble is that the moment a drifting lure sinks, the influences which result in drag promptly become three-dimensional. A floating dry fly is affected by forces which are confined to a single plane, but to drift naturally a sunken nymph must respond without visible signs of restraint to impulses coming from all directions. Trout are as critical of the lack of conformity in depth as they are with respect to floating objects, and the problem of convincing presentation becomes ever so much more complex.

As for depth, about the only way to get a nymph down deep in a stream is to take advantage of plunging currents. Since these occur with but slight regard for the fisherman's convenience, his nymph usually rides just under the surface and seldom gets down to the pay-dirt level. A sinking line or a split shot will *drag* the nymph down, but this introduces the very element that must be avoided.

So, although nymph fishing enjoys a rather exalted reputation, results usually fall far short of the advance advertising, which is a pity, for the thrill of taking a trout on a sunken nymph is as great, if not greater, than that of taking a trout on a dry fly. One watches his floating line for signs of a check which will indicate a strike, and usually the strike will be accompanied by the barely visible flash of the striking trout. The response must be instantaneous, and if the rod fetches up against a good fish the angler is flooded by the smug feeling of having pulled off a mighty clever caper. Which he has, indeed.

It is possible to take trout on artificial nymphs by twitching them against the current, or otherwise imparting motion, but this has always seemed to me to smack of cheating. The proposition is to effect a natural drift, and every trout fisherman should face up to it at one time or another — for the rare quality of whatever success he may achieve, and for a better appreciation of his limitations.

It should be added that under ideal conditions nymphs can be used with deadly effect in lakes and ponds in the absence of the difficulties encountered in stream fishing. Using a sinking line, make long casts from an anchored boat or canoe. When the nymph has reached bottom, retrieve it *very* slowly. The trick is to barely inch it along the bottom to simulate the crawling motion of a live nymph, in which guise it will win plenty of attention if it is among bottom-hugging trout.

But this doesn't solve the problem of fishing nymphs in streams with consistent success. I've read all the directions and testimony, but I'm still waiting to meet the angler who qualifies as an expert nymph fisherman.

My greatest love of fly fishing extends to only that phase in which the aim is to imitate the behavior and appearance of natural insects, and I might as well admit to this prejudice. The moment the goal becomes that of inducing strikes by yanking and twitching something around, it ranks several notches down on my scale of values. The distinction is only relative, of course. Tell me where I can take landlocked salmon on streamers, or bass on popping bugs, and I'll wear out a pair of shoes to get there. It's just that it's impossible to admire all good things with the same intensity.

Justified or not, my preference is prompted by the feeling that in imitative fly fishing the outcome is largely determined by the quality of my presentation. When fishing a dry fly, under favorable conditions, I am confident that I can take fish if I can manage to fish properly. Furthermore, I know the essentials of the basic requirements — even though my efforts may fall short by a considerable margin.

When I'm casting a streamer or a popping bug this confidence is lacking, for it is impossible to identify that perfection of presentation which will assure success. In all probability, none exists, with the result that strikes are more a reflection of the mood which happens to prevail among the fish than testimony of my skill as a fisherman.

The refinements by which a fish can be convinced that a fly is a genuine article of food are open to logical deduction, and while compliance with these refinements may be difficult, their identification furnishes a definite and recognizable goal. Provocative fly fishing, on the other hand, aims at inducing irrational responses, and there is no logical way of establishing definite means by which this may be done. One searches for the indication of understandable cause and effect, but in vain; fish strike because of impulses induced by stimuli which lie outside the field of human experience.

The streamer fly is generally regarded as an imitation of a bait fish, despite the considerable strain which this belief places on the imagination. Accordingly, it is fished with a twitching action, which supposedly simulates the swimming motions of the small fish which it is alleged to imitate. The total result, insofar as the aspect of imitation is concerned, is about as convincing as a rubber half-dollar, and the fish which hits a streamer in the belief that it is actually a small fish has most certainly taken leave of its marbles.

This fact is beside the point, for fish will hit a streamer fished in this manner, if only for reasons known solely to them. Yet the theory that an imitative effect is the determinant is belied by what often happens.

The streamer fisherman works a pool in the conventional manner, and when no strikes are forthcoming he decides to move on. He makes one last cast as a parting gesture, but gives up midway through his retrieve and reels in rapidly. The streamer zips up the pool at a steady pace, utterly devoid of whatever imitative action may, or may not, have been implicit in its previous action. Wham! A fish zooms up and smacks it, triggered into attack by the very antithesis of the "imitative" action upon which a streamer's appeal allegedly depends.

All game fish are more or less susceptible to the strange fascination of a rapidly reeled streamer, and I have found that landlocked salmon are particularly responsive to this unorthodox measure. Wherever stream conditions permit, I often let the current carry out all of my fly line, and even part of the backing. Then I simply reel in at a steady pace — and there is always a good chance that the streamer will take a belt from a salmon before I have it wound in.

Much the same thing often happens when two fishermen are trolling for salmon from the same canoe. One hooks a fish, and the other reels in as quickly as possible to avoid a tangle. But on the way to the canoe, the streamer that is being "fished" with no objective but to bring it aboard in the least possible time gets socked by a salmon that probably would have ignored it otherwise.

It is this inconsistency, and the resulting lack of orderliness, which, in my opinion, detracts from the charm of provocative fly fishing. This doesn't mean that I'm unhappy when a salmon grabs my fly while I'm reeling in, or when a fish hits my streamer under other circumstances which preclude logical accounting for the act. It's simply a matter of being denied credit. There is a solid satisfaction in taking fish when one can attribute his success to his preconception of what had to be done, plus sufficient skill to implement his plan of attack. But how the devil can one take credit for taking a fish when he is at a loss to account for its decision to strike?

There is always the temptation to fabricate the lacking credit by ascribing success to particularly clever lure manipulation, but the validity of such claims are ever dubious. Bass bugging serves as a handy example.

Much has been made of the subtle effect to be achieved by allowing a bass bug to remain motionless after it lands. At one time it was popular among fishing writers to recommend that the fisherman light a cigarette and finish smoking it before giving the bug its first twitch. Nowadays the same advice persists, but in revised form: "Let the bug lie motionless for a minute or more." Easy to say, but usually impossible to do!

Most bass bugging is done from either a boat or a canoe, and it is seldom, indeed, that the motion of the craft fails to tighten the line, thus moving the bug, long before the specified minute is up.

This long wait appeals to the imagination, for it suggests a subtle cunning on the part of the fisherman. I doubt, however, that it has any significant practical application, and while, in theory, it is regarded as axiomatic, it is generally ignored in practice. I have yet to see a fisherman let a bug lie motionless for a full minute, much less the time it takes to smoke a cigarette.

It is true that bass will hit a motionless bug, but it probably would be nearer the truth to say that they do so in spite of its lack of motion, rather than because of it. In my opinion, the fisherman who begins an erratic retrieve the instant his bass bug strikes the water will take as many, and probably more, bass than the fisherman who uses up time watching a resting bug. Actually, when bass are in the mood to come to popping bugs, it is as impossible to hit on a presentation to which they won't respond as it is to arrive at one which is demonstrably superior.

Thus, the distinction between imitative and provocative fly fishing persists. In the first, since the chain of cause and effect is discernible, the successful fisherman can take credit for having executed a plan of action born of logic and perception. In the second, the governing principles are never clearly evident, and the satisfaction of success is diluted by the doubt that it is truly a manifestation of skill.

5

The Dry Fly and the

Third Dimension

BACK IN THE DAYS of his first administration, the late President Dwight D. Eisenhower made a public appearance at a shindig in Rutland, Vermont, and at a nearby mountain resort. Because Ike was a fisherman, as well as a golfer, arrangements were made for him to fish the headwaters of Furnace Brook early the following morning.

There is a federal trout hatchery situated on the banks of the stream, so it goes without saying that the "arrangements" included a heavy stocking of large trout in the stretch which the President was to fish. I had long been a close friend of Ben Schley, then superintendent of the hatchery, and Ben asked me to help distribute the fish.

As Ike's intention to fish the brook came on short notice, the stocking was a crash program which had to be carried out at night if the trout were to be positioned for the President come morning. So we stumbled around in the dark, spotting two, three and even four-pound rainbows along the stream, and it was well after midnight when the job was finished.

Needless to say, the President caught none of the hefty trout. They were fat, hatchery-reared slobs, and were undoubtedly terrified by the sudden transfer to a harsher environment. It can be added that local fishermen fared considerably better after the big trout had become at least partially acclimated. Unaware of the nocturnal stocking, and prepared for fish only a few inches over the legal length limit, these fishermen left the stream in a happy daze, toting trout that wouldn't fit in their creels.

Although I know for a fact that Ike never caught a single fish, much was written about his efforts to do so. And, of course, every concession was made in an attempt to identify the President as a fisherman of prowess. Much was also made of the fact that the President, in spite of the grandeur of his office, was a regular fellow when it came to fishing. This feeling was neither misplaced nor an exaggeration, for Ike charmed all those who made up the party with his unaffected warmth and geniality.

Striving to make this particular point, one reporter combined hearsay and a personal ignorance of subject to contrive an outlandish observation. At the close of the morning's fishing, he wrote, Ike democratically insisted on "oiling his own dry flies" instead of delegating this menial chore to an attendant. The reporter had Ike pegged correctly, for the President was friendly and democratic to a degree which kept the attending phalanx of Secret Service men in a constant state of apprehension. But the reporter had a hazy concept of dry fly fishing, for he obviously was under the impression that dry flies required lubrication with use, possibly to eliminate squeaks.

Although ignorance of the law is deemed to be no excuse, misconceptions concerning dry fly fishing which result from ignorance should probably be regarded as pardonable. At best, dry fly fishing is nothing more than a frivolity about which certain individuals permit themselves to become serious. One can avail himself of its pleasures by observing dogmas which have no basis in fact. As an example, the popular theory that fish lie facing upstream because food appears from that direction, and that it is easier for them to take in and expel water, is generally accepted as gospel. This "accounts" for a known circumstance, for fish do face upstream, but the reasoning involved is probably false.

Picture what would happen if all the fish in a stream suddenly swapped ends. The kit and boodle of them would be carried downstream promptly, for fish simply aren't designed to swim *backward* to any significant extent. In the final analysis, they face upstream because they *must* do so in order to hold their positions.

As another example, the use of leaders tapered to fine terminal diameters is often believed to increase one's chances in dry fly fishing by reducing the leader's visibility. Again, the basis for this belief, whether true or false, is of secondary importance. A fine tippet is a must for the dry fly fisherman, and even the finest is visible to the fish and would serve to alarm them if they associated leaders directly with danger. To repeat a previous observation, what makes them suspicious is any unnatural influence the leader has on the fly's drift. The greater the flexibility of the leader point, the less influence it exerts on the fly, and it is obvious that maximum flexibility is to be gained by using the finest tippets.

To most enthusiasts, dry fly fishing is a framework in which the delights of angling are brought into the sharpest possible focus. Since this is the consensus of fishermen who are thoroughly familiar with all angling methods, it is reasonable to conclude that this opinion is genuine and innocent of affectation. This being the case, dry fly fishing deserves recognition as the method by which a majority of experienced anglers attempt to get the most for their money.

But because certain refinements are essential — light rods, tapered lines, wispy leaders, tiny lures — the notion prevails that fishermen deliberately adopt these compromises to give fish a "sporting chance." It is further conceded that dry fly fishermen are entitled to exaltation by reason of this apparent sacrifice, and it must be admitted that they have made little effort to disclaim the adulation thrust upon them. That fishing could give rise to anything approaching a caste system seems nothing short of ludicrous, yet this actually has happened. Anglers of moderate skill acquire inhibitions which dissuade them from attempting to invade the social sanctities with which they imagine dry fly fishing to be surrounded.

On various occasions I have met fishermen, on one stream or another, who have shown interest in the trappings of dry fly fishing, but who, after hefting a two-ounce rod, inspecting a leader that tests a mere two pounds and squinting at a No. 14 or 16 fly, shake their heads and declare that such an outfit is okay for those of great skill but much too delicate for ordinary fishermen like themselves.

Since nothing could be more farfetched or sillier, and since belief in this sophistry does deter many deserving fishermen from experiencing the best that sport fishing has to offer, there seems to be need for a convincing refutation. In what follows I intend to identify dry fly fishing for what it is: just another fishing method, but one which many consider to be the most rewarding and exciting.

Actually, a dry fly fisherman uses delicate tackle for exactly the same reason a poacher employs dynamite. In each instance, the means best calculated to achieve the desired goal has been selected as the most efficient and practical. To shove this around a bit, the dry fly fisherman who wanted to make it hard on himself — and it is by virtue of this image that he is accorded prestige — would immediately switch to heavier tackle. He would use a stiff, heavy rod to make a delicate presentation that much more difficult. He would give fish fairer warning by using heavier leaders. Finally, he would scorn the use of the tiny flies that are the trout's undoing and make a more sporting game of it by using large flies that would draw fewer rises and strikes. Show me a dry fly fisherman who deliberately handicaps himself in this way and I'll be the first to admit that he is honestly trying to give fish a break.

So far, I have never encountered so much as a hint of this type of benevolence among dry fly fishermen: we are as passionately determined to victimize as many fish as possible, as are bait fishermen, spin fishermen and bait casters. Every last refinement of tackle and technique which we employ is hopefully intended to deceive the poor fish and designed for no other purpose whatsoever.

The fact that many of us may release our fish is of no relevance at the moment; the question is whether we fish as we do for "sporting" reasons, or to catch as many as possible. Our intent, believe me, is to get a hook into every last fish that can be persuaded to rise, and we will use every means available within the limits of dry fly fishing to increase our chances.

To be more specific, let's examine the matter of fly rods. My heaviest fly rod weighs less than five ounces, and I do much of my dry fly fishing with rods which weigh a mere couple of ounces. Unenlightened fishermen tend to regard the use of a two-ounce rod as evidence of self-imposed restraint, but nothing could be wider of the truth.

In the average situation it would be hard to pick a rod that would give a hooked fish *less* chance to escape. Once I get a hook in a fish I don't figure on losing him, and I base most of my confidence in the knowledge that my rod is diabolically designed to thwart his efforts to get loose. Fish often whittle me down to size by coming off, of course, but this is invariably due to my bungling, or to other circumstances, and never because of shortcomings inherent in the use of a light rod.

Actually, the difference between playing and landing fish on a two-ounce rod and a five-ounce rod is purely academic. A fly rod by design is the most efficient tool ever devised for capturing fish. On the rare occasions when I'm lucky enough to hook a big fish, my only aim is to bring him to the net. Whenever I hang one on a spinning or bait casting rod, I am tortured by marked apprehension. I am uneasy about the stiffness of the rod, and particularly about drag tension. I am at the mercy of mechanical safeguards which cannot make thinking responses, and I know that a sudden surge can result in disaster. Dammit to hell, I always think to myself, why couldn't I have hung this fish on a fly rod!

Never is this feeling inspired by the desire to give the hooked fish a better chance. On the contrary, I would like nothing better than to eliminate all possibility of escape, which is exactly why I would be much happier had I hooked the same fish on a fly rod of only a few ounces.

Fighting against a fly rod, a fish finds itself in much the same predicament as a rabbit caught by a snare affixed to a limber sapling. Because of the sapling's flexibility, the poor rabbit can never throw its weight against solid resistance, and it dies from exhaustion and strangulation while vainly attempting to do so.

The cards are stacked against the fish to an even greater degree, for the fisherman can always avert undue strain against his rod by letting the fish run the reel. When this is done with proper discretion the fish's plight becomes all but hopeless. He is doomed to eventual exhaustion because the fly rod, while constantly imposing mild but inexorable restraint, denies him the opportunity to force a showdown of strength.

While a fly rod may appear to be a weak and untrustworthy means of subduing strong fish, it is actually a device of deadly efficiency. Therefore, the fisherman who uses a fly rod is no more entitled to special distinction than is the deer hunter who deliberately, and wisely, hunts with a rifle of sufficient shocking power to assure clean kills.

As further illustration of the fly rod's unique efficiency, it would be next to impossible to land sizable fish on light leaders and tiny dry flies with the help of any other type of rod. Only the fly rod has sufficient sensitivity and flexibility to cushion sudden surges and thus enable the fisherman to release line in time to prevent breakage.

Of course, there are fishermen who foolishly feel obliged to pit their strength against that of any big fish they hook, and their doubts concerning the fly rod arise because it is obviously a poor instrument with which to snub heavy fish. Its use does indeed preclude the indulgence of this unfortunate habit. But it is only necessary to adopt the more reasonable strategy of give and take to discover that the fly rod, fragile though it may seem, is actually no less than a devastating fish killer.

It is equally important, however, to demolish the notion that dry fly fishing is a game strictly for the "experts." One does not have to be an angling wizard to fish with a dry fly and enjoy the sport with reasonable success. All that's actually required is a modest investment in equipment and the ability to cast a fly a moderate distance.

In fact, I doubt that a beginner will go wrong if he simply walks into a reliable tackle shop and buys the following items without fuss and bother: a fly rod designed to handle a No. 6 line, a double taper floating line of this weight (DT6F), a single action fly reel made by any company which advertises regularly, two-dozen dry flies of any standard patterns tied on

No. 12 and No. 14 hooks, a few nine-foot leaders tapered to 3X and 4X, plus a spool of monofilament in each size to renew the tips, a bottle of dry fly floatant and a pad of line dressing if one doesn't come with the line.

I probably should add a note for the beginner who may question my failure to recommend a rod of a particular length. Actually, the weight of the line a rod is designed to handle is more indicative of its action than is its length. A rod which requires a No. 6 line will have an action which will give the beginner the least trouble. Whether it be 7, 7½ or 8 feet long is of secondary importance.

As for fly casting itself, the principles and mechanics involved are too obvious to warrant the many solemn words of explanation that have been written about them. To explain that the necessary casting weight is supplied by the line is almost to insult the beginner's intelligence; people no smarter than fishermen are not likely to conclude that this weight is provided by the *fly* (the only alternative) whose density is in a class with that of thistledown. It is equally obvious that the line must be tossed to the rear before it can be cast forward. Acquiring the proper timing is quite another matter. But here, where pertinent advice would be most helpful, it is almost impossible to contrive.

In spite of all that has been written on the subject, the beginner must rely on his sense of coordination to discover the timing which is the whole secret of fly casting. Fortunately, the "feel" comes naturally with practice, and nothing more than confidence in this eventuality is needed to learn fly casting by trial and error. Actually, there isn't isn't any other way.

The important point is that no fisherman need deny himself the pleasures of dry fly fishing beause of apprehensions concerning his ability to meet its skill requirements. Just as it is a relatively simple matter to learn the moves of chess, it is easy to pick up the fundamentals of dry fly fishing. In each instance, the joys of the game become evident at the moment of initial participation.

On the other hand, these introductory delights immediately suggest even more profound pleasures to be gained by study and increased proficiency, and the beginner finds himself drawn down trails which grow increasingly enticing, and which are without end. Dry fly fishing is thus a source of deep pleasure, the gateway to which is open to one and all. Inside lie mysteries compatible with all degrees of curiosity, among which can be found those to challenge the talents of the most determined and gifted.

To look upon dry fly fishing as both noble and ennobling because of these virtues is rather silly. More properly, dry fly fishing is a classical example of man's atonishing propensity to become preoccupied with matters of little or no real consequence.

A trout, a creature hardly to be counted as a major evolutionary triumph, is going about the prosaic business of sucking mayflies from the surface of a stream. A human being, whose self-declared claim to evolutionary nobility seems equally suspect, is inexplicably excited by this common phenomenon. By carefully observing rituals which he holds sacred, but which are ridiculously childish when appraised objectively, he contrives to float over the unsuspecting trout a lure which he hopes is a convincing imitation of the flies upon which the fish is feeding. If the trout, in whom intelligence can be conceded only by the most charitable application of the term, makes the mistake of grabbing the imitation, the fisherman is instantly flooded by feelings of exultation that are incredibly disproportionate.

If the trout is a particularly large specimen, its carefully mounted form will be treasured (and conspicuously exhibited) as a symbol of great achievement. Even if the fisherman is a man of widespread fame and vast accomplishment, he will count the taking of such a trout among his greatest triumphs.

Should the trout scorn the fly, or break the leader while struggling to escape, the man will preserve his dignity and self-esteem by the curious process of equating himself with the unintelligent fish. By establishing an ostensible equality in his adversary, he will manage to create the satisfying illusion of honorable defeat.

Fishermen must do all of these things, to greater or lesser degrees, in order to make fishing worth the effort. It is only when they do so self-righteously, and without introspection, that they tend to become insufferable.

Fortunately, it is both possible and pleasant to indulge in the necessary whimsy with full awareness. There is an altogether splendid sense of escape and freedom which results from deliberately making a fool of oneself, and the man who can fish a dry fly with both deadly seriousness and the knowledge that his seriousness is ridiculously misplaced enjoys the full blessing of this relief. Accordingly, he comes to love dry fly fishing for what it is: an absurdity upon which he can focus his full powers of concentration with only superficial concern for the outcome. Whether a man raises a trout to his fly matters as much as it matters little, and as little as it matters much. It is because dry fly fishing proffers this comfortable option that it is both a field of battle and a blessed haven of peace.

I think it is safe to say that fishermen are people who not only take pleasure in catching fish, but who are instinctively fascinated by the fish themselves. Such people miss no opportunity to study and observe fish under any and all circumstances, and their curiosity is largely inspired by the romantic feeling that fish are mysterious creatures of an alien world, which in truth they are. Fishermen study fish, not in search of truth for its own sake as does the biologist, but because truth in this instance represents the exotic. I can account in no other way for the strange fascination fish have always had for me, and I assume this to be true of others with a similar leaning. I also believe that this reason helps to account for the intense dedication which dry fly fishing so often inspires, for it is by far the most romantic way of making personal identification with the truths in question.

Since the dry fly fisherman's approach is almost completely subjective, it is not surprising that notions concerning the many whys and wherefores of the sport are of wide variety, nor is it to be desired that things be otherwise. Uniformity of opinion would only ruin the fun.

But because among contrasting opinions there is usually one truth and many misconceptions, one cannot resist the urge to seek out the lone truth, even though he may attempt to do so with only small chance of success. Also, should he by any chance succeed, there is always reason to doubt that his success will result in any significant advantage. He may learn the truth, only to find himself outfished by those who have the incredible knack of always doing the right thing for the wrong reason.

Several years ago, Pete and I wound up one afternoon at the dam on Maine's Moosehead Lake which is known as the West Outlet. The gates were wide open, and the stream below the dam was an unfishable torrent. As the gates were to be closed soon, we decided to hang around until it became possible to fish the stream.

In the meantime, it was possible to walk out on the dam and twitch a streamer against the current in the big pool below, and we joined the several fishermen who were killing time in this manner.

Nobody had had a strike, but suddenly a good landlocked salmon zoomed up through all the turbulence and nailed the streamer of a fellow who was fishing beside us. He whooped and hollered in great style, and finally maneuvered the fish to the base of the retaining wall at the edge of the pool. There, with a long-handled net obviously designed for that purpose, a friend reached down and scooped up the fish.

After feasting his eyes on his glistening prize, the lucky fisherman removed the streamer from the salmon's mouth and held it high over his head for all to see.

"The old Black Ghost has done it again!" he shouted, and the overtones of reverence in his voice were unmistakable.

Since I am perversely intrigued by manifestations of blind faith, I gently egged him into expanding on the unique virtues of that particular pattern. This didn't take much doing, for the proponents of unquestioning faith are seldom disposed toward reticence.

He was a guest at a nearby fishing camp, he said, and confined his fishing to trailing a streamer from the dam. He fished both mornings and afternoons, and on most days he managed to take a fish. For what he looked on as a rather impressive record he gave full credit to the "Old Black Ghost," and completely overlooked a perseverance which should have won him a fish a day had he dangled a hook baited with raisins. Not only did he scorn all other patterns, but by some strange logic he viewed the rather meager returns from the Black Ghost's exclusive use as proof of its infallibility.

It is easy to write off a fellow like that as a nut, but the fact remains that he was the only fisherman who caught a salmon, and a good one at that. While his faith in a Black Ghost may seem naive, who can say definitely that he would have done as well or better with any other pattern?

Many dry fly fishermen are equally loyal to a single pattern, and equally certain that their particular favorite possesses magical qualities. As an example, certain Pittsford friends and acquaintances of mine, including two lady schoolteachers, swear by a dry fly of local invention. In what must have been a burst of chauvinism it was named "Spirit of Pittsford Mills," a touch of flag-waving that seemingly should have excluded it from all serious consideration.

Lo and behold, however, the Spirit of Pittsford Mills heads the list of favorite dry fly patterns in *"McClane's Standard Fishing Encyclopedia and International Angling Guide,"* a puzzling circumstance that I am at a loss to explain. To the best of my knowledge, this pattern is known to only a few dozen fishermen at the most, and its use has been almost completely confined to Furnace Brook.

At any rate, aside from its unlikely name, the pattern has no readily discerned claim to distinction. I feel quite certain that the *truth* in this instance is that this particular fly is neither more nor less effective than dozens of similar patterns. Yet this is not "truth" for those who believe the pattern to be something special. Although the reasons for their faith may be imaginary, they can undoubtedly take more trout with a Spirit of Pittsford Mills than with a pattern in which they have less confidence.

The fisherman who attempts to determine the truths of dry fly fishing by sheer logic soon is thwarted. He soon discovers that he must deal with "truths" of two entirely different kinds: those which can be deduced by logic and those which defy all the rules of logic without loss of validity.

One evening last summer I moved into a long, smooth stretch of the Battenkill in which numerous trout were dimpling the surface. I had been fishing broken water farther downstream and doing fairly well with a No. 14 Adams on a 4X tippet. I offered the Adams to the trout rising in the quiet stretch, and none would have anything to do with it.

I waded ashore, tied on a 6X tippet and a No. 20 fly, then went back to work. I drifted the tiny fly over a brown that had been the last to refuse the Adams, and who had continued to rise in one spot while I changed flies. He took on the first try. I didn't take all the trout rising in the stretch by any means, but I managed to get a rise out of nearly all that I cast to.

That trout feeding in flat water often necessitates a change to a very fine leader point and an extremely small fly is a well-known fact. One needs no additional knowledge to take trout under these conditions, yet this, by itself, does not satisfy the curiosity. Why do the trout insist on tiny flies? Can it be that they actually prefer barely visible midges to larger flies which would most certainly provide more nourishment? Do they shun the larger fly because it is an anomaly and therefore reason for suspicion? Or, in slick water, can they discern drag in a large fly and fail to detect it in the tiny one? What is the *real* reason? In other words, what is the "truth"?

Last summer I entertained a young fisherman as a houseguest. He was quite inexperienced in dry fly fishing, but he had discovered the fun of it and was going at it enthusiastically. He regarded me as an authority on the subject, a travesty which I took no steps to deny, and he expressed the hope that I could find time to give him the benefit of streamside instructions.

The next morning we visited a stretch of Furnace Brook which had been particularly productive, and even as we approached the stream we could see a trout rising tight against the far bank, which was a high, sheer wall of raw soil. I have already discussed this common situation at some length and have pointed out the almost absolute necessity of dropping a fly so that it literally bumps along the bank as it drifts.

I advised my guest of this requirement, but it was obvious that he didn't take me literally. In spite of repeated urging to "get it against the bank" he persisted in floating his fly a foot or more on the stream side of the feeding trout, plainly confident that the fish would move that short distance to gather in any fly which appeared to his liking. No such thing happened, and after much repeated casting he gave up on a fish which he regarded as hopelessly critical, but which should have been a pushover.

We smoked cigarettes, during which time he asked my opinion of his newly purchased rod and suggested that I try a few casts with it. This gave me a perfect opportunity to play the smart aleck, for the trout was still rising against the bank directly across the stream from us. It was an easy matter to drop the fly where the current would sweep it against the bank, and the trout — a foot-long brown —sucked it in unsuspectingly when it came abeam of his nose. Although my behavior was certainly in poor taste, nothing else could have impressed my young friend more favorably. He had expected to see genius at work, and in his opinion his expectations had been realized.

But the fact that my "genius" consisted of knowing that the trout would accept no flies other than those which bounced along the bank does not explain why this was so. Why wouldn't the fish move a mere foot to grab a fly which gave him no cause for suspicion? Knowing merely that he wouldn't enabled me to catch him, but did not answer the question. Again, what was the "truth"?

On trout streams it is reasonable to expect a hatch of mayflies to result in rising fish, and also to expect mass participation in this surface feeding. In other words, trout can generally be counted on to become surface-minded collectively, and one need only observe the beginning of a hatch to appreciate this circumstance. The hitherto unbroken surface is suddenly dappled with the rings of rising fish, and this continues until the action ends as abruptly as it began. One is tempted to conclude that this unanimous response is merely due to the equally spontaneous beginning and ending of the mayfly hatch, but there is some reason to doubt that this is all there is to it.

Under ideal fishing conditions, when water levels and temperatures are optimum for both trout and hatching mayflies, this aspect of simple cause and effect seems unassailable. Hatches and rises begin and end concurrently, and there seems to be no particular mystery involved, at least none connected with the behavior of the fish. There is reason to wonder what mysterious signal prompts the mayflies to emerge simultaneously, but the surface feeding in the wake of this happening seems a natural response which can be taken for granted.

Yet there are times and conditions when observation indicates that the situation is not that cut and dried. There are periods when water temperatures are marginal, high enough to trigger a hatch, but not quite high enough to move trout to the top. Or if temperature is not the critical factor, some other requirement remains unsatisfied. Although it happens quite rarely, mayflies do sometimes emerge in large numbers without eliciting the usual response from the trout.

Perhaps the most curious part about such interludes is that

a lone trout may suddenly get the urge to go on the feed. Once he does, and stations himself in a productive current, he will go on rising steadily. This lone, steadily feeding trout attests to the abundance of surface food. The failure of all his relatives to take advantage of the opportunity suggests that surface feeding is not necessarily precipitated directly by the *appearance* of mayflies. Instead, it seems likely that trout are sensitive to stimuli which usually, but not always, prompt them to become surface-minded during those periods when some *other* combination of conditions brings on a hatch.

The occasional exception, the lone trout who "gets the signal," seems to support this theory. The flies on the surface are certainly as visible to all other trout in the pool as they are to him, and the fact that only he rises to them strongly suggests that trout rise because of a compulsion of mysterious origin. Although they rely on vision when picking off mayflies, of course, the urge to set about feeding on these insects is not, in my opinion, the direct consequence of their visibility, but due to obscure factors which await identification.

As further evidence, I submit the difficulty of raising trout to a dry fly when they are not disposed toward surface feeding. The alleged trick of "creating a hatch" by repeated casting provides fine typewriter fodder and has helped fill pages of copy for me, as well as for writers of greater distinction. But the truth is that it is largely bunk, and to float a dry fly over trout when they are indifferent to everything on the surface is pretty much a waste of fishing time.

It is tempting and natural to conclude that trout at such times are not interested in the surface because no hatching insects are in evidence. Yet when this lack is remedied by repeated casting over the same water, why does their indifference persist? A fly, which trout will take readily when surface-minded, appears over and over again and is certainly clearly visible to the fish. Yet it is steadfastly ignored.

While I have had little success in interesting fish in a "created hatch," I have had excellent dry fly fishing, on rare occasions, when no insects were hatching and no trout showing on the surface save those that came to my fly. What seems likely is that trout and mayflies are attuned to similar, but not identical, influences, one a composite of particular conditions which causes mayflies to emerge, and the other a somewhat different composite which usually, but not always, draws trout interest to the surface at those times when hatches are imminent. It is therefore quite possible, and I believe probable, that a hatch is no more responsible for trout "looking up" than the hatch is the result of this sudden and instinctive interest in the surface on the part of the trout. Each comes about spontaneously because of related, but separate, influences, a distinction which is disguised by the general tendency of both to occur simultaneously. They do not always do so, however, and it is by happening singly, even though rarely, that they betray their independence of origin.

The secrets of fish nature are hidden in truths that are profound and not apparent. If one searches earnestly for these truths he discovers that quite often they contradict traditional concepts and beliefs. Please be charitable enough to accept for the moment my premise that a trout, at a given moment, is a creature bound by an imposed behavioral pattern of stringent rigidity. Accept also my contention that this pattern, although temporarily fixed, is open to almost infinite variation.

Things of substance are necessarily three-dimensional, and this concept of trout behavior can be said to constitute dry fly fishing's third dimension. If it is not taken into account, one sees only the two-dimensional surface of the sport, which prompts the conviction that to take a trout on a dry fly is almost entirely a matter of fishing the fly in a manner which gives the trout no cause for alarm or suspicion. Yet this, by itself, is not enough, for too often it achieves what I think of as "tolerance." I mean that frustrating standoff during which the trout calmly continues to rise, undisturbed by the artificial fly which drifts over him repeatedly, but completely indifferent to its bid for attention.

For instance, water tumbles into a pool via a long chute, then quickly loses its speed and turbulence as it sweeps toward the center of the pool. A trout has stationed himself somewhat downstream from the fastest water and is rising steadily. Precisely what he is rising to cannot be determined, but in such a location a trout is not likely to be highly selective; a No. 14 in any standard pattern should fill the bill. It is easy to drop the fly a short distance above the fish, and it rides jauntily on the uncomplicated current with no sign of drag. Nevertheless, the trout ignores a dozen seemingly perfect presentations while continuing to pick off naturals.

On the theory that rejection may be due to drag, the fisherman wisely alters his position. He moves a bit upstream in order to cast more from the side and avoid any drag that may have resulted from line and leader piling up on themselves.

This move achieves additional refinement by keeping all but the terminal end of the leader away from the fish. But in spite of this measure the trout refuses to take.

As a last resort, the fisherman adds a finer tippet and changes to a very small fly. With this stock response he has exhausted the resources of the two-dimensional approach. He has carefully indulged the more obvious facets of trout sensitivity — but to no avail. The trout continues to refuse, his reluctance a baffling refutation of seemingly perfect presentation.

It is at this point that the trout must be regarded as an individual if a solution is to be reached. Since all known niceties of presentation have been observed, the fisherman can only conclude that his flawlessly presented fly has been ignored because it has somehow failed to penetrate the critical area upon which the trout's attention is exclusively focused.

In this case, and I speak from much experience which I believe to be honestly evaluated, the trout is interested only in those flies which first appear at the extreme limit of his vision and will ignore any which suddenly alight at relatively close range. In other words, his pattern of behavior is such that he will accept only those flies which drift to within view and will ignore all others.

By dropping his fly only a short distance above the trout, our hypothetical fisherman failed to satisfy this eccentricity. Had he been alert to this ostensibly illogical requirement, he would have dropped his fly much farther above the trout than the too short distance which common sense prescribed. And in all probability he would have taken the trout, for then his fly would have satisfied the trout's sense of propriety by traversing the one and only area to which his attention was devoted.

Many will find it hard, and perhaps impossible, to believe that trout are bound by such finely drawn, and seemingly purposeless, behavioral distinctions. Yet in this rather typical situation I have caught hundreds of trout that were not to be interested except by dropping a fly that seemed to be an unnecessarily great distance above their position.

Other stock situations can be used to illustrate this utter devotion to one-track behavior. One, already mentioned, is the trout who has eyes only for flies which drift along the very edge of a steep bank. One might reason that this trout, because of his preoccupation with the shoreline, is literally blind to flies in all other areas, but I'm positive that this is incorrect. Trout are keenly aware of what goes on around them, and that a fly could pass within a foot or two of them and escape notice is highly unlikely. Yet, as previously noted, the trout intent on gathering in shoreline insects simply will not turn aside to snap up any others, even though they come within easy reach.

Unfortunately, in most instances, this area of dedication is not as easily deduced. It occurs in many variations, but it is always there. Since the fish is a trout, he can be expected to manifest all the furtive traits characteristic of his species. But above and beyond that, he will follow a narrowly defined pattern of behavior which, to the fisherman, may seem quite without reason. Yet this seemingly senseless restraint serves a purpose, for it makes the trout less vulnerable by rendering him impervious to distraction. On the other hand, it lays him open to exploitation by fishermen who can envision the routine to which he is temporarily committed. No angler will solve all the mysteries of trout nature, but eventually he will be able to fish with the conviction that he has at least some idea of how trout "think."

It is at this stage that trout fishing becomes most enjoyable, and it is by dry fly fishing that it is best reached. There is very little luck in dry fly fishing, for the terms of the problem (a rising fish) are usually clearly stated before a solution is attempted. The outcome is then determined by the insight the fisherman can bring to bear upon the task.

Although dry fly fishing is easily entered upon, and can be enjoyed by fishermen of modest skill, it is perhaps the most exacting test to which angling ability can be subjected — not because it requires great physical skill, but because it tests the angler's understanding of fish as does no other method. If you can bring yourself to believe what I have had to say, the biggest test of understanding lies in trying to determine just what characteristics are prompting a given trout at a given time.

6

Bait Fishing, A Source
of Insight

*I*F A FISHERMAN has gone on to fly fishing after an apprenticeship in bait fishing, he can probably catch more fish on flies than a beginner can catch on bait. But let him revert to bait, if he is truly a master at the game, and I'll back him to outfish any fly fisherman over the long haul, or any bait caster or spin fisherman for that matter.

Can I prove this contention? Not to everybody's satisfaction, perhaps, but I can support it on the grounds of percentage. First, there are times when it is virtually impossible to take fish on anything. Next, there are periods during which fish will respond to bait but will show almost no interest in flies, plugs or hardware. Finally, there are those interludes when they will hit both bait and artificials. In other words, there are times when fish will take bait and refuse artificials, but never a time when they will hit artificial lures and scorn bait.

Some dry fly fishermen are likely to insist that this is not true; that when fish are rising to mayflies they cannot be interested in bait. It is quite true that at such times they are not to be taken by the casual worm dunker. But all bait fishermen are not mere worm dunkers.

Several years ago, Pete and I were fishing the Clyde River in northern Vermont. Pete came on a rising fish which he took to be a whopping trout and promptly went to work on him with a dry fly. His careful casting did not put the fish down, but neither did it result in a strike. After dozens of fruitless casts, Pete decided that the size of the fish warranted other measures.

He removed his fly and tied on a No. 14 hook. Then he scrounged around until he found a stick caddis, shucked the larva from its case and threaded it on the tiny hook. Returning to the still-rising fish, he made a soft cast to a spot above its station. The fish took the dab of bait the instant it came over him and shot nearly a yard into the air when Pete gently set the hook. Instead of the anticipated trout, it was a dandy landlocked salmon.

So I happen to know that surface-feeding fish will take bait as well as dry flies, and sometimes, as in this case, even more readily. It all depends on the bait — and the fisherman.

Now, what about my contention that at times fish can be caught on bait but cannot be persuaded to hit flies or hardware? (Pete's salmon, a rising fish, did not fall in this category; although Pete couldn't fool him with a dry fly, it can be assumed that he would have gone for any dry fly in which he saw no cause for suspicion.) The question, of course, is whether I know what I'm talking about. Quite possibly I don't.

There have been many times when I could catch fish on bait, but not on artificial lures. Perhaps fishermen of greater skill could have taken the same fish on flies, at the same time and under identical conditions. I must confess, however, that I'm brash enough to doubt it. This isn't because I have an exaggerated opinion of my skill as a fisherman. It's because of the honest conviction that there are times and conditions when even the most skillful fishermen cannot take any appreciable number of fish on artificials.

Lynn and Nina Tanner own and operate a fishing camp on Long Pond in Jackman, Maine. Their wilderness location is so remote that it cannot be reached by road. To get there, guests must run down a stretch of the Moose River by boat or canoe and then cross a section of the pond itself. Pete and I made our headquarters at this camp during a series of annual trips to the Jackman region.

During our first trip, before we had learned enough of the country to shift for ourselves, Lynn spent considerable time showing us around.

The first spot to which he took us was a stretch of quickwater a couple of miles up the Moose River from where it entered Long Pond. The stretch is called the "Cattle Beat," probably because the first settlers used it as a ford for their livestock. No cattle have crossed there for many years, and the name no longer conveys a literal implication. Instead, at least to fishermen, it denotes trout and salmon, for the Cattle Beat is one of the fishing hot spots of the Moose River.

It was early spring, the water was still high and the weather unseasonably cold, even for Maine. Lynn anchored the boat near the head of the fast water, and Pete and I began working streamers across the slick where the current first picked up speed. If I remember correctly, we took one short landlocked salmon and that seemed to be the end of it.

When we couldn't get another fish to come to our streamers, we switched to spinning rods and deep-running spoons and wobblers. Results were almost identical: one lone nine-inch brook trout, and then not another strike.

Lynn, compared to whom the most taciturn Indian would seem to be a chatterbox, watched our fruitless efforts in silence. Finally, he reached under the stern seat and came up with a can of worms.

"Try these," he said to Pete.

I went through the motions of protesting that we hadn't come all that distance to catch trout and salmon on worms, but Pete took a more practical view of the situation. He soon had a worm-baited hook and a couple of split shot on his spinning line, and a moment later the squirming worm was drifting down the slick, bumping bottom as it went. On the very first drift a two-pound salmon snapped up the worm and then leaped high when the hook stung him.

Pete's next drift produced a brilliantly marked brook trout which weighed more than a pound. Pete continued to take fish after fish, and it was obvious that the spot was teeming with trout and salmon, all apparently waiting in line to grab a sunken worm.

136

I redoubled my efforts with spinning lures. But if I was stubborn, the trout and salmon were more than a match for me. Try as I might, and while Pete landed fish after fish, I couldn't so much as draw a strike.

Unfortunately, I cannot prove that a better fisherman couldn't have found ways to take some of those fish on streamers and spoons. I admit the possibility, but cling to the belief that it simply couldn't have been done. The fish were hugging bottom, as they invariably do in high, cold water. But even though I bumped the bottom with my spinning lures, and weighted my streamers by pinching shot on my leader, my efforts went for naught. Both Pete and I fished at the same level. But my lures were ignored while Pete's worms were a surefire bet.

There was a time when I wasn't as stubborn about such matters. When trout refused my flies and lures I didn't hesitate to offer them something more to their liking. And although there were plenty of times when I couldn't take them on artificials, I could usually manage to tempt at least a few with bait.

In Otter Creek there is a long stretch of fast water which in past days was heavily populated with hefty rainbows and held a lesser number of even larger browns. Whenever a hatch developed the stretch would fairly boil with feeding fish, and the fishing at such times was the answer to a dry fly fisherman's dreams.

But when no hatch was in progress, it was almost impossible to raise a fish to a dry fly. Nymphs, sunken wet flies and streamers? One, or all, of the three *should* have turned the trick, but I tried them repeatedly to but trivial avail.

I was not alone in my frustration. Seasoned anglers of my acquaintance were plagued by the same enigma, and we often commiserated. Here was a stretch of water which we knew held many large trout. Yet to all intents and purposes, at least for the fly fisherman, it might as well have been barren of fish save for the all-too-short intervals when hatches were going on. Did those confounded fish feed only on mayflies?

You may be sure that they didn't. At the head of the stretch was a shallow rips, and under rocks in the rips were hellgrammites nearly as large as a man's little finger. After vainly working the run with flies, I'd move upstream and turn over a few rocks. I'd soon have one of the big hellgrammites, hook it under its "collar" and return to the run.

I'd lob the bait upstream, and it would settle toward bottom as it drifted back. Usually the line would check during the very first drift, and almost always this signaled a bite from a rainbow in the two-pound bracket. Very seldom did a hellgrammite fail to produce a trout after a long and vain effort with flies.

I submit that this is a test which few fishermen apply; most either do or die with flies, or use bait in the first place. I've done it enough times, and in enough different places, to shatter any belief that flies are inherently more deadly than appropriate natural bait.

In recent years I have become more and more reluctant to resort to bait when fishing for trout and seldom do so except on streams and beaver dams where a tangle of brush and trees makes it impossible to fish in any other way. One reason for my objections to the use of bait for trout is that bait-caught trout are often so deeply hooked that they cannot be released with a real chance of survival. Since I return many of the trout I catch, the fact that those caught on flies suffer nothing more serious than a superficial prick is an important consideration.

Yet I suppose the truth of the matter is that I'm even more strongly influenced by pride and stubbornness. My primary goal in trout fishing is to take trout on dry flies. This is an obsession which undoubtedly helps to hold down the number of fish I take. Nevertheless, I can't shake the notion that to resort to nymphs, wet flies or streamers is a concession to weakness, a matter of "giving in" instead of standing firm.

This doesn't mean that I don't fish with sunken flies when there seems to be no alternative, but only because I lack the willpower to remain loyal to my cockeyed ideals. The same weakness of character may prompt me to turn to spinning, but by so doing I always suffer the guilty feeling of having lost face with myself. All of which indicates nothing, of course, other than that I am vain.

It is on such subjective grounds, however, that bait fishing is frequently condemned. There is nothing extraordinary about this; man instinctively condemns those pursuits which do not conform to his personal persuasions, and we live in a country which guarantees us the right to so indulge. But the point I would like to make, in the interest of accuracy, is that it is a violation of fact to brand bait fishing with the mark of inferiority because of any imaginary inefficiency. It may be the least-refined method of taking fish, but in all fairness it should be recognized as the one which is most generally reliable and effective. And it affords insights into the art of angling not to be gained in any other way.

The truth is that while fish may be "foolish" enough to grab a metal spoon, they are often "wise" enough to refuse a poorly presented worm or minnow. Bait fishing reveals this paradox and enables the fisherman to see fish for what they really are: creatures in which stupidity and shrewdness coexist in a curious alliance. Because of these contrasting characteristics, fish can be expected to behave cautiously under certain conditions, and to throw caution to the winds in other circumstances.

It is quite possible, for example, to wire a hook to a beer can opener and catch a northern pike on this outrageous "lure." This, by itself, would seem to prove that northerns are mentally incompetent and totally unfit to look out for themselves. Their willingness to grab a red-and-white spoon denotes little more by way of intelligence, and the fisherman who confines his pike fishing to the use of metal lures has little reason to credit northerns with any marked powers of discrimination.

Yet this biased view is misleading. If one fishes for northerns with live minnows, careful observation will disclose a rather curious contrast. The very fish that "knows" no better than to launch an unthinking attack on an undisguised can opener is very likely to study a live chub or sucker on a hook with all the shrewdness of a red fox surveying a baited trap. The parallel does not dissolve with projection, for the suspicious pike and the sly fox are equally good bets to escape capture by prudently resisting temptation.

It is not surprising that the fox avoids the trap, for Reynard is well known as a shrewd operator who has his wits about him at all times and seldom makes a rash move. But the pike's behavior gives cause for considerable wonder. How can he be such a blockhead in one situation and sly as a fox in another?

This question becomes more provocative when the pike's inconsistency is analyzed in more detail. First, let us concentrate on the situation in which, like an idiot, he commits suicide by grabbing the can opener.

Here, if he had the slightest sense of caution, it seems that he would most certainly turn tail and flee for his life. Not only is he confronted with a contraption completely foreign to his experience, but one whose crude design and unnatural behavior fairly shriek of danger. But because the pike is a fish, and fish are schizophrenic, he is done in by the brasher side of his nature which often prompts him to ignore glaring signs of peril.

It seems almost inconceivable that the very same fish may eye a live sucker with cautious reservation and eventually decide against grabbing it. He is face to face with a familiar and tempting item of food, and one which he knows to be absolutely genuine. In addition, the hunger which inspires his interest in the bait is a powerful advocate of indiscretion. It is hard to believe that a critter rash enough to smack a beer can opener may see cause for alarm in the slight eccentricities of behavior displayed by a live sucker that is hampered only by a hook and leader.

Yet this is precisely what happens more often than not.

The drama is usually enacted outside the fisherman's range of vision, and therefore without his knowledge, but it can be observed with sufficient frequency to warrant the conclusion that it is a common occurrence. I have watched big pike study my bait enough times to know that they are far more likely to glide off disdainfully than to close in and grab it. So observed, northern pike seem anything but stupid.

Full understanding of this duality of character which exists among fish helps greatly to engender the empathy which plays such a big part in determining the extent of a fisherman's success. This empathy can be gained only by peering through keyholes, so to speak, for we and the fish live in mutually exclusive worlds. The more keyholes we peer through, the greater our understanding, and the view to be seen through the bait fishing "keyhole" is apparent through no other.

As an example, the use of bait will support a claim made in a previous chapter: that taking fish on genuine items of food, or on their close imitations, is an altogether different matter from that of taking them on lures designed to arouse excitement. In the first instance, the fisherman pits his skill against the conservative and calculating side of fish nature, and he can win out only by employing all possible refinement of presentation. As a matter of fact, skill is more important in bait fishing than it often is in the use of lures that are essentially provocative. Let's assume that we are dealing with a rank beginner and compare the requirement for early success in each of the two fields.

If we start him off with a spinning outfit, he must first learn to cast. This he can do quickly and easily. Probably the reason for spinning's great popularity is that any beginner can learn to cast reasonably well with a spinning rig by practicing no more than an hour on his lawn.

We then take him to a stream and start him off with a lure of proven appeal. What must he do to take fish? Nothing more artful than to cast downstream and crank his lure against the current. The fact that he may know almost nothing of the nature of the fish he is after will not be a prohibitive handicap. He is absolved of the necessity of presenting his lure so that it will appear innocent of incongruity. If he merely turns the reel handle, his lure will promptly exhibit the peculiar powers of fascination which it owes to its design. Even though our tyro has never caught a fish in his life, he is likely to make a fairly good showing on his first attempt — granting, of course, that we have taken him where there are fish to be caught.

Should we start our beginner with a fly rod, he would need to spend considerably more time learning to cast. But even then, he should be ready after a few practice sessions.

We take him to the same stream, tie a streamer fly to his leader and instruct him almost exactly as before: cast downstream and retrieve against the current. Again, if conditions are equally favorable, there is little to prevent him from making a reasonably good catch. A streamer, like a spinning lure, is designed to do its own "catching," and he would have no need to make it appear innocent. On the contrary, he would need only to flaunt its incongruity to win strikes.

Had we chosen to introduce our beginner to bait fishing,

such simple directions would not have sufficed. Perhaps I can illustrate this difference by the following example.

My friend Vic Gladski operates a thriving grocery store which overlooks Furnace Brook, and the adjacent stretch of stream is always heavily stocked with trout prior to the opening of each fishing season. Since this circumstance is common knowledge, a steady procession of fishermen passes in review on opening day. Vic, who is a fisherman himself, keeps as close tab on what goes on as business will permit.

"Last opening day," he told me, "I bet thirty or forty fishermen had fished down through by ten o'clock. Most of the ones I talked to told me that they had been fishing since daylight. One fellow had four trout, but most of them had only one or two.

"Then, after the rush was over, Pete Terwilliger parked his car in front of the store and began fishing upstream. You wouldn't have believed that anybody could have caught a trout after that army had gone through, but darned if Pete didn't take fish almost as fast as he could haul them in. He was back in less than an hour with his limit of twelve trout."

Most of the trout in question were rainbows fresh out of the hatchery and seemingly should have been easy pickings for anybody who took the trouble to dangle a worm in the stream. But the water was high and cold, as is usually the case on opening day, and in that icy water the trout were anything but ravenous. Also, although they were hatchery products, they retained a measure of that aversion to suicide for which trout of all kinds are justifiably noted.

They were certainly interested in food — Pete's success with bait proved that — but their hunger was too mild to be indulged at the cost of serious indiscretion. The dozen trout which Pete caught had undoubtedly seen, and refused, dozens of baited hooks before falling for his. Since all the fishermen, Pete included, had fished with worms, the enormous difference in results could only have been due to greater skill on Pete's part.

As Pete is my long-time fishing partner, I know how he fishes and can account for his success. In spite of the early season and the high water, he rigged up almost as though for dry fly fishing: fly rod, tapered line (for easier casting) and a leader tapered to at least 3X. His hook was a light wire No. 12, and this he baited with only the pinched-off tail of a small worm. In spite of the heavy current he clamped no more than a small split shot to his leader, or he may have elected to fish with no sinker at all.

Finally, Pete fished upstream, whereas all the others fished downstream. By making careful soft casts he could lob his tiny bait to the heads of pools and runs and then let it trickle back toward him under no tension from his line. Thanks to the light, flexible leader and tippet, the small hook and the minimal bulk of his bait, the dab of worm drifted so naturally that the trout found it indistinguishable from the customary tidbits upon which they normally fed. And this was all they asked!

As for the others, they fished downstream with much heavier terminal gear: shorter and stiffer leaders, much heavier sinkers and far larger hooks. Most probably draped on several large worms, and the result was a combination which, instead of yielding to the whims of the heavy current, openly defied them. It was this unnatural behavior which advertised the artificiality of the whole lash-up.

These unsuccessful fishermen were not beginners in the strict sense of the word, but their efforts were typical of a beginner's and are a valid basis for comparison. Our imaginary beginner would probably have proceeded in much the same manner, and with much the same results. Had we advised him to fish as Pete did, he would have found his skill unequal to the job. Also, I'm sure, he would have questioned the necessity of adopting such measures.

Eventually, if he fished seriously with bait, he would come to realize that it has insufficient appeal to carry the day by itself. It would be brought forcefully to his attention that bait is truly effective only when fetchingly presented, and gradually he would discover, and learn to apply, the necessary refinements.

As already stated, the fellow who begins fishing with provocative lures is not bound by any such protocol, and he may eventually attempt dry fly fishing with insufficient enlightenment. He is immediately in for some surprises which he will find difficult to understand. When he finds himself on a stream during a heavy hatch of mayflies, with trout rising all around him, he is all too likely to assume that the rising trout will regard imitation flies with the same lack of discrimination they displayed in hitting his spoons and streamers. Confident that they will fall for anything which roughly approximates a drifting mayfly, he is amazed to have his offerings

146

scorned, even when they seem to imitate the natural insects to perfection.

At long last he comes face to face with the bugaboo of "drag." But because his previous experience has not been well rounded, he is likely to conclude that drag is a factor peculiar to dry fly fishing.

The man who has first fished with bait will see this phenomenon in more realistic perspective. Having witnessed the rejection of natural food items for trivial violations of natural behavior, he sees little reason for surprise in the rejection of imitative items on the same grounds. In fact, this even more critical attitude toward imitative offerings is exactly what he has been conditioned by experience to expect.

Thanks to his bait fishing, he knows that drag is the villain that must be put down whenever the intent is to persuade fish to accept real food, and he automatically accepts the fact that this requirement carries over to food imitations. Furthermore, he knows that the need to avoid drag exists whether the bait or artificial is fished along the bottom, in the middle depths or at the surface. Thus the man who has first fished with bait identifies drag correctly as an angling factor of broad application. The fellow who has used only artificial lures tends to see it as an isolated oddity, and the limitations of his understanding place him at a disadvantage in coping with it.

Since the effectiveness of provocative lures is largely determined by their design, some are unquestionably more deadly than others. The fisherman who launches his fishing career with the use of lures of this type soon notes this distinction. He comes to believe, and his belief is not entirely misplaced, that success is often largely a matter of choosing the proper lure. This is all well and good as long as he sticks to hardware, but he is likely to believe that the same holds true in imitative fishing.

The fisherman familiar with the problems of bait fishing has learned better than to depend so disproportionately on a choice of offering. He knows that some baits are superior to others, but he also knows that the difference is relatively unimportant compared to the importance of striving for natural presentation. When he turns to dry fly fishing his trust will be based on realism, rather than on notion.

It is therefore my belief that opinions concerning bait fishing should not be formed until after its lessons have been learned. I think a beginning fisherman should indulge in bait fishing if for no other reason than to gain full appreciation of the extent to which fish tend to resist temptation.

I was first enlightened in this matter while still very young, and under rather unique circumstances. In my hometown, water was drawn from a man-made reservoir situated high above the village. It was an object of great curiosity to all the kids in the village, but our yearning to inspect the installation at close hand was thwarted by a high and impregnable fence of closely strung barbed wire.

But on one memorable Saturday, several other lads and I were surprised and delighted to find the gate open and unattended. We immediately invaded the forbidden territory, of course, but with every expectation of being chased off just as promptly. Instead, we were greeted by a couple of boys, only a few years our senior, who had been given the job of cutting the grass which had grown high inside the enclosure. We were welcomed as witnesses to this evidence of budding maturity.

We solidified our status as welcome visitors by adopting the proper air of deference, then set out on a tour of inspection. We climbed the embankment which surrounded the reservoir, and discovered that it dropped off to depths that seemed bottomless. Water boiled to the surface in the center of the reservoir, seething as it entered under pressure from a hidden conduit. I knew exactly where the water came from — a dam on a brook some five or six miles away — and marveled at the engineering miracle which made this possible.

After an initial survey, our interest came to focus on a small wooden structure which rose above the water about twenty feet from shore. The small building rested on a concrete foundation which rose several feet above the water, and a plank bridge or ramp led from the shore to the door of the building. The door was open, and inside we could see the wheels and levers by which the flow of water was controlled.

We were inside in a matter of seconds, gazing at an array of gadgets which invited experimental manipulation. It is quite probable that indignant townspeople would have noted a disconcerting fluctuation of water pressure shortly thereafter had not one of the group made an interesting discovery — a trapdoor in the center of the building's floor.

When the door was raised, which is to say immediately, we found ourselves peering down into a well of green water of substantial depth. At the bottom, an arched opening in one of the concrete walls admitted water and light, and presently it admitted something vastly more interesting — a brook trout of ponderous bulk and majestic bearing. The big trout had no sooner glided through the arch than it was followed by what seemed its twin. A third trout soon joined the first two, and we could make out the shadowy forms of still more leviathans drifting back and forth just outside the opening.

We hastily deployed in search of worms, and a few overturned rocks soon provided us with a supply. A worm was dropped through the trapdoor, and each of us held his breath as the worm sank slowly into the green depths, its frantic writhing a futile defense against the Archimedean law to which it had so unexpectedly become subject.

Unfortunately for the hapless worm, it was soon overtaken by an even greater catastrophe. One of the big trout finally spotted it and zoomed up to take it with a roll that was a breathtaking display of fluid grace. We proceeded to shower the trout with worms, with small regard for the sensitivities of the town's water consumers, and the hollow interior of the buildings's foundation soon became packed with wildly excited jumbo trout.

Our next step was decided swiftly, and with no time wasted debating the pros and cons of its ethics. The youngest among us was ordered to depart immediately and to return with a line, hook and sinker in the shortest possible time. In the meantime, the rest of us would keep the trout at their present feverish state by feeding them additional worms.

Excitement filled the little shack when a coarse line, heavy sinker and large baited hook were finally lowered into the midst of the milling trout. It is safe to say that each of us looked forward to removing every big trout from the reservoir.

Yet, right from the start, it was very evident that the trout did not regard our baited hook in the favorable light in which they had viewed the unencumbered worms which preceded it. One after another dashed at the bait as though intent on grabbing it, only to swerve at the last moment and pass on by. This drama was repeated time and again as we watched in an agony of suspense, but finally one of the big fish made the mistake of actually seizing the worm. He was promptly hauled clear of the water amid loud commotion which echoed hollowly in the concrete shaft. Unfortunately, at least from our viewpoint, the surface of the water was six or more feet below us, and the mighty flopping of the big fish during its aerial ascent tore the hook free and the trout fell to its freedom with a thunderous splash.

The lad handling the line was loudly reprimanded, but not with the bitterness reserved for one guilty of critical failure. The enclosure was still filled with hungry trout, and none of us believed that the plan to remove them one by one had suffered anything more serious than a temporary setback. The hook was rebaited and then lowered with undiminished confidence.

Yet things did not work out as we anticipated. Try as we might, we could not persuade another one of the big square-tails to bite. This was probably almost as fortunate for us as for them. There were undoubtedly those who held the trout in high esteem, and who would have tracked down the guilty parties — a job which, in this case, wouldn't have required any great amount of detective work. Parents would have been informed, and in those days parents who received such reports quickly did what they saw as their duty by administering extremely painful punishment.

Perhaps evidence gained by fishing in the forbidden waters of a municipal reservoir should be ruled inadmissible, but it illustrates what the fisherman is up against. Although the trout in this case had never been fished for, no more than one made the mistake of snapping up a worm which was presented without any accompanying effort to make its appearance and behavior seem natural.

In all public waters, where fish are even more wary, the incidence of success is undoubtedly much lower. In other words, and contrary to popular opinion, the bait fisherman who uses but little skill in presenting his bait will catch mighty few of the many fish who see it.

7

Where the Grass
Is Really Greener

ROTARY CLUBS are habitually hard up for speakers, at least this seems to be the case in my neck of the woods. I'm basing this opinion on the fact that they sometimes ask me to give a talk on fishing.

My shortcomings as a public speaker are sufficient to make me apprehensive about such assignments, but my queasiness is compounded by the knowledge that not all Rotarians are fishermen. In my audience are bound to be those who look on fishing as a foolish enterprise, and an acute awareness of them dampens any small enthusiasm I might otherwise have for the job. Even when speaking to groups made up entirely of fishermen, I never feel confident of hitting on any common denominator of interest. To the many people who fish, fishing is a great many different things, and what one fisherman sees as

153

its greatest charms may be in sharp contrast to the views of other anglers of equal enthusiasm.

One beautiful June day, several years ago, Pete Terwilliger and I were fishing Attean Rips, a stretch of rapids on the Moose River near Jackman, Maine. Fishing at the head of the rips, or the "top of the pitch" as it is called in Maine, we took brook trout up to a two-pound top, plus several land-locked salmon which weighed between two and three pounds. All had risen to dry flies, so it was fishing that left little to be desired.

Our guide was a hardened veteran of the Maine woods named Walter Wilson. Walter had guided me on several previous trips, and I had come to value and appreciate his expert services.

But Walter wasn't one you'd pick as your guide on the strength of appearances. He was well past seventy, and his lined and angular face seemed to bespeak a deep-seated cynicism toward everything and everybody, giving the impression that he was patiently waiting for the world to get the comeuppance he believed it richly deserved.

Just to watch him paddle a canoe was enough to bring on strong feelings of depression. He hunched himself over his paddle in a manner which seemed to reflect the accumulated weariness of more than a half century of paddling, while his face took on the dour expression of a man who has just discovered a leak in his waders. To anyone the least bit sensitive to human suffering, the idea of pursuing pleasure in the presence of such abject misery seemed almost indecent.

I hadn't fished long from Walter's canoe, however, before

discovering that I was always exactly where I wanted to be: in comfortable casting range of the most likely places. In the meantime, although in the manner of one discharging an odious duty, Walter drew on decades of experience to point out the precise spots where I should drop my fly. By the end of the first day I knew that he had done his darndest to put me on fish. When I got to know him better, I came to realize that he actually got a big kick out of doing so.

That morning, however, Pete and I needed no help from Walter. We fished in waders, the fish were on the move and all we had to do was to lay about us with high-riding dry flies. Walter watched us a spell, then ambled downstream to the big pool at the base of the rips where we had beached the canoe. He'd holler when lunch was ready, he told us.

There was a rustic table and shelter overlooking the pool, and I can think of no pleasanter setting for a noon cookout. This, plus the exuberance brought about by the splendid fishing, impelled Pete and me to praise Walter's culinary efforts to the skies. The broiled chops were delicious beyond all previous experience, the pan-fried potatoes and onions superb and the heady flavor of the boiled coffee — which only Maine guides seem able to achieve — was out of this world.

If Walter reacted to our praise, it was without visible sign. He stared out over the broad pool in silence, and then, if such were possible, his face took on a more pained expression than usual.

"There was a feller I used to guide years ago," he said, plunking down each word as though glad to be rid of it. "He wanted to catch a trout of five pounds or more. Had his heart set on having one that big mounted, but wouldn't settle for anything smaller. He caught quite a few trout that weighed over four pounds, but darned if I could ever get him one that weighed five.

"One spring he showed up with his uncle, an old feller who had never caught a trout in his life. We came up here to the rips, and the young feller told me to look out for the old man while he fished the top of the pitch.

"I put the uncle in the canoe and paddled up to the head of this pool in front of us. Tied on a streamer for him, stripped out some line and then handed him the rod and told him to keep twitching it.

"Pretty soon a fish hit that streamer a helluva belt, and I finally managed to net it. It was a trout that weighed five pounds and two ounces. I worked out line again and gave the old man the rod. Another helluva wallop, and *another* trout of over five pounds!

"You should have seen the young feller's face when he saw that pair of fish. But before he could say anything, the uncle wanted to know where I planned to have him fish after lunch.

" 'You and I are going right back where we were this morning,' I told him.

" 'What for?' he wanted to know. 'We fished there all morning and only caught two.' "

Walter continued to stare out over the pool, tortured by the resurrection of irony too painful for a man to bear. Finally, still lost in glum reflection, he silently went about gathering up dishes and the few leftovers from our lunch.

If nothing else, this yarn illustrates the degree to which the charm of fishing lies in the eye of the beholder. Although some see it clearly, others see it not at all, raising for philosophical debate the question of whether it is real or imaginary.

Even among those who dearly love to fish, a divergence of viewpoint has developed in recent years, threatening to alter the traditional concept of the sport. This new concept has evolved, I suspect, as a result of the quickening tempo of life with which we seem obliged to keep pace.

What I have chosen to call the traditional point of view or concept is that which concerns itself largely with nearby waters and the problems involved in taking fish that have been well educated by persistent attempts on their lives. Within this framework the gross thrill of taking large numbers of big fish is not a paramount goal. Instead, the principal objective is to achieve modest success under circumstances sufficiently demanding to make this a reliable and gratifying reflection of angling skill.

The modern concept has little patience with this quiet challenge. The foremost goal, to its swelling ranks of adherents, has become that of reaching remote waters which have seen little or no fishing, and where even the tyro can expect to catch more fish than he can carry.

It is both natural and practical for editors and writers to capitalize on the glamour of far-off places, and much that is published about fishing nowadays has to do with the spectacular fishing which can be found only in the most remote regions. Such material has its effect on the reader. Local attractions have less appeal as he reads of virgin fishing and big fish, and his angling ambitions come to include little else than the desire to fish the romantic waters he reads about.

How well does this modern concept serve the fisherman's

need? If he was bitten by the same fishing bug that long ago bit me, it tends to tantalize far more than to satisfy.

When I was a kid, a small group of men in my hometown made annual trips to a wilderness pond in northern Vermont, which involved a drive of less than a hundred miles, plus a hike through the woods of a dozen more. For these modest efforts they were rewarded with virginal fishing. They never failed to return with big catches of trout that ran up to three and four pounds in weight, to say nothing of yarns calculated to make a youngster squirm with envy. Needless to say, a good road now leads straight to the pond, and the fishing has been a put and take proposition for many years.

Years later I enjoyed somewhat the same kind of fishing in Maine. The demands had become greater, however: a drive of nearly four hundred miles, then plane flights to wilderness ponds and lakes. A few years later, Pete and I drove over a good road to a pond I had previously visited by plane. Where my friends and I had caught a trout on about every fourth cast, Pete and I worked an entire afternoon to catch a dozen.

Three years ago, Pete and I drove four hundred miles to Bangor, Maine. From there we flew nearly a thousand miles to a camp in western Labrador. From the base camp, we hopped another two hundred and fifty miles northeast to a river on the Labrador coast. With that distance behind us, we finally stood where few men have fished. In a huge pool which teemed with big arctic char, fresh from the sea, we finally found fishing which matched our wildest dreams.

But that was three long years ago. We haven't returned to that wild and wonderful river, and the chances are good that we never will. The memories of that trip still make my scalp prickle, but they are no answer to my basic fishing need which, above all else, is to fish as frequently as the mood strikes. This is likely to be on any balmy evening, and by the time I have eaten dinner and assembled my fishing gear there is scarcely time to reach the northern coast of Labrador.

For this reason alone, the theory that the answer to a fisherman's needs can be found in the blessings of modern transportation is largely an illusion. Anybody who hopes to find virgin fishing that can be easily reached, even by plane, is entertaining a pipe dream. Any easily approached fishing is soon reduced to mediocrity, and only those places which can be reached with difficulty remain truly beyond the frontier.

This does not detract from the thrills to be found beyond these frontiers, but it does compress them into the infrequency with which the necessary trips can be made — if they can be made at all. And what fisherman can be at peace with the world if he must confine his fishing to an occasional trip, or even worse, to dreams of making such a trip?

There is a bit more to it than that. Once the fisherman reaches waters that are everything he has dreamed of, he finds that the game suddenly changes. Big fish that are easily caught tend to lose significance, just as gold would lose its glamour if gold nuggets were as common as pebbles.

Two years ago Pete and I fished the George River in northern Quebec. We were after Atlantic salmon, and we were lucky enough to arrive when the run of these dynamic fish was on. But along with the salmon, brook trout of several pounds rose to our flies, as did lake trout that weighed up to ten pounds. The composite result was fishing that was as close to the ultimate as any fisherman could hope for.

But Pete and I came to look on strikes from big brookies and lake trout almost as intrusions, even though we do most of our fishing where a foot-long brook trout is a rare prize, and the fisherman who takes a ten-pound laker gets his picture in the papers. With eyes only for salmon, fish that normally would set our hearts to pounding became victims of a sliding scale of values.

This feeling suggests that the thrills of fishing are not tied in directly with the size and number of fish, caught, but are determined by the relativity fish have to the context in which they are encountered. In other words, spectacular success in an atmosphere of extravagance is not necessarily more satisfying than substantially lesser achievements made under more modest circumstances.

There is a stream only a few miles from my home in which there is a long stretch of quiet water which is perfect for dry fly fishing. It teems with wild brookies, and the only disparaging thing to be said about it is that the trout run to small size. I have caught as many as forty in a single evening, not one of which was more than nine inches long.

One evening last summer I reached the upstream limit of this stretch before darkness had closed in and decided to fish downstream toward my car. I tied on a fairly large Cooper Bug, and as I sloshed my way back I skittered this fly across some of the better holes.

Small trout made abortive passes at the thing, but none had the courage to grab it. Suddenly, in a particularly deep hole, a fish broke behind it with a tremendous swirl. I could feel my hackles rise, for I knew by the size of the swirl that the trout was *fully a foot long!* Adding to my excitement was the feeling that the "lunker" would take on the next cast.

Sure enough, he attacked the bug almost the instant it hit the water a second time, and I'm completely honest in saying that my heart hammered for fear that he would come off before I could get him in the net. Although he proved to be a wee bit short of the estimated twelve inches, he was one of the "biggest" brook trout I have ever taken.

Was I kidding myself? Does fishing admit a line of demarcation between those thrills which are somehow absolute and those which are merely affectations? I doubt that any such line can be drawn that will stand the test of objectivity.

In support of this contention I'll pass along a yarn told to me by Bev Weatherby of Grand Lake Stream, Maine. Bev and his wife Alice own and operate a popular fishing camp on Grand Lake, and for a string of years I have enjoyed wonderful fishing for both smallmouth bass and landlocked salmon with their camp as my headquarters. In addition, I've been privileged to listen to Bev tell stories, and thanks to his rare talent for yarning, this has been no small consideration.

According to Bev, there was this fisherman of advanced age who, for years, had tried in vain to hang an Atlantic salmon in the Maine rivers which still have limited salmon runs. At long last the miracle came to pass; a big salmon rose to his fly and was securely hooked.

The water was low and the shoreline a jumble of large boulders. And since the salmon made many long runs, the old fellow was forced to chase upstream and down to avoid the calamity of a cleaned reel.

This went on for some time, during which the angler showed increasing signs of wear and tear. He had fallen several times, shedding patches of skin and some blood as the result of rough contact with raw granite. Eventually he seemed on the verge of collapse, from exertion and from his high state of excitement.

At this point a native, who had watched the proceedings with interest and amusement, felt obliged to intercede. He arose, drew up alongside the battered and wildly excited fisherman and pointed toward the salmon with the stem of his pipe.

"It ain't really none of my business," he said, "but before you kill yourself I want to remind you that the thing out there on the end of your line ain't nothing but a fish."

It can be argued that the man with the pipe missed the point, that, to a fisherman, an Atlantic salmon is not "just a fish" but a thing of enormous worth. While this may be true, the salmon's magnificence is a reality only in the sense that it is an emotional conviction which fishermen happen to share.

Many years ago I helped land a bluefin tuna which weighed nearly seven hundred pounds. The power and speed of this huge fish were incredible to behold, and perhaps they should have made me contemptuous of the relatively puny fighting qualities of freshwater fish. Actually, the epic battle with the huge fish had no such effect. Although I still remember how the tuna all but yanked three of us over the stern — this was in the days when tuna fishing off the coast of Maine was in its experimental stages — I can refer to the "terrific" battle put up by a trout or salmon without feeling the slightest bit ridiculous.

This story brings into focus what I believe to be the fisherman's salvation: his ability to adjust to the situation at hand, and to realize through relativity the satisfactions which otherwise lie beyond his reach. Fishing is such that the ultimate becomes a mirage for those who seek it deliberately and exists as an attainable reality only for those who do not consciously engage in its pursuit. The man who fishes with only modest expectations experiences the ultimate whenever these are exceeded. This tends to happen quite frequently, for it takes no more than a fifteen-inch trout or a three-pound bass to turn the trick. The fisherman who sets loftier goals not only renounces his principal source of triumph, but dooms himself to almost constant disappointment.

There is a limit, of course, to the kind of fishing that will furnish the satisfaction the fisherman craves. I like to fish for bluegills, crappies, perch and bullheads, but I would be the last to suggest that panfish are a satisfactory substitute for game fish. Fortunately, few fishermen are so compromised that they have only panfish to turn to. All of us have a much greater area within easy reach than is generally realized, and this area almost always holds unappreciated potential.

In this day and age a distance of fifty miles has become trivial — a mere hour's drive. The Battenkill is that distance from my home, and I don't hesitate to drive to it for the evening fishing — whenever I get the vain and foolish notion that my skill is a match for its sophisticated trout.

Actually, most fishermen, myself included, think nothing of driving much farther to fish, but to be on the conservative side, let's assume that all waters within fifty miles constitute a fisherman's home base. This base establishes an imaginary circle of rather surprising area. Applying the formula $A = \pi r^2$, the area of a circle of fifty-mile radius comes out to be 7857 plus square miles!

There is no denying the inroads made upon fishing by pollution, construction, urbanization and other forces, but an area of nearly 8000 square miles is a mighty large chunk of territory. In spite of the many negative factors, I believe it would be next to impossible to find an area of this size which didn't contain at least some worthwhile fishing.

But proximity, like familiarity, breeds both contempt and indifference, and the more one associates glamour with remoteness, the more he is inclined to dismiss the potential of that to which he has easy access. As a result, local opportunities often go begging simply because of the widespread assumption that they cannot, and therefore do not, exist.

Several years ago a colony of beavers set up housekeeping on a tiny stream only five miles from my home, almost within sight of heavily traveled U.S. Route 7. Long before their appearance, I had checked out the stream, hardly more than a trickle, and came away convinced that it held no fish of any description, let alone trout. So, although aware of the beaver flowage, I wrote it off as unworthy of investigation. Others who knew about it apparently did the same, for it existed for several years, without attracting the attention of a single fisherman.

In the meantime, brook trout somehow became established in the pond, prospering and fattening without interference from the fishermen who sped along the nearby highway. I'm sure that among these were many who, like myself, have kicked themselves since for not taking the trouble to investigate.

Finally, on last opening day, one angler who refused to take things for granted gave the flowage an off-chance try. He was richly rewarded for this slight effort with brookies which were as deep bellied as bass and which had reached lengths as great as eighteen inches.

Inconceivable as it seems, this lucky fisherman blabbed of his discovery, and hordes of eager citizens converged on the flowage. It took only a week to rid it of its trout, but they totaled several hundred, almost none of which was under a foot long.

Where did those trout come from? The question is rendered pointless by virtue of the fact that they were there awaiting discovery. The fellow who found them made out gloriously while the rest of us were either headed for or dreaming of more distant places.

Although I goofed this chance, I have made comparable finds. About ten years ago beavers dammed another nearby stream. The resulting flowage covered many acres and was so large that it could be explored by canoe. The stream had always catered to a population of brook trout, and this led Pete and me to believe that a concentration of brookies existed somewhere in the expanse, brookies that would be growing steadily bigger and fatter. But although we acted on our hunch and probed all sections of the flooded area on successive years, we never found our dreamed-of bonanza. Two or three small trout per trip were the best we could do.

Eventually the flowage threatened to flood the nearby highway, and apprehensive town fathers dynamited the dam repeatedly until the beavers finally gave up and moved. This action left our unsolved mystery dangling, and whenever I had nothing better to do, and often when I had, I'd fret about the trout we'd never been able to track down but in whose existence I had never lost faith.

Then one spring evening, I took my setter out for some exercise and decided to see if the woodcock had returned to some of our favorite covers. The route home took me along the border of what had been the beaver flowage, but what was now a stark expanse of dead trees which rose above a tangle of weeds and vines. With the remote hope of finding signs of reconstruction, I pulled off the road and forced my way through the tangle to the remains of the dam.

There was no evidence of rebuilding, but the dynamiting had not destroyed the dam so completely but that a pool of some size and depth remained. As I morosely surveyed the wreckage of the dam, a trout rolled up to suck in a mayfly only a few yards up the pool. This rise was followed by another, and the pool soon boiled with rises as a hatch developed. These were the deliberate, bulging rises of bulky fish — trout that had grown sleek and fat somewhere in the flowage, exactly as Pete and I had suspected. Now, they had been forced to take up residence in the only remaining pool large enough to accommodate them.

Needless to say, I was back there the following evening with the appropriate tools. Although cars buzzed steadily past, no more than a couple of hundred yards away, not a boot print marred the border of the trout-jammed pool. As for the trout, they were as gullible and unsophisticated as those of unfished wilderness waters. So what followed was almost too easy; my dry fly hardly had time to settle on the water before one of those fat squaretails had it.

As a consequence, I actually got a bigger kick from finding those trout than I did from catching them. The rare chance to take trout after trout without changing position was a pleasant experience, but sole possession of the knowledge of their whereabouts was a source of even greater pleasure.

Strange as it may seem, and I presume in much the same way that a miser is ever reluctant to dip into his hoard, I found myself reluctant to press the advantage of my discovery. I never did return to that trout-filled pool throughout the remainder of the season, and from this asceticism I derived unaccountable pleasure and satisfaction.

My mood had become more realistic by the beginning of the next fishing season. Unfortunately, however, I returned to find the pool filled with silt and the trout long gone. In accord with the old saying, I had my cake for quite a spell, but without getting to eat much of it.

To continue with the same metaphor, the rare finds such as I have mentioned are but frosting on a cake which is usually thoroughly palatable by itself. In other words, one need not discover secret pockets of fish to enjoy good fishing in local waters. The extent to which fishermen neglect nearby fishing opportunities is often nothing short of amazing.

Until recent years, certain stretches of fast water in Vermont's Otter Creek furnished some of the finest trout fishing in New England. These stretches, in the vicinity of Middlebury, are only twenty-five miles from Pittsford, so for many years Pete and I were able to pay them the attention they deserved. Along these stretches we enjoyed some of the most glorious dry fly fishing we have ever had anywhere.

The fish were predominantly rainbows, intermixed with a scattering of browns. Their forage was so rich that scale samplings revealed that they grew to lengths as great as eighteen inches over a period which included only three winters. They were crammed to the gills with energy, as is the case with rainbows that have grown rapidly in big water, and we took as many as two hundred of these gorgeous fish per season — practically all of which we released.

Yet in spite of such fishing it was not uncommon to fish an entire afternoon and evening and never see another fisherman. Most of those we did encounter were out-of-state anglers who drove hundreds of miles to fish waters neglected by local fishermen. We got to know several who regularly made long trips to fish there, and they never failed to marvel at the lack of competition. Most of them erroneously accounted for it by picturing Vermont fishermen as a quaint subspecies which angling evolution had passed by. They attributed their absence to a lack of interest in fly fishing and visualized them as worm dunkers who stuck to pasture brooks.

Nothing could have been further from the truth. Skillful and dedicated fly fishermen are not lacking among Vermont anglers, all of whom would have found the fishing every bit as rewarding as we did. The only reason they stayed away was that they simply didn't know that that particular fishing existed. Otter Creek is the longest stream contained wholly within Vermont, and over most of its length it is sluggish and virtually devoid of trout. Consequently, most fishermen wrote it off without investigation. Very, very few knew that it contained stretches of fast water which teemed with wild trout. As binding proof of the extent of this oversight, these stretches, which furnished some of the finest trout fishing in the east, were classed as open (nontrout) water by the Vermont Fish and Game Service. They are still classed as such, and to the best of my knowledge no effort has been made to restore the once heavy populations of trout.

Although the number of trout has dwindled, the same stretches afford another possibility that is virtually ignored. They always held large numbers of smallmouth bass, even when the trout were abundant, and the bass are still there. One afternoon last summer Mike and I caught over fifty smallmouths on fly rod poppers in only a short stretch of river. We never saw another fisherman.

Although I mourn the trout's passing too much to take comfort in the undiminished bass population, I'm sure that less prejudiced fishermen would be happy with a spot that yielded fifty bass in a single afternoon. Yet such spots go largely unattended, on the theory that there is little of value to be found in that which is readily accessible.

For a substantial number of years I have done a fair amount of fishing in Maine. Typically enough, most of my efforts have been aimed at reaching waters as remote as possible. Trips have involved plane flights, wilderness canoe trips and long hikes to get "back in" to where fishing pressure is minimal. The result has been many memorable experiences, and sometimes, but by no means always, fishing which has lived up to expectations.

As far as expectancy is concerned, probably nothing builds it up as does a flight over miles of seemingly impenetrable wilderness before dropping down to a forest-rimmed lake that shows no sign of habitation. The romantic promise of wild, virgin fishing is implicit in such a circumstance. Pete and I have experienced it many times — enough to know that it can be very misleading and disappointing. We have racked up big scores in such places, but we have also had our high hopes shattered.

Any fishing enterprise which involves a reasonable hope of getting "beyond the beyond" induces an excitement which justifies the attempt, even when results are abortive. In line with the intent of this chapter, however, it is significant to point out that some of the best fishing Pete and I have had in Maine has been along the outskirts, and in the very center, of the village of Bingham.

This village is situated on the banks of the Kennebec River, a few miles below the Wyman Dam. I don't know the population, but it is a community with a business section which boasts several restaurants, a concentration of stores, garages, filling stations, motels and the like. It is not an outpost which marks a jumping-off place for wilderness fishing.

On our return trips from Jackman — which is precisely such an outpost — Pete and I often dined in a modern restaurant and then had wonderful fishing by driving no more than a few hundred yards to the river.

The rainbow is something of a rarity in Maine, but this

section of the Kennebec holds an established and self-sustaining population of these fish. Like all big water rainbows, they are fairly bursting with strength and energy. The river also holds enough landlocked salmon to make a strike from one of these wild leapers an interesting possibility. Neither Pete nor I have ever taken a brown trout there, but huge browns are snagged by lucky fishermen on rare occasion, and there is a scattering of brook trout to complete the picture.

Pete and I have discovered several good spots along the river, and as I have indicated, one is smack in the center of town. There, in the community's backyard, Pete and I have stood among rising fish, busted our leaders on whoppers and enjoyed wild and woolly fishing without seeing another fisherman.

Is this because State of Mainers are not interested in trout fishing? Hardly! Unless I miss my guess, while Pete and I fished in the center of town, any number of resident fishermen were battling black flies on wilderness ponds and bogs that could be reached only by punishing a jeep to the limit and then walking miles beyond the jeeping-off place.

This contention was borne out by gabbing with local fishermen. Few shared our enthusiasm for the nearby river, but most were ready with suggestions concerning spots that could be reached only with difficulty. We were even gullible enough to act on one particularly strong recommendation and spent an entire morning getting ourselves and our canoe to a bog where we were assured our sweating and straining would be rewarded by a hefty catch of squaretails. Instead, while we could have been fighting reel-running fish almost in sight of our car, we caught two trout that were all of eight inches long.

Indifference to that which lies handy seems to be typical of fishermen. As a result, many of those who bemoan the lack of good fishing do so without good reason and actually are victims of this strange form of blindness.

Otter Creek passes through the town of Pittsford, and within less than a mile of my home. Here it is slow-moving, snag-infested and overhung by the soft maples and willows which line its high, steep banks. Among the snags, and in the shaded pockets, northern pike lie in wait for fish, frogs and other forms of life to come within easy reach of their long snouts. The setup is ideal for float fishing and, over the years, Mike, Pete and I have taken hundreds of these pike by casting to them from a canoe.

Although northerns do not enjoy a favorable reputation in all quarters, I have yet to see a fisherman react with anything but excitement when a big pike savagely assaults his lure. This is particularly true if the lure is an oversize popping bug. We have bugged and landed pike of over ten pounds in weight and have lost larger ones. Most important of all, pike fishing tends to be at its best during the low water periods when trout fishing is poorest. We have come to hold pike in high esteem, if for no other reason than that they keep us in business when trout fishing falls off.

But in spite of this opportunity, I know of only one or two other local fishermen who fish Otter Creek seriously for pike. I have written articles about it which have appeared in national magazines, and these have inspired a substantial number of fishermen to drive long distances to fish Otter

Creek for pike — usually with good results. Nevertheless, the creek doesn't exist as far as most local fishermen are concerned. Naturally, I am not unhappy with this state of affairs. Yet I cannot help but feel sorry for those who don't know what they're missing.

If all this seems to identify me as a wise and crafty character who profits because of a human failing to which he is immune, let me hasten to admit that I can be, and often am, as blind and blockheaded as the next fellow. If I have learned to take fuller advantage of nearby opportunities, it is only because I have lived long enough for the obvious to finally penetrate my thick skull, at least to a degree.

For the past twenty years I have lived almost within sight and sound of that remarkable little trout stream, Furnace Brook. It rises high in the mountains and is fed by bountiful springs which keep its water cool and maintain a trout-sustaining level of flow during even the hottest and driest months of the year. A couple of miles before joining Otter Creek it tumbles down a gorge carved from solid rock, furnishing a waterpower potential which attracted Pittsford's first settlers.

Only the barest traces of ancient dams and mills remain, and the Furnace has long since ceased to be of industrial significance. But because of its past attractions in this respect, a very happy and fortunate state of affairs exists for those who now live in the community: a magnificent little trout stream flowing through the center of town, providing a recreational facility which no expenditure of effort and money could duplicate.

I moved to Pittsford at the end of World War II and like many other recently discharged G.I.'s at the time found that cars were completely unavailable. I was without private means of transportation throughout an entire spring and summer, and for that reason my trout fishing was confined almost completely to Furnace Brook. As a result, I probably caught more trout than I have caught in any season since.

Most were rainbows, all wild fish that ran from eight-inchers to a top limit of around sixteen inches; twelve-inch fish were common. Fish of that size are not exactly lunkers, but I submit that happiness is to be found wherever foot-long rainbows come regularly to a dry fly. The stream also held a lesser number of brown trout, and some of these grew to considerably larger size. During that summer I took a few browns that measured more than twenty inches.

I owned a car by the following spring, but one might conclude that I saw little need to burn gasoline in search of trout fishing. Yet this was not the case. To all intents and purposes I ignored Furnace Brook and drove far afield with the instinctive conviction that I could better my lot simply by putting distance behind me.

This ridiculous notion persisted for years. On many occasions I returned from all-day jaunts with little to show for my efforts, when, as my wife always took it upon herself to point out, I could have filled my limit on the Furnace in a fraction of the time and with far less effort.

Actually, this was precisely why I *didn't* fish Furnace Brook, but I could never explain this to my wife's satisfaction. Now, when I perhaps have a bit more common sense than I did then, I can appreciate her inability to understand.

I have also learned to appreciate Furnace Brook. This has been due in part to the fact that while trout fishing has declined in general, the Furnace has remained almost as productive as ever. Also, I have revised my formerly held opinion that the only way to fish for trout was to set out at daylight, or before, and fish until dark.

I suppose that this turnabout is an involuntary concession to the aging process. At any rate, my goal now is to enjoy the best hours without wearing myself out long before they arrive.

The best hours of trout fishing, at least in my opinion, are those between sundown and darkness. This is the best part of the trout fishing day, but it is impossible to enjoy it to the fullest if one is already weary from hours of wading and casting. But it can be a truly wonderful period to the fellow who is just starting out.

This is particularly true when an evening's fishing comes at the close of a trying day. One thing after another may have gone wrong until life seems nothing more than a hopeless assault of insurmountable obstacles. But if one can step into a stream that evening, just as the trout are beginning to rise, the next few hours will make life seem worth living after all.

This feeling of rejuvenation seldom can be gained on opening day, or even for several weeks thereafter. Magazine articles appear each spring which purport to reveal the secrets of taking trout during April and early May, and I have written several such pieces myself. But the truth is that early spring trout fishing is usually a slow, cold business, distinguished largely by excesses of enthuiasm and apathy manifested respectively by fishermen and trout.

For me, the real opening day arrives when streams finally

come to life, an event that is not tied in with any date set by law. This day of transformation cannot be circled on the calendar, but its arrival can be felt instantly in the bones.

There is that period following the formal opening of trout fishing when harsh traces of winter linger in the air. Streams are open and fishable, and angling enthusiasm is at fever pitch. But the water has a hard and brittle look to it, and an experienced hand can tell by its appearance that his prospects are slim.

Finally, there comes a day that is as soft as a down pillow, and this is the day that trout fishing turns a corner. Water temperatures rise, trout metabolism shoots upward, mayflies begin to hatch and pools that seemed to hold nothing but ice water are suddenly dotted with the rings of rising fish.

This phenomenon is worthy of special mention, for it illustrates the mistake one makes by judging streams against early season results. April skunkings are often blamed on a lack of trout, but a stream that appears to be fishless in April can break out in a rash of fish a few weeks later when the water has warmed and insects have begun to hatch.

Last spring, the soft day I had been waiting for fell in the middle of the week. Warm air had begun drifting in from the south the previous afternoon, and the temperature had risen steadily during the night. By morning it was easy to tell that the looked-for time had come; trout would be gorging on mayflies that evening as surely as the sun would set.

After supper I drove to a favorite stretch of Furnace Brook, a drive which took all of five minutes. From where I entered the stream I could see a church spire bathed by the last rays of the setting sun, a golden beacon above surrounding homes already overtaken by the soft neutrality of dusk. I could see cars passing along the street on which I live and hear the cheers of a crowd watching a ball game at the school's ball field. As I tied on a fly, I heard Nimrod, my big Bluetick coonhound, bawl his approval as Mike brought him his supper. I was that close to home.

I make a point of stressing the proximity, for it was this very factor which had once made me contemptuous of the Furnace; that and confidence that I could take trout without any great difficulty. To show the extent to which this prejudice robbed me of good fishing, I'll recount the highlights of the evening.

Even as I looped on a leader, a nine-footer tapered to 4X, and tied on a No. 12 Nearenuf, I could see a good fish rising. He had taken cover under an apron of debris that had lodged against a fallen tree and was busily gulping flies along the edge of this cover. This is a situation that is both easy and difficult. On the easy side, the trout is effortlessly approached and is very likely to gather in any dry fly which bumps along the edge of the debris. What makes it hard is that the fly *must* trickle along this edge, and in so doing it runs a fifty-fifty chance of snagging.

My fly was fresh out of the box and high riding, so it nudged along the border of the debris without hanging. The trout was lying with his nose only inches from the barrier and scarcely had to move to suck in my fly. But while the rise was a very quiet affair, that which immediately followed was quite the opposite. I jabbed the barb home, and an estimated fourteen inches of rainbow trout promptly went berserk. He made one wild leap after another, and by the time I brought him to the net he was utterly exhausted.

I removed the fly and held the helpless fish upright until he regained sufficient strength to take off. I looked on it as a particularly grand beginning, for I have a special love and respect for the rainbow. It is sometimes argued that the rainbow is not particularly distinguished as a scrapper, that the smallmouth actually packs more punch, and so on. I have always suspected that those who hold this view have never caught rainbows under ideal conditions, or perhaps have never caught wild rainbows at all. It has been my experience that naturally propagated rainbow trout, taken while at their physical peak — just as water temperatures are becoming optimum, will dish out more thrills per inch of fish than any brown, brookie or smallmouth that ever swam. In fact, I rate them ahead of the landlocked salmon, although the landlocked is admittedly the more spectacular leaper.

Feeling real good, I worked on upstream. Trout showed in almost every pool and run, and I took several nice browns — eleven- and twelve-inch fish — in pleasantly swift succession. Then, in a long, flat pool which usually gave me trouble, I came up against a better fish that wasn't so easily fooled.

He was rising steadily in the glassy flat near the tail of the pool, and although my fly seemed to drift over him faultlessly, he would have none of it. In the meantime, he continued to feed on the abundant naturals with tantalizing regularity.

I was reluctant to spend time on an obstinate fish when there were plenty of more willing takers, so I marked the trout down for future reference and continued upstream. I ran my total up to ten fish, and with my yen for quantity somewhat satisfied my thoughts returned to the difficult trout I had given up on. Nagged by challenge, I reeled up and returned to the long, flat pool.

The trout was rising steadily in the very same location, and now I had the patience to tie on a 6X tippet and a No. 16 fly. These refinements had no immediate effect; the fish went on ignoring my fly as before.

Yet this time I fished with considerable confidence. Doing so was more than a hunch, for it was conditioned by much past experience in similar situations. I wouldn't have been at all confident earlier in the day, but time was working in my favor. Light was dwindling rapidly, and the time would soon come when the finicky trout would no longer be able to distinguish the small flaws of presentation which, to this point, had accounted for his steady refusal. If I just kept putting the fly over him . . .

I could no longer see my fly when the trout finally took it, as indeed he did, but I could see the boil of the rise. I set the hook gently, a discretion which I do not always observe, and the reel buzzed as the trout ran the length of the pool. Then things settled down to a dogged, rod-thumping struggle which seemed to leave no doubt that the fish was a brown. When I finally had him in the net I was surprised to find that he was a beautiful, heavy-bodied squaretail. I laid him on the grass, still in the net, and held the tape of my De-Liar above him before releasing him. I needed the help of my flashlight to see that he was fully fifteen inches long.

A squaretail is a rarity in Furnace Brook, and particularly a fifteen-incher. I had additional reasons to prize this particular fish, however, for the previous year I had caught and released a half-dozen brookies in the same spot. Investigation disclosed that cold spring water seeped and trickled into the pool along one bank, and this undoubtedly accounted for the presence of brook trout. At any rate, it pleased me to think that the fifteen-inch fish was one of those I had put back the year before. (I caught three more during the season, and all were larger than the six I had released a year earlier.)

It was almost completely dark by that time, and perhaps I should have deemed the brookie the fitting close of a perfect evening. But I wasn't quite ready to call it quits. Instead, I replaced my tapered leader with a six-foot strand of eight-pound test monofilament and tied on a big rubber-hackled fly about which I shall have more to say in a later chapter.

The rubber monstrosity would have scared the wits out of any sensible trout in daylight, but trout, particularly browns, become bold under cover of darkness to a degree that many fishermen fail to appreciate. I spatted the big fly down on the calm surface of the pool and retrieved it with erratic jerks. Nothing happened during the first half-dozen retrieves, but I gradually lengthened line and when it finally landed near the tail of the pool I felt the electrifying yank of a savage strike. The big hook took its bite, and all was commotion for a spell thereafter. After a dingdong battle — always an exciting and uncertain bit of business in pitch darkness — I brought the trout into the beam of my light and netted him. He was a beautiful brown of well over two pounds in weight.

Had I chosen to stick at it, perhaps I could have donged up more, and possibly bigger, browns with my after-dark prescription, but suddenly I felt the urge to call a halt and bask in the culmination of perfection. The delights of the past few hours simmered within me as I made my way back to my car, giving rise to a feeling of well-being and contentment that nothing but a perfect evening of fishing could have aroused.

In only a short time I had caught what must have been nearly ten pounds of wild trout. They were all back in the stream, little the worse for wear, with plenty of others to keep them company. Most of them would be there when I next decided to fish, and best of all, only five minutes away from my front door. How could I have once been so stupid that I was blind to such a blessing!

Before counting me as specially lucky — few fishermen have a stream like Furnace Brook almost in sight of their homes — remember that all who live within twenty-five miles of the same stream are equally fortunate. All could be on the Furnace in a half-hour or less. The city of Rutland is a mere ten miles from Pittsford, and its population of over 25,000 — a metropolis by Vermont standards — includes many fishermen. Yet all the time I was busy taking trout I *never met another fisherman!*

This is a circumstance which I in no way deplore. In fact, if I thought what I wrote here would bring fishermen flocking to Furnace Brook, I wouldn't set down a word. I'm sure it will have no such effect. But to be on the safe side, I hasten to add that the Furnace doesn't give up its trout as easily as reported except when conditions are unusually favorable.

Like all other streams it usually makes a fisherman work for his trout, and once the peak of the season is past it yields fish grudgingly only to those who know their business.

Actually, what I have written about Furnace Brook hasn't been about the Furnace at all. Instead, it has been about the many "Furnace Brooks" that are largely neglected by the fishermen who live closest to them. They need not be trout streams. They can be bass ponds, pickerel bogs, pike waters, catfish holes, panfish hotspots and opportunity in other guises.

In my own case, although I greatly prefer trout fishing, I depend on the totality of local opportunity to satisfy my inborn hankering to fish. Each year, between ice-out and freeze-up, I figure to get in my licks at trout, landlocked salmon, smallmouths, largemouths, walleyes, northern pike, bullheads, catfish, yellow perch, calicoes and any other species I can track down in nearby waters.

As a result, I have come to know a good many "Furnace Brooks." I value all of them highly, for while I often relive the more spectacular fishing I've had elsewhere, it is upon these close-to-home spots that I depend for sustenance. I find it far more satisfying to fish frequently for whatever lies within easy reach than to reconstruct glorious experiences of the past, or try to live on the uncertain hope that they can be repeated.

8

Some Lethal Lures

I REMEMBER READING a short story years ago in which the hero came into possession of a fishing lure so magical that it brought a strike with every cast. He obtained it from natives of an imaginary island in the South Pacific who seemed strangely eager to rid themselves of the contraption. The lure, hand carved from bone, proved to have universal appeal for every kind of fish in every possible location, but its new owner soon found it to be a curse rather than a blessing. He couldn't bring himself to use less effective lures, yet the complete infallibility of the bone gadget took all the joy out of his fishing.

It is safe to say that no real-life fisherman has had to cope with this dilemma. Although thousands of different lures have been designed and new ones pop up regularly, the lure that no fish can resist still awaits invention. No two look or behave alike, yet all achieve the same results: they trigger fish into striking because of subtle properties which create excitement.

The true subtlety of these elusive qualities became apparent to me during a period in which I experimented with spinning lures of my own making. Because my methods were crude, I could never turn out two lures that were exactly alike. Whenever I tried to follow a certain pattern, each of the resulting batch would be slightly different from all the others. It is significant that these slight differences inadvertently resulted in a few real killers.

One of these is still treasured among my spinning lures, and I dread the day when I break it off. It is a small spoon, sawed and hammered from a sheet of bronze, which no fisherman would think of buying if he saw it in a tackle shop. To add to its rough appearance, its convex side is haphazardly pitted, an effect achieved with the point of a drill out of pure whimsy. But although this little spoon looks like something a youngster might turn out, some elusive quality was accidentally incorporated in its design that causes fish to react to it with exceptional excitement. It has been deadly on brookies, rainbows and browns. Smallmouths hit it as eagerly, and in spite of its small size, it has accounted for many northern pike. But for all its effectiveness, the reasons for its appeal stem from properties too subtle to permit identification.

Furthermore, these mysterious qualities have defied my efforts at duplication. I have made dozens of lures that appear to be all but identical, but they have been no better than mediocre. The spoon in question outfishes all "imitations," its superiority achieved only by chance — an inadvertent combination of sawing, hammering and drilling that is sadly beyond recall.

Home manufacture of spinning lures is a tedious job that would have little to recommend it were it not for the fact that, as in this case, there is always the chance of turning out one of exceptional appeal. In addition to the small spoon just described, I have made others of different designs that were almost as deadly. However, these exceptions are discouragingly rare.

But the possibility does exist, and for those who want to try their hand at it, the following may be of help. Cut blanks from sheet metal of the desired thickness — brass, copper or bronze. Make a cardboard pattern of the desired shape, and scribe its outline on the metal. Clamp the metal in a vise and use a hacksaw with a round blade to cut out the blank. (It is virtually impossible to follow a curve with a conventional flat blade, but the round blade makes it quite simple.) Drill holes at opposite ends of the blank for line attachment and the placement of split ring and treble hook. Now comes the step that will tell the story: giving the lure a concavity which will largely determine its action.

To make the flat blank concave (unless you can think of a better way) lay it on a block of hard wood, hold the rounded face of a ball peen hammer against the metal and strike the upturned flat face of the peen hammer with a second hammer. The process requires considerable pounding, but it has the virtue of permitting a gradual shaping to any desired degree of curvature. When the shaping is finished, smooth any rough edges with a file and then scrub the lure with fine steel wool until it shines.

That's all there is to it. The whole business would be pretty drab were it not for the fact that just the right combination of shape and curvature can result in a lure with that extra something which will make fish pile into it. One never knows until the finished lure has been tested.

That fish can be aroused by a curved piece of metal defies satisfactory explanation, and it seems even more improbable that slight differences in essentially similar designs determine the degree to which excitement is induced. Yet to appreciate that this is indeed the case, one need look no farther than the Eppinger Dardevle.

Most experienced fishermen, if they had to pick a single, all-purpose lure, would choose the Dardevle — and the choice would be a wise one. I have been taking fish on Dardevles since I was a kid, and its reputation is so well established that no point would be served by dwelling on its unique virtues here. But although the Dardevle's sweeping effectiveness is well known, the reason for its success remains a mystery; like all lures which provoke fish it exerts its peculiar influence without disclosing the reason for its strange appeal.

In subarctic waters, where it is still possible to fish for fish that have never seen a lure of any description, the one-ounce Dardevle is looked on as a specific for almost every species of fish — brook trout, lake trout, ouananiche and arctic char. Many of these fish are of trophy size, so perhaps it is not too surprising that the larger ones do not hesitate to pile into a big Dardevle. It does come as something of a shock when a twelve-inch, or smaller, brook trout assaults the same lure.

The small brook trout of subarctic waters have few inhibitions, but those in an eastern trout stream will not hit big Dardevles. Unlike northern fish they are deeply inhibited, and their instinctive urge to strike is counteracted by their exaggerated sense of caution. Yet even these extra-cautious fish will indulge this irrational urge whenever the source of attraction makes concessions to their keener sensitivity.

It was as a means to this end that ultralight spinning evolved several years ago. It enjoyed a brief period of popularity, then interest waned. This is rather strange, for ultralight spinning provides a means of using lures that are extremely provocative, but which are so small that they do not seriously alarm the highly sensitive fish with which most of us must cope.

I have used an ultralight spinning outfit off and on for at least ten years and can vouch for the effectiveness of tiny lures and wispy lines in hard-fished trout streams. I have tried many different kinds of lures — good, bad and indifferent. I have discovered one, however, that has those exceptional qualities to which this chapter is devoted. It is not well known for some strange reason and is relatively hard to come by.

I learned of this lure from H. G. Tapply. Tap is always eager to try anything new in the line of fishing, and he was quick to investigate the possibilities of ultralight spinning. His reports were enthusiastic, then one day I received a few of the lures from him with a note urging me to try them to see if they would do for me all that they had done for him.

I tried them, and they did. Tap and I compare notes regularly, and while we do not always agree on all things, we have long shared the opinion that this particular lure has built-in qualities which place it in a class by itself. We also agree that its failure to win widespread recognition is a minor mystery. I have given samples to friends who use ultralight spinning tackle, and none will be without the lures after once testing them. Yet in spite of the fact that the lure quickly demonstrates its superior effectiveness with use, it remains relatively unknown.

The lure is called the "Panther Martin." It is made in Italy, which perhaps accounts in part for its lack of recognition. But it is such a remarkable fish-getter that it is difficult to account for the lack of demand, regardless of where it is made.

It is of rather simple construction, consisting of a shaft upon which are mounted a tiny lead body and a spinner blade. The design and manner of mounting of the blade are rather unconventional, however, and undoubtedly account for the lure's unique effectiveness.

The spinner blade is of distinctive shape, in that it features a reverse curvature: the bottom part is concave on its underside, while the top, to a lesser degree, is concave on the upper side. Unlike most blades, which are mounted on the shaft by a clevis, the shaft of the Panther Martin goes through the blade itself, at the point where the curvature is reversed which is about a quarter of the way from the top.

The result is a blade which not only spins rapidly, even when retrieved slowly, but which creates an extraordinary turbulence. In spite of its very small size, the lure sets up a vibration which the fisherman can feel throughout the retrieve.

It seems reasonable to assume that the Panther Martin excites fish largely because of the pulsations which it creates.

Spinning lures are usually most effective when retrieved erratically, but no tricks of manipulation seem to be necessary with this lure. The best policy seems to be to cast either downstream or across and then retrieve at a slow, steady pace.

I have caught many trout on this lure, but I have never taken any really large ones. Its appeal seems to apply mostly to fish up to fifteen inches in length, and not, at least to the same degree, to fish that weigh several pounds. At least I cannot remember any belts from big trout while using it. But among trout of the size common to most hard-fished streams it is extremely deadly, and it is equally surefire when used on stream smallmouths.

Why do fish hit this oddity? Why are they provoked to belligerence by vibrations which have no natural counterparts? Finally, why are they drawn to a gadget so patently anomalous when they are so often alarmed by anything strange or different?

These are questions which I cannot answer. All that seems clear is that it is possible, if only by trial and error, to devise unorthodox stimuli which will cause fish to strike by awakening compulsive passions which normally lie dormant. Among existing lures are those which are sufficiently hypnotic to confirm the fact that this mysterious vulnerability is characteristic of all game fish.

Yet, as previously asserted, there seems to be no common denominator. The Cooper Bug wins my nomination as a lure of exceptional effectiveness. But although it can be fished provocatively with marked success, its power to trigger impulsive strikes derives from characteristics which seem to have nothing in common with the Panther Martin or the Dardevle.

The Cooper Bug is nothing more than a humpbacked fly tied mainly with deer hair. The body is wound on the hook — peacock herl, chenille, dubbing or what have you — and a small bunch of deer body hair is tied near the bend of the hook with the tips of the hair forming the tail. The bulky part of the hair is then drawn forward along the top of the hook shank and bound down near the eye. The flared butts are trimmed to form a small head, and the lure is finished.

The completed fly looks anything but impressive, but it is a lure of rather remarkable properties. It can be fished on the surface as a dry fly. It is an excellent producer when fished in this manner and is undoubtedly mistaken for an item of food.

But the surprising thing about this fly is that although a dragless float may not bring a rise, a walloping strike often results when the pretense of imitation is dropped and the bug is twitched along the surface. This sometimes happens when the same trick is tried with an ordinary dry fly, but it is the exception rather than the rule. With the Cooper Bug, it is just the opposite; it is usually much more killing when twitched than when fished with a dead drift.

Why will trout ignore this fly as it drifts over them, then attack it savagely when it is skittered along the surface? They must see it in an altogether different light when it takes on movement. As a suggested item of food it tempts only their appetite, and in this role it may be found wanting. When it ceases to be passive, and plays directly on their emotions, the same fish flash to attack.

Some Lethal Lures

I have said that the Dardevle, the Panther Martin and the Cooper Bug have almost nothing in common, yet this viewpoint may be superficial and grossly incorrect. Perhaps they do have a common denominator which we cannot recognize but which is clearly manifest to the fish. I'm convinced that fish hit these widely different lures because all three, although by seemingly different means, generate the same compulsion. Perhaps what seem to us to be marked differences are actually isotopes of a single element of provocation which awaits identification.

For want of a more satisfactory explanation, it has long been common practice to attribute a lure's effectiveness to imitative qualities which can be acknowledged only by the wildest stretch of the imagination. Fish are presumed to strike lures because the lures suggest edibility, when in reality they strike for reasons in which hunger plays no part at all. The theory that they are motivated by hunger offers an easy answer to an otherwise perplexing problem, but the perceptive fisherman cannot fail to recognize the specious and naive quality of such reasoning.

The same perceptive angler recognizes the sharp line between imitative and provocative fishing. He knows that when fish take his dry fly or artificial nymph they do so with every intention of eating it. He also realizes that when they hit his spoon or plug they are motivated by stimuli which he can administer, but to which he cannot assign positive identification. And in this mystery he finds delights which enlightenment would only destroy.

A complete listing of specially effective lures would include a number of longtime favorites, which like the Dardevle, have gained widespread recognition for their clearly demonstrated excellence. They are so well known that their mention here would serve no purpose, so I shall pass them by in favor of a few other lures which have impressed me, but which are relatively unknown.

One is the Calcasieu Pig Boat, designed by my friend Tom Nixon of Maplewood, Louisiana. Tom is an ardent and accomplished fisherman, an extremely skillful fly tier, and an angler whose many talents are augmented by a marked flair for invention.

The Pig Boat is a huge fly with a body of black chenille which is palmered with black hackle. The wings, if they can be called that, consist of some forty strands of black rubber, tied in so as to form a fluttering skirt which envelopes the fly when it is retrieved. The head is built up with the working thread and lacquered black, and the only departure from the all-black motif are two yellow eyes which Tom paints on the head.

The Pig Boat was designed to take largemouth bass, which it does with marked distinction. Tom Nixon ties it with wire weedguards, and equipped with these it can be soused among lily pads and weeds with very killing effect. It is equally effective along open shorelines, fished as is or behind a small spinner.

But I have come to value the Pig Boat for an effectiveness not anticipated by its inventor. At night, it is a remarkable killer of big brown trout.

If one studies the habits of brown trout, he finds that up to a point they are not substantially different from other trout. Much has been written and said about the brown's exceptional wariness, but I have never detected it to any great degree among browns of small and medium size. Browns from two pounds on up are difficult critters to cope with, however, but for reasons which derive more from peculiarities of temperament than from any deliberate exercise of shrewdness.

During the day, big browns have a frustrating habit of retiring behind an impregnable wall of indifference. (Whether this habit is conditioned by hard fishing I cannot say; I have had no experience with brown trout in other than heavily fished waters.) They ignore hatches that bring lesser fish to the surface, and they seldom station themselves in the path of drifting food as do other trout. Instead, they tend to withdraw to some safe retreat and go into a defensive trance which renders them immune to all ordinary temptations. During a sudden rise of water they will gorge on the resulting abundance of food, and they are then easy to take with night crawlers. A heavy hatch of exceptionally large mayflies may bring them to the surface, and at such times they pose no exceptional problems for the dry fly fisherman. These conditions arise all too infrequently, however, and a good share of the time big browns are beyond human reach for the simple reason that they have taken refuge in a lethargy from which they cannot be aroused by the fisherman.

At night, large browns become entirely different creatures. They come out of their daytime trance, cruise about in search of food and become bold and aggressive to a greater degree than is generally realized. This turnabout tends to escape attention largely because most surface feeding ceases with the arrival of darkness, and fishermen usually depart with the impression that the show is over. The few that linger on are likely to be startled by awesome commotions made by big brown trout that have just come alive.

Since I was aware of this circumstance, I took my first look at a Calcasieu Pig Boat and immediately had a hunch that it would be strong medicine for after-dark browns. A couple of nights later I gave it a try on a pool which I suspected of harboring likely candidates.

I had made perhaps a dozen casts and was beginning to fear that my hunch was unjustified, when a fish hit like a thunderbolt and then tore line from my reel. Some five or ten minutes later I netted a brown that weighed two and a half pounds. I moved upstream a bit and resumed casting. I had twitched the big fly through no more than six or eight retrieves when it was slammed again, this time even harder than before. The fly was only a few feet beyond the tip of my rod, and the fish hit so violently that I actually felt water splash against my face. I managed to weather what followed by feel and finally landed a brown that was a full pound heavier than the first.

It goes without saying that I have never since been without one or two Calcasieu Pig Boats while trout fishing. Whenever I fish until dark, which is frequently, I switch to a heavy leader, tie on one of the big flies and give a pool or two a working over before calling it quits. Needless to say, I don't always come away with a big trout. But the Pig Boat has accounted for a substantial number of hefty browns over the years, all of them fish I'm sure I wouldn't have caught without the big fly's help.

Discounting rare exceptions, the fly fisherman, particularly the dry fly fisherman, has but little chance of taking trophy-size trout from hard-fished waters. This is no great tragedy, for a fly fisherman can be very happy wherever fish of moderate size come well to his fly. But most of us like the thrill of feeling the rushes of a heavy fish once in a while, and we like to drop an occasional twenty-incher in the kitchen sink with a splat that brings the rest of the family on the run. The Calcasieu Pig Boat, used as directed, will make such moments a reality.

At night, big browns are prone to gobble any living thing they can swallow, so it is possible that they look on the Pig Boat as edible prey. Yet I suspect that they strike from aggravation, rather than from hunger. Fish shorter than fifteen inches very seldom strike the Pig Boat, but they often boil the water in its vicinity as they make abortive passes at it. This, to me, indicates an excitement not to be aroused by the suggestion of food.

Another crude-looking fly which is endowed with special powers of provocation is one I ran into in Labrador, and again on the George River in northern Quebec. Norm Hathaway used it in Labrador with telling effect on big brook trout and ouananiche. On the George River, it took Atlantic salmon that showed little interest in conventional salmon flies.

I plan to refer to this lure in another chapter, but it seems appropriate to discuss it here as well. It is made entirely of the body hair of either deer or caribou. A tuft of the hair is tied in for the tail, then a thick bunch is laid along the top of the hook shank and crisscrossed with the working thread to form a buoyant body. A sprig of body hair is tied in as wings and should stand away from the shank. More hair is spun on the hook ahead of the wings, then clipped to form a large head. The finished product should be rough and shaggy, and the fewer pains taken with the tying the better.

The fly is a floater, and I have since discovered that it is very effective on smallmouths when fished as a bass bug. Norm Hathaway fooled brookies and ouananiche by fishing it as a dry fly. On the George, Atlantic salmon smashed it when it was cast across heavy currents and allowed to swing through a wake-cutting arc on a tight line.

This response on the part of the salmon led me to wonder if perhaps I couldn't con the trout back home by presenting the same fly in much the same manner. I suspected that some intangible quality of appeal resulted from the fly's rough construction and appearance, and experimentation among Vermont trout has borne me out. In fact, the hair creation has become a "secret weapon" to which I resort in specialized times of need.

This need arises at dusk, when good trout are showing but when the lack of light makes it exasperating to try to take them on a dry fly that cannot be seen. Such trout are not yet large and bold enough to tangle with a Pig Boat, but like large browns, they become less cautious in the gathering darkness. Because of this, they are open to the same sort of exploitation when concessions are made for their lesser size.

The hair fly, in a scaled-down version on a No. 8 hook,

offers just the right degree of challenge. Trout of around a pound in weight will not accept this challenge if it is presented in broad daylight, but they will respond to it boldly when dusk is changing to darkness.

On a typical evening, trout become more and more in evidence as darkness approaches. This would be fine were it not for the fact that as activity increases the fisherman is burdened by a steadily increasing handicap. By the time the water is fairly boiling with rises the fisherman can no longer follow his fly, and to all intents and purposes he is fishing blind. To add to his woes, there are so many naturals on the water that his fly stands an ever-diminishing chance of being taken. It is all very demoralizing, much like the dream in which one finds himself surrounded by opportunity of which he cannot take advantage.

In such a situation, when my chances have been reduced almost to the vanishing point, I find that I can reestablish them by snipping back my leader and tying on one of the floating hair flies. Wherever possible, I do nothing more than let the current swing it over the fish; if current is lacking, I retrieve it as smoothly and steadily as possible.

In many instances, this turns the tide in my favor. Trout that have been calmly plucking off drifting mayflies (and scorning my dry fly for flaws of presentation) suddenly find their tranquillity shattered by an exciting distraction. One moment they are intent on gathering in food and are carefully selecting only those items which seem conventional and innocuous. A moment later they are faced with temptation which they cannot assess with the same dispassion. The provocative qualities of the skittering hair fly arouse them to a state of aggression, and moved to boldness by darkness, they imprudently attack.

I am sure that most fishermen are unaware of the advantages to be gained by so drastic a turnabout of technique in this particular situation. As long as fish go on feeding, there seems to be no alternative but to continue the attempt to fool them with imitations, even after this has become little better than hopeless. The hair fly I have described is an effective means of proving that deepening dusk has made them ripe for an approach from an altogether different angle.

I believe that the effectiveness of all provocative lures depends upon their ability to inflame passions which lie dormant in all game fish, and which, when sufficiently aroused, quite exceed all normal powers of discretion and restraint. Fish strike these lures because, for a fatal moment, they become creatures of blind impulse, victimized by stimuli mysteriously capable of inducing involuntary response. Due to differences in design, lures elicit this response with varying degrees of success. I have described a few I have found to have exceptional provocative powers, but I am sure there are others of which I am unaware.

I am certain that not all the most effective lures have come to my attention, for it is strangely true that some of the most deadly are among the least known. More than a dozen years ago I wrote a book entitled *Tricks That Take Fish* in which I listed the spinning lures that had done best by me: the Eppinger Dardevle, the Stuart Goldfish and the Swiss Kneubuhler Long Spoon, Normal Spoon and Broad Spoon. Time has not altered my respect for these lures, for they continue to demonstrate that "extra something" that keeps them at the top of my list. But while most fishermen are familiar with the Dardevle and the Goldfish, how many know about the Kneubuhler lures?

Very few, apparently, for I still get letters from readers who have searched for these lures in vain and want to know where they can be bought. In spite of the fact that these spoons are among the deadliest of spinning lures, the fact that they are generally unavailable clearly indicates that they remain virtually unknown.

Fortunately, for those who may be interested, I can name a source: The Orvis Company, Inc., Manchester, Vermont.

New lures appear on the market in such numbers that it is virtually impossible for a single fisherman to keep track of them all. Yet I think it is safe to say that the ratio of truly distinguished lures to all those newly developed is exceptionally low. New lures of great value do appear, however, and a recent newcomer which seems to have special provocative powers is the long, slim plug which has quickly gained widespread popularity. Several versions are available, but they are of the same basic design and feature the same rolling and darting action when retrieved.

My experience with these lures has been limited, but during such use as I have made of them they have demonstrated great effectiveness.

One evening last summer, Pete, Mike and I were trolling for walleyes in Lake Champlain, bouncing worm and spinner combinations along the bottom in forty to fifty feet of water.

We were having fair fishing, snagging enough fish to indicate that they were hugging the bottom and that we were going about our business in an appropriate manner.

A stiff breeze kept the surface choppy until nearly dusk, but then it subsided and the bay in which we were fishing suddenly became glassy smooth. Shortly thereafter, fish which we knew to be walleyes began to show at the surface. We killed the motor and began casting to the rising fish with shallow running lures. The lure I picked happened to be one of the long, slim plugs — the only one in the tackle box.

It proved to be a happy choice, for almost every time I could drop it near a breaking walleye it promptly drew a strike. In the meantime, Mike and Pete ran through lure after lure with very little success. A walleye would break within range of Mike or Pete and ignore the lure which instantly dropped nearby. Whenever I was permitted to take a crack at the same fish, darned if he wouldn't hit after only a few turns of the reel. The evidence of so brief a test is anything but conclusive. Yet the marked difference in results seemed to be too great for coincidence, and I'm inclined to attribute it to the lure's design and action.

Later, in the Grand Lake region, Mike and I tested lures of the same type on smallmouths, and we had outstanding success with these slender plugs. Of more significance was a consensus among the local guides that the lures were uniquely superior bass-getters.

Since then I have heard and read many reports of success with these plugs on many different species of fish, which suggests a basic quality of provocation which acts upon all fish, and which is the mark of the truly distinguished lure.

But even with the most outstanding lures, the fisherman is still but a poor match for the fish. Lacking a clear understanding of how and why they "work," he must content himself with nothing more than the knowledge that, by some mysterious means, they cause fish to strike. And perhaps it would only ruin his fun if he knew more.

9

Tools of the Trade

MORE THAN THIRTY years ago I taught school in a small community in northern Vermont, and although the pay was small the quality of the trout fishing more than made up for it. Nearby streams and ponds teemed with fat native trout, and there was little competition from other fishermen. In spite of these happy circumstances there were certain drawbacks which are pertinent to this chapter, and which the following bit of reminiscence will serve to identify.

Much of the surrounding region was near wilderness, and it contained a large number of obscure pondlets, bogs and potholes. Many of these held trout, but they were largely ignored by the few local fishermen.

I wasn't long in the community before joining forces with a fisherman whose enthusiasm for trout fishing matched mine, and for whose skill my own was no match at all. He introduced me to local streams and ponds, and also to the intriguing business of prospecting for pockets of virginal fishing in the many obscure spots.

One Saturday afternoon we decided to forgo the proven fishing of our favorite stream in order to check out a pothole we had happened on the previous winter while rabbit hunting. It was less than a mile from a bumpy, but passable, back road, but it lay in the very center of a quaking bog. The approach to the pond was so treacherous that it discouraged investigation and was, therefore, an unknown quantity, and this circumstance inspired us to look it over.

When we arrived at the bog we discovered that beavers had dammed the outlet. While this had not increased the area of open water, it had flooded the shaky ground which surrounded it and had made it even less trustworthy. We also discovered that the circular pocket of black water in the center of the morass was full of trout. Bulging rises showed all over its surface, and we made a determined effort to get within range. But it was no go; the spongy footing sank ominously beneath our weight, and soon we were waist deep in water with many yards still to be covered.

The next evening we returned with axes and attempted to construct an approach by cutting scrub spruces and using them for bearing. Results were scarcely better. No matter how many spruces we cut and piled on top of each other, they sank slowly under our feet when we climbed on them. We gave it a determined try, but we finally gave up when it became plain that we could go on cutting and piling spruces until doomsday without getting closer to the pond. We had located trout — two-pounders that rolled and bulged in plain sight — but for all the good it did us those trout might as well have been a thousand miles away instead of a mere fifty yards.

Today, I would gladly give a week's pay for an identical chance. I own a thirteen-foot Grumman canoe which weighs only forty pounds, and toting it to the bog would be no chore at all. It would be equally easy to slide it out through the flooded brush. Once it was on the tiny pond, amid big brookies that had never seen a lure, the fishing would be no less than glorious.

Therefore, while I look back on the good old days with nostalgia, it is also with certain reservations. Like all other fishermen I would like to be able to return to the fishing that once was, but I'm sure I would suffer acute feelings of frustration if I could not take back with me the tackle and equipment to which I have become accustomed. I'd find myself with many more fish around me, no question about that, but if I had to return to my meager equipment of three decades ago I'd be unable to take more than partial advantage of the opportunity.

I know this to be true from experience, for the above incident was only one of many. It was not hard to find waters that held plenty of fish, but coming to grips with them was another matter. All too often, we were compromised by the limitations of our tackle and equipment.

We were not conscious of this compromise, of course, for we could not foresee the great increase in angling efficiency which invention and improvement would eventually bring about. Tackle and equipment are of great importance to the fisherman, yet I can think of very few fishing friends and acquaintances who systematically equip themselves to take full advantage of all existing opportunities. Most go overboard in one or more directions and stint themselves in others. This leaves gaps in their outfits which make it impossible to cash in on all the chances which occur during the fishing year.

Perhaps the commonest mistake is to become overly concerned with rods, reels and lures while neglecting equipment which may seem less directly connected with fishing, but which is often of the greatest importance. Last summer, Mike and I discovered a weedy bay in Lake Champlain where calicoes nearly as large as dinner plates had congregated. Unfortunately, we had only a half-dozen minnows in our bait bucket at the time, and streamers, small spoons and spinners proved ineffective after the few minnows had quickly been snapped up.

All of my family are especially fond of calicoes, and we felt certain that we could catch a boodle of these fine food fish for the freezer if we could return with a large supply of minnows. But as it so often happens in such cases, all the bait dealers we knew were fresh out of minnows.

We have a seine for just such emergencies, and we know a brook where a few drags of the seine will yield all the minnows needed for a day's fishing. The next morning we detoured to the brook on our way to the lake, and in only a few minutes we had dozens of small minnows that were just the right size for calicoes.

The calicoes were still there in the bay and hungry for minnows. We enjoyed many delicious meals of broiled fish last winter as a result of that day's fishing. More important, we had a day of lively fun only because we had a simple item of equipment when it was needed. We had a boat, motor and trailer, of course, and all the necessary fishing tackle. But the fact remains that we never would have caught those calicoes if my outfit hadn't included a minnow seine.

It is for this reason that I believe the dominant concern in building up a fishing outfit should be to achieve readiness on as broad a front as local opportunities require, plus additional breadth to cover any trips that are anticipated. Once that has been done, one can indulge in duplicity and refinement if it pleases him. But until a fisherman has acquired one of everything which he is in a position to use, it seems ill-advised to me to build up at one point — rods, for instance — while doing without anywhere along the line.

To the best of my knowledge, I am equipped to fish for anything in Vermont that wears fins, at all seasons of the year and in all types of waters. This doesn't mean that I'm rigged out lavishly in all departments, nor that I have avoided unnecessary extravagance in others. My boat and motor are rugged, dependable and adequate for my needs, but they look antiquated alongside the sleek outfits that are common nowadays. On the other hand, I have a rack of custom quality bamboo rods. It would break my heart to part with a single one, but I certainly could make out with fewer and less costly rods.

I make no claim for my equipment other than it is sufficient in scope to enable me to capitalize on all existing possibilities. Each year I take advantage of just about every type of fishing Vermont affords. This includes stream fishing for rainbows, browns and brook trout and lake fishing for landlocked salmon and lakers; trolling for walleyes in Lake Champlain during the spring runs, plus periodic trips to the same lake later in the season to take potluck among the many species which the lake holds; bass and northern pike fishing in creeks, ponds and lakes; early spring fishing for bullheads, yellow perch and other panfish; and ice fishing for walleyes, northerns, perch and smelt. In opportune years there have been trips to Maine for landlocked salmon, trout and smallmouths, and to Labrador and northern Quebec for Atlantic salmon, arctic char, ouananiche, brook trout and lakers. Since my outfit has stood the test of meeting these various requirements, perhaps it can serve as a guide to rounded adequacy.

Like most fishermen, I have more tackle than I need, at least in certain categories, and I want to hold the list down to only those items which are necessary. To do so, I am going to try to imagine what my gear would consist of if stripped of all items but those required for adequacy. I'd hate to be with so "little" equipment, but if I had to cut my outfit to the bone it would shape up about as follows.

Fly Rods

One 7½-footer with an action suitable for general fly fishing. One 8-ft. rod powerful enough to handle large popping bugs. The same rod would see duty trolling streamers for landlocks and would serve as an Atlantic salmon rod should this need happily arise.

Fly Reels

One good quality single-action reel capable of holding a DT6F line plus 50 yards of 20-lb. test backing.

One top quality reel large enough to hold a WF8F line and at least 100 yards of 20-lb. test backing.

A spare spool for each reel to allow a choice between floating and sinking lines.

Spinning Rods

One 6½-ft. rod designed to handle ¼-ounce through ½-ounce lures.

One 7-ft. or 7½-ft. rod capable of handling ¾-ounce and 1-ounce lures.

One 5-ft. ultralight rod designed to cast lures as light as ⅟₃₂ of an ounce.

Spinning Reels

One top quality open-faced reel with a capacity of approximately 150 yards of 10-lb. test line.

Two extra spools for the same reel. (Filled with line of appropriate weights, the spare spools will enable the one reel to serve on both the medium and heavy-duty rods.)

One miniature reel to go with the ultralight rod. This reel must be of the best workmanship and design to give satisfactory service. Because of the small spool, a five-to-one gear ratio is to be desired.

Bait Casting Rods

One 5½ or 6-ft. designed for heavy duty, to be used for trolling and for casting where the requirements are too rugged for the spinning rods.

Bait Casting Reels

One level wind reel, the best that one can afford. Casting reels come in for much mechanical wear, and only those of top quality will give prolonged service.

Tools of the Trade

Trolling Reels

One trolling reel capable of holding at least 100 yards of 25-lb. test lead core line. This can be a single-action reel designed for lead line trolling, or a multiplying reel designed for the same purpose.

If trolling with wire line is contemplated, another spare spool for the larger fly reel will convert it to a trolling reel. (I use my heavy-duty spinning and bait casting rods for metal line trolling so have not listed a special trolling rod as a necessity.)

Lines

One double taper floating line for the lighter fly rod, probably a DT6F.

One sinking line for the same rod, a forward taper in the same weight — WF6S.

One forward taper floating line, WF8F, for the 8-ft. fly rod.

One forward taper sinking line, WF8S, for the same rod.

Monofilament of either 2- or 3-lb. test for the ultralight spinning outfit.

Monofilament of 6- or 8-lb. test for the medium-action spinning rod.

Monofilament of both 10- and 15-lb. test for the heavy-duty spinning rig.

Braided line of 12-lb. test for the bait casting outfit.

One 20-lb. test lead core line (100 yards).

Squidding line of 20-lb. test for fly reel backing.

Wading Gear

One pair of chest high waders, boot footed and with felt soles.
One pair of hip boots.

Fishing Vest

One, with both large and small pockets. Zipper closings will prevent loss of equipment when vest is tossed in a car trunk, a canoe or stowed in a plane. Vest should be short to avoid wetting during deep wading.

Landing Nets and Gaffs

One wooden frame net for stream fishing.
One long-handled boat net.
One gaff, approximately 2 inches across the bend, 3-ft. handle.

Tackle Boxes

Two, of the type with multiple trays. (I need the pair to avoid carrying around the big lures I use for pike when I'm fishing for bass, walleyes, etc. Pike fishing needs go in one box, all else in the other.)
I have at least two dozen plastic boxes of various sizes, but all small enough to be carried in a fishing vest. All are filled with flies, bugs, spinning lures, etc., and I could fill more if I had them.

Boats and Motors

One 13-ft. lightweight aluminum canoe with motor bracket.
One 1.7 hp. motor.
One 14-ft. boat and trailer.
One 12 hp. motor.

Fly Tying Equipment

All necessary tools.
Materials for all types of flies, bugs, etc.
A large cabinet to hold tools and materials.

Ice Fishing Gear

A fishing shanty equipped with stove.
One ice auger.
One spud.

Three dozen tilts.

One jig stick, rigged with monofilament, for jigging perch and smelt.

Skimmer, minnow bucket, sounding weight and extra lines and hooks.

Miscellaneous

Lures (flies, bugs, plugs, spoons, spinners, etc., which total far into the hundreds), hooks, swivels, sinkers, anchors, paddles, minnow traps, seines, bait buckets, fish bags, stringers, creels, knives, pliers, flashlights, thermometers, leader materials, leader pouches, bobbers, rain gear, line dressing, fly floatants, insect repellents and undoubtedly other significant items I have overlooked.

Although this list is lengthy, I have tried to include only those items which I could not dispense with without reducing the scope of my fishing. If I have been realistic, which I believe I have, the list reveals the broad front along which one must tool up in order to capitalize on all which lies around him.

If this list seems excessive to some who doubt that I have tried to be as conservative as possible, allow me to state that a *complete* listing of my tackle and equipment would quickly allay this distrust. The sum total of my fishing effects represents what I *pretend* to be necessary, and to reveal it in its entirety would cause me considerable embarrassment.

Advice on fishing tackle usually centers around fine distinctions, real or imaginary, and the reader may be disappointed by the general way in which I have approached the matter. It is the custom to be more specific, and as an example, advise prospective fly rod purchasers on the matter of choosing a fly rod which will have precisely the desired action. Honesty forces me to admit that I am of no help to anybody when lines of choice become so finely drawn.

I have read (many more times than once) that the respective actions of rods of identical lengths can be assessed by holding the butts and letting the tips rest on the floor. It is alleged that when the rods are held side by side, differences of flexibility will become manifest as differences of curvature, and meaningful deductions regarding action can be made by comparing the sag of one rod with that of the others. This is pleasant stuff to write, and also to read; it sounds so very logical. But in my opinion, it is nothing more than a gem of sophistry; one could make as good a choice by flipping a coin.

I may be wrong, of course; other rods may behave more logically than mine, three of which flunked this test ignominiously. The three rods are all Orvis 7½-footers. The first is a No. 11 ferrule with a sweet blend of softness and guts which makes it one of the pleasantest of my rods to cast. The second is an Orvis "Midge," also a No. 11 ferrule, but with a built-in slowness designed for casting a light line where delicacy of presentation is of the utmost importance. The third is a No. 12 ferrule, and of an altogether different character. This is a hard-driving, spiky rod that is no dream to cast, but which has a great reserve of power. It will handle large bass bugs, and it has accounted for Atlantic salmon.

As further indication of their dissimilarities, the "Midge" will respond to a No. 4 line. The next stiffer rod requires a No. 6 line, whereas the one in No. 12 ferrule takes at least a No. 7 and is not overloaded by a No. 8.

But although these rods have nothing in common save their length, I cannot detect the slightest difference in curvature when I place their tips on the floor and let them sag of their own weight.

Even if there were visible differences, I doubt if they would be of any great help in choosing a rod. As far as I'm concerned, the only practical way to determine a fly rod's feel and action is to put a line on it and try it. In the meantime, however, there are matters of more importance to the fisherman than that of picking a fly rod of a particular and narrowly defined action.

As an example, there is a waterway about fifteen miles from my home consisting of a channel of dark water which winds through a wide and impenetrable bog. It holds both brook trout and browns. They seem to come and go in cycles, but during the years of plenty this stretch furnishes some excellent fishing.

The trout that live in that channel cannot be approached on foot, and the problem of putting a fly over them is not to be solved by acquiring a rod that sags in a certain way when its tip rests on the floor. By the same token, one can try to honor every refinement known to the world of fishing tackle and not be a bit better able to cash in on those trout.

But if one has a canoe which he can tote on his car, the problem is solved instantly. The channel is such that a fisherman can paddle its three-mile length with ease and be among rising trout when conditions are right. To me, this is the concern that rates top priority: to get to where there are fish. If I can do that, I'll settle for tackle that will do the job with reasonable efficiency. I'll leave it to those who are at home, with nothing better to do, to argue the fine points of tackle perfection.

It is with good reason that I use a canoe as an example of equipment that often means the difference between fishing attractive and productive waters and not fishing them at all. I have used my thirteen-foot Grumman for over twenty years, and I estimate that it has at least doubled the scope of my fishing over that period. I am confident that a canoe can do the same for most fishermen, yet canoes are owned by only a small minority of anglers. Those without canoes include many whose inventories of conventional tackle can be considered to be lavish.

The lack of a canoe is probably due to a couple of common misconceptions. First, those who have had but little experience with canoes tend to doubt and underestimate their stability, and they instinctively conclude that a serious risk of personal safety is inherent in their use. Yet a canoe is much like a bicycle in this respect; the bicycle's design seems to preclude the possibility of stability, yet this illusion vanishes completely once the knack of bike riding is learned. The same is true of a canoe; until one gains the knack of balance, every move seems likely to capsize it. With practice, exactly as with the bicycle, the fear of turning turtle gives way to an easy confidence that is entirely justified.

Another dissuader is the feeling that difficulties of transportation would make a canoe more bother than it would be worth. This is true only if the fisherman, unduly apprehensive about stability, buys a canoe that is longer and heavier than he actually needs. If my canoe were a seventeen-footer, I'd think twice before I loaded it on my car, and in many cases probably would decide against it. But a craft which weighs only forty pounds virtually invites itself along on each trip. Quite often I toss it on the car just in case I may need it before the day is over.

Convictions are hard to change, so I doubt that my opinion that a thirteen-foot canoe is ideal for freshwater prospecting will win more than partial acceptance. But after more than twenty years of bog-prowling, creek-running and general small water fishing, I am sincere in my belief that additional length and weight would be no more than unnecessary handicaps.

If I sing the praises of a canoe with what seems to be undue enthusiasm, it is only because I firmly believe that it can do more to enhance a fisherman's chances than any other item of auxiliary equipment. I am certain that almost every region has good fishing that can be reached by no other means, and this fishing has the unique virtue of being beyond the limits of general competition. It may lie buried in swamps and other hard-to-reach places, but possibilities are by no means confined to obscure and hidden pockets.

For an example, I need only draw on one of the most famous and hardest fished trout streams in the east — the Battenkill in southwestern Vermont. Most of this stream takes a pounding from hundreds of fishermen, from opening day to the end of the trout season. Yet there is a stretch of this stream, north of Arlington, which escapes this beating. It is generally too deep to wade, and so thickly grown along the banks that it discourages all but a few from fishing from shore.

Here is a mile or more of beautiful fly fishing water which is oftened dimpled by the rises of many trout. One can fish it from a canoe for an entire evening with a good chance of not seeing another fisherman. The competition will be hard at work, above and below the stretch, and the steady hum of traffic on nearby Route 7 will be plainly audible. Yet to all outward appearances, the scene could be lifted from a wilderness setting.

Several years ago, Pete and I were fishing in the Jackman, Maine, region and receiving very little cooperation from the trout and landlocked salmon. It was rather late in the season, the water was low and we made a circuit of favorite spots with very little success. Bud Dillihunt, secretary of the Jackman Chamber of Commerce, wanted to show us fishing worth writing about, so he sought advice from Eddie Comber who operates a flying service for fishermen.

Eddie knew of a remote wilderness lake where he felt we could get some good fishing — if we had some way to fish once he flew us to it. Fortunately, we had brought along my canoe. It was soon lashed to one of the pontoons of Eddie's plane, and not long thereafter we were waving "so long" to Eddie from the little craft as he took off after flying us to the lake.

We took enough trout during the bright hours of the day to make things interesting, but the fishing picked up tremendously as dusk came on. Soon after sundown we had brookies rolling all around the canoe, and we were nailing them almost as fast as we could lay out our lines.

Tools of the Trade

Eddie Comber returned to pick us up when the fishing was at its peak. He is an ardent fisherman himself, and when he saw our happy circumstance he held off the return flight for as long as possible. Not until barely enough daylight remained for the trip back did he ask us to quit, and by that time we had caught many more trout than were needed to make the day memorable. It must be admitted, of course, that we couldn't have reached that wilderness lake without the help of a plane, an item of "equipment" considerably beyond the means of most fishermen. The fact remains, however, that there would have been no point in flying to the lake had we not had the canoe.

Although canoes are owned by relatively few fishermen, the opposite is now true with respect to boats. Because of the widespread popularity of water skiing, and a passion for speed and power, many of these craft are better suited for joyriding than for fishing. Although they may not be ideal for the purpose, most of these boats are also used for fishing, and the result is increased utilization of the larger fishing waters.

In any event, a fisherman should have either a cartop boat or a boat and trailer in order to take advantage of the waters for which a canoe is not suitable. In my case, nearby Lake Champlain provides a wide variety of fishing which I would be unable to enjoy if I lacked a boat, motor and trailer.

Boat ownership is rapidly becoming so general that its advantages for the fisherman needs little emphasis. What should be stressed is that a boat designed for general use will provide access to only a part of the fishing waters in a given region. The others require a canoe, and these less accessible places are generally the most productive and interesting. The fisherman who is determined to make the most of his chances will not limit himself to a single craft. He needs both a boat and a canoe, and for my money he has greater need of the canoe.

Under certain circumstances, nevertheless, it is possible to put too much reliance on a canoe. Fishing guides have a tendency to do this, frequently to the point of discouraging clients from bringing along waders on trips where it later turns out that waders could be used to great advantage. I have learned from experience to reject this advice on any river trip; my waders go in the canoe, even at the risk of offending the guide.

Inevitably, on such trips, there are stretches of fast water that cannot be fished satisfactorily from the canoe, no matter how skilled the guide may be with setting pole and paddle. It is sometimes a touchy matter to ask the guide to put me ashore, but most guides soon recover from the blow to their pride when it is demonstrated that many rapids and riffles are best fished by wading.

The mention of wading gear focuses attention on an important matter that is skipped over much too lightly by a surprising number of fishermen. Although no longer as true as in the recent past, many anglers limit their wading gear to a pair of hip boots. This sharply restricts the scope of their fishing in all but the smallest streams. In streams of significant size, chest-high waders are a must if one expects to cover more than a fraction of the most likely spots.

Waders are available in a wide variety of weights and styles, and choice is largely a matter of personal preference. Those of lightweight construction permit the greatest ease of

movement but at the sacrifice of ruggedness and durability.
My own choice is canvas waders with boot feet that are soled
with felt. This type is sturdy and long-lasting, and the weight,
which seems excessive on land, is of no consequence in water.
This style is merely my personal preference however. The
important thing is to have waders of one kind or another
in order to extend the range of one's fishing.

I wish I could make recommendations among specific items
of tackle with the same conviction that I have concerning the
importance of striving for scope. But here I can offer no more
helpful advice than to avoid cheap equipment, and having
done that, let practicality be the guide. Try to acquire an adequate tool to meet each need, until all needs are met.

As an example, I have a couple of 6-ft., 2-oz. fly rods from
which I derive much pleasure. They are a delight to cast, if
for no other reason than that their considerable power seems
miraculous in view of their short length and slight weight.
Because of my affection for these two rods it would be easy
for me to persuade myself that they meet an unfilled need in
certain situations — on small streams, for instance. Much as I
hate to admit it, this simply isn't true. The rods represent a
personal indulgence, pure and simple. If I had stinted elsewhere in order to acquire them, they would be definite detri-
ments.

I can think of no situation in which it is of any *practical*
advantage to use an ultralight fly rod. This is particularly true
on small streams where, contrary to popular notion, a 6-ft. rod
imposes disadvantages. To be of any practical worth a 6-ft.
rod must be relatively powerful. It is therefore a rather unsat-

isfactory tool where fishing is limited to short casts, for a longer rod of slower and softer action will handle a short line much more satisfactorily. The lower back casts which tend to result from the use of a short rod may seem to be an advantage in small stream fishing, but in actual practice I have found the opposite to be more generally true. Most small streams are bordered more by brush than by trees, and the predominant need is to keep back casts as *high* as possible in order that they clear this brush.

The joy of owning fine tackle is so great that it is often difficult to distinguish between basic needs and the urge to possess that which delights the sensitivities. But to the best of his ability, one should resist the urge to splurge on such items as ultralight fly rods if this indulgence means doing without equipment that meets one or more practical needs.

The reader may wonder why I have excluded ultralight fly rods from my list of essential equipment, but included an ultralight spinning outfit in the same list. The reason is very simple. Nothing can be done with an ultralight fly rod that can't be done as well with the 7½-ft. rod named in the list, whereas the ultralight spinning outfit provides a unique and specialized means of fooling fish that cannot be implemented with conventional spinning tackle.

I have used ultralight spinning tackle over the past ten or more years and have taken trout with it at times when they would have been almost impossible to take by fly fishing or by spinning with lures of customary size. As already observed, ultralight spinning has failed to gain widespread popularity in spite of its deadly potential, and I think that this is because fishermen tend to put the cart before the horse in evaluating it.

My ultralight spinning rod is 4½ feet long, weighs only 1½ ounces and feels hardly more substantial than a broom straw. The reel is correspondingly tiny and light, and the 2-lb. test line adds to the general appearance of impractical fragility. Finally, the lures which I use with the outfit range in weight from ⅟₃₂ oz. through ⅛ oz.

I cite these dimensions and weights only because I have yet to show this rod to a fisherman unfamiliar with ultralight spinning who has not used reverse reason in appraising it. To be more specific, each concludes that the extremely light rod, tiny reel and wispy line are the objectives, and the tiny lures nothing more or less than necessary concessions to the outfit's frailty. Actually, of course, the midget lures are the items of functional significance, and the rod, reel and line the only practical means by which lures of such slight weight can be cast.

Finally, the reason for using such tiny lures is not to resort to exotic methodology as a means of demonstrating one's fishing skill, but to take advantage of the fact that the miniature spinners and spoons are extremely deadly in today's hard-fished waters. The fact that care must be exercised in handling fish on such fragile tackle adds spice to the game, but I can assure you that I value my ultralight spinning outfit solely for its ability to take fish. It is for this reason that I have included ultralight tackle in my list of basic equipment — it affords a specialized means of taking fish for which there is no adequate substitute.

I have preached against indulgence, but in truth I am a sentimental moron when it comes to fishing tackle. I find this very strange, for my attitude toward rifles and shotguns, after hunting most of my life, is quite the opposite. My guns, although mechanically sound, are battered and scratched — and I couldn't care less. They are quite adequate for my hunting needs; consequently, I have no desire to add to them, or to replace them with new and handsomer models.

Reason does not serve me as well when it comes to fishing tackle. Although I know that domestic fly reels will do everything fly reels can do, I fork over hard-earned money for English reels which cost nearly three times as much. I have more rods than I need, yet I'm sure that if I had a hundred I would still itch to own more. I don't kid myself that I could catch more fish if I had more and fancier tackle; I just hanker for it for the pure pleasure of possession.

Several years ago I developed a hernia which I neglected until it began to interfere with my stream fishing. Wading provoked it, for some unknown reason, and when it began forcing me out of streams you may be sure that I lost no time arranging for the necessary surgery.

For the comfort of any who may be facing similar repairs, the operation itself is hardly more to be dreaded than a haircut. In atmosphere, as a matter of fact, the affair strongly resembled a visit to the barber shop, and I rather enjoyed it. Like my barber, both the surgeon and the anesthetist were fishermen, and we were well into a discussion of fishing before my lower half was numb enough for the surgeon to begin his labors.

Oddly enough, I presently found myself trying to defend the merits of expensive bamboo rods, an ironic situation because I was arguing with people, who, unlike me, could *afford* such rods. Nevertheless, the two doctors took the position that glass rods could do everything that bamboo rods could do, and that the love of bamboo was nothing more than a snobbish affectation.

Having already admitted to owning a battery of rods of impregnated bamboo, I had no alternative but to try to refute this claim. I could have lied, of course, and stoutly insisted that I could take more fish on my Orvis rods than I could take on rods made of glass. But I stuck to the truth and foolishly admitted that in all probability I couldn't. With this admission behind me, my attempt to justify my preference was reduced to floundering.

How can one find adequate words to describe the sweet feel of a rod that makes casting an esthetic delight, yet which adds little to one's ability to catch fish? Or how can he explain the satisfaction of using a reel of exquisite workmanship, a distinction that is apparent only to the fisherman and utterly wasted on the fish?

Although these are very real considerations, their relative importance is determined by the value one places upon them, which, in turn, depends upon the nature of the individual fisherman. If he happens to be one to whom the possession of fine tackle is a source of rare joy, then the indulgence of this passion for ownership is almost as important to him as the degree of success he enjoys on the streams and lakes he fishes.

Since my inclinations seem to run in both directions — toward the practical matter of making the most of my fishing on the one hand, and toward the possession of tackle for its own sake on the other — I can weigh the respective worths of both.

As I have tried to make evident in this chapter, I believe that the fisherman best serves his own interests by adopting adequacy as his goal until he is equipped to cope successfully with all the angling variations that are open to him. When this goal has been reached, he can, and for the good of his soul he should, indulge in duplicity, refinement and unabashed lavishness to the full extent of his resources. But to do so prematurely, which is a very common failing, will be to the detriment of his sport.

10

Landlocked Salmon

*I*T IS GENERALLY CONCEDED that the Atlantic salmon is the noblest fish the freshwater angler can aspire to catch, and the vision of some day hanging one probably is the one dream most widely shared by fly fishermen. Unfortunately, this dream comes true for all too few, for a composite barrier of scarcity, expense, distance and proper timing places Atlantic salmon fishing beyond the reach of the majority of fishermen.

The landlocked salmon is virtually indistinguishable from the Atlantic in all respects but size and is probably second on the list of most wanted trophies. The landlock is rare enough to be rated as exotic, yet not to the point that landlocked salmon are unattainable to fishermen of average means. As a result, dreams of catching this species have a much better chance of coming true. This applies, at least, in the northeastern part of the country, where the northern New England states, Maine in particular, have accessible lakes and streams which provide reasonably good early season fishing for land-locks.

Unfortunately, most family vacations are taken much too late in the season for good salmon fishing. This poses a problem for fishing camp proprietors, for guests who arrive in July and August often entertain high hopes of taking their first landlocked salmon and are unaware of the difficulty with which these fish are caught after hot weather sets in. More often than not, the latecomer does his salmon fishing in vain and finds little consolation in his host's explanation that salmon move into deep water as soon as the surface becomes warm and are mighty hard to extract from the cool depths in which they take refuge.

There are exceptions, however. Sometimes a stray fish ventures near the surface and grabs the lure of a fisherman lucky enough to be in the right spot at the right time — a cause for rejoicing on the part of both guest and host. The fisherman is ecstatic because of the realization of his ambition, and the host is happy and relieved to get off the hook.

It may seem to be an exaggeration to imply that a fishing vacation can be turned into an unqualified success by the taking of a single fish, but I can assure you that this is sometimes the case. A couple of years ago I unconsciously contributed to the happiness of a fisherman interested in just one fish, and although I can take no credit for the assist, I take great delight in the quaint nature of my involvement.

My wife Edna, my son Mike and I were spending a week at Weatherby's Camps in Grand Lake Stream, Maine. It was

August, and the sensible thing would have been to concentrate on the smallmouths which abound in a wide choice of surrounding waters. Instead, since Mike shares my special love for trout and salmon, he and I elected to troll for landlocks in Grand Lake. We knew our chances were slim, but we also knew that the lake held plenty of salmon. The knowledge that they were there enabled us to whip up enthusiasm, even in the absence of any real hope of success.

We ran up the lake about three miles to what I knew to be good salmon grounds and then began trolling. Mike was using a lead core line on a stiff bait casting rod. My line was less orthodox, for it was of the fine stainless steel wire which orthodontists use to bring children's teeth into line. I obtained a large spool of it years ago, from the specialist who straightened Mike's teeth, and have used it since for deep trolling.

The wire, which tests about eight pounds, is of such small diameter that hundreds of yards of it will fit on a fly reel. I mount the fly reel on a spinning rod, which gives me an outfit that is somewhat unconventional but one which allows me to troll small lures through the lower depths with a minimum of resistance.

We snapped on small wobbling spoons, payed out line until our lures bumped bottom at trolling speed, then reeled in enough line to provide clearance. Mike could gauge the length of his line by noting the distinctive colors of each ten-yard section, but I could only count the pulls as I stripped wire from my reel. I felt bottom after 150 yanks and estimated that I had let out about 400 feet of line.

We trolled all morning and had exactly two strikes, both of

which fell to Mike. One came from a salmon of keeper size, but which came off as I was reaching for him with the net. The other strike came from a short salmon which we released after handling as gently as possible.

After lunch the pace became even slower. We dragged back and forth, and around and around, for several hours, with nothing to break the monotony but an occasional hang-up on the bottom. It was a pleasant day, the boat rockabyed in the slight chop and by late afternoon I was more nearly asleep than awake. I completed a turn at the end of a run and was tucking myself back into my comfortable coma when a fish all but yanked the rod from my hand. One thing can be said for a wire line: lacking any elasticity, it transmits the full force of every strike directly to the rod, which results in a shock that is particularly electrifying if the fisherman is half asleep at the time.

Since the salmon was some 400 feet astern, it took a fair amount of time to work him to the boat. Gained line was lost repeatedly as the fish made short, but lightning fast, runs. These explosive dashes caused me some uneasy moments, for I knew that a kink in the fine wire line would be fatal. But I finally got the fish in where Mike could net it — a salmon of nearly five pounds in weight.

Sad to relate, the average size of landlocked salmon has diminished over the years in nearly all New England waters. But as a result, our fish — which would have attracted no more than passing interest two decades earlier — created quite a stir when we brought it back to camp. I gave it to Bev Weatherby for freezing and suggested that he give it to some deserving, but unsuccessful fisherman who would like to take home a salmon.

I thought that was the end of it, but I had failed to take Bev Weatherby's wry sense of humor into account. Like all geniuses of native wit, Bev instantly recognizes the subtle logic which lies hidden in all absurdities, and he put this talent to work in disposing of the salmon. I learned the details from a letter which I received later in the year.

After we had left, he wrote, a fisherman had arrived who had no other objective but to catch a landlocked salmon. One fish would suffice, he declared, and he would leave happy and satisfied if only he could catch it.

By prodigious effort, and with luck, he finally managed to land a salmon. His catch resulted in a situation of some delicacy, for although the fish was only a two-pounder, the ecstatic fisherman looked on it as a trophy of a lifetime. It required considerable tact to honor this viewpoint without betraying the employment of pretense, and even more when the fisherman commissioned Bev to have the small salmon mounted and shipped to him when the job was finished.

Ordinary mortals of small inspiration merely would have carried out this order, but not Bev. Instead, he sent the fish I had caught to the taxidermist, and eventually to the fisherman. Just as Bev expected, it was accepted without question and with great pride and delight. As Bev explained in his letter, the fellow was fully prepared to receive a fish which in his eyes was twice its actual size.

At any rate, it delights me greatly to know that my salmon graces the wall of some nice chap who takes great pride in its possession. Just as Bev Weatherby "reasoned," it was only appropriate that the fellow should receive a fish every bit as big as he thought the one which he caught was.

Actually, as already noted, the concept of what constitutes trophy size among landlocked salmon has been revised downward steadily over the past half century. The rod and reel record for landlocked salmon was set in 1907 at Sebago Lake, Maine, with the landing of a salmon which weighed more than twenty-two pounds. Here in Vermont, within my memory, large salmon from Lake Memphremagog made annual runs up the Clyde River at Newport, and fish weighing as much as fifteen pounds were sometimes caught. I have talked with Maine guides who remember the days when ten-pound salmon, if not exactly common, were not too much to hope for. But, for the most part, landlocked salmon of such regal sizes have disappeared from the scene. In most, if not all, salmon waters, a fish of five pounds or more is a rare trophy. Three-pounders are considered good fish, and the majority run between keeper size (and less) and the three-pound mark.

Smaller fish do not mean that today's landlocked salmon fishing is anything but exciting, for the landlocks are still salmon with their full quota of the dynamic energy which marks salmon of all species. This vitality is almost always manifested by a series of wild and startling leaps which begins with the first feel of the hook, and a two-pounder, on suitable tackle, will give the fisherman plenty of thrills.

This statement is particularly true if the fish is hooked in the fast water of a stream, and it is for this reason that I prefer, when possible, to fish for landlocks in rivers rather than in lakes. Not only do river fish give better accounts of themselves, thanks to an assist from the current, but stream fishing is open to variations of technique which enhance the attending pleasures.

The most thrilling day of landlocked salmon fishing I ever enjoyed was a day spent on Maine's Moose River in the Jackman region. The exact locale was a stretch of rapids below the outlet of Long Pond.

The river was high — it rained bullets much of the day — but the stretch was full of salmon. Pete Terwilliger was with me as usual, and as our guide poled us toward the head of the fast water we saw several salmon shoot high in the air. This is always an encouraging sign, but not because the high leaps are associated with feeding; salmon that climb high into the air for no apparent reason are simply showing their muscle and exuberance for the sheer pleasure of it. Needless to say, their exuberance quickly rubbed off on Pete and me, and we piled out of the canoe almost before our guide could ease it into an eddy along the shore.

The heavy rain and high water seemed to make a streamer the most sensible choice, and I spotted the swirl of a breaking fish as I was tying one on. I put the streamer above and beyond the fish with every expectation that it would be walloped when I twitched it over him — but no such thing happened. The streamer swam untouched through more than a dozen retrieves, and another dozen casts later I was still hoping for my first strike.

Fish were showing all around me, so I marked down another potential customer and moved to within range. The second fish showed no more interest in my streamer than had the first, and I had no better luck when I tried to sell it to others. This seemed almost incredible. The river was full of moving fish, and the landlocked salmon has earned the reputation of showing especially keen interest in streamers.

Fish kept on breaking and rolling. I looked for emerging insects, but could see none. Yet something was making those salmon surface-minded. Also, it was clearly evident that they weren't to be taken on streamers. I changed leaders, tied on a No. 12 dry fly and floated it over the first fish to show within reach. The salmon ignored it.

Fortunately, I had done enough landlocked salmon fishing to get to know some of their eccentricities, one of which is to chase after dry flies that are deliberately skated and skittered along the surface. Rainbows will sometimes fall for this ploy, brook trout even less frequently and browns almost never. But a skittering dry fly is one of the surest ways of triggering landlocks into action, even when dragless floats bring no response.

After several conventional drifts had gone untouched, I moved upstream from the steadily rising fish and cast straight across the current. The line tightened, drawing the fly through an arc which would bring it over the lie of the fish. When the fly came over him, I gave it a few twitches. The water behind the fly boiled, then boiled again. This was typical; salmon often make several swirls behind a skating fly before nailing it, a habit that makes dry fly skittering doubly exciting. I gave the fly a few more twitches, which brought a third swirl that was for the money. I felt the line go tight, and a salmon of at least five pounds showed himself in a magnificent leap.

The salmon went on to exhaust himself by his own acrobatics. When the show finally was over the fish lay helplessly on his side, exerting no force against the rod but that supplied by the strong current. I reached out with the net, and at that moment the tiny hook simply let go.

The loss of such a fish would have taken the shine off any ordinary day, but not that one. Once we discovered that a skittered dry fly was the answer, Pete and I went on to hook more than thirty salmon in that glorious, fish-filled stretch. We didn't land all of them by any means, and I didn't take one as big as the fish I hooked and lost at the outset. Pete hooked one which was even bigger, but this fish stayed stuck only long enough to make a single tremendous leap. Apart from those minor tragedies, it was one of those days that stand out in a lifetime of fishing experiences. About the only undistinguished thing about it was that, as usual, the biggest ones got away.

The experienced trout fisherman learns to sense where trout are most likely to lie in a stream, and this ability will stand him in good stead on a landlocked salmon river. Any spot that bespeaks trout is likely to hold landlocked salmon, but the fisherman should also bear in mind the fact that he may find salmon where trout wouldn't choose to hang out ordinarily. One reason for this is that salmon tend to change locations to a much greater extent than trout. Streams which hold landlocks often flow through a chain of lakes, and when the temperature in the streams becomes too high the fish leave for the cool depths of the lakes. A rise of water or dropping temperatures are likely to cause them to move back into the streams once more, and this cycle is more or less continuous.

I cannot back up this contention with scientific proof, but I regard it as a logical deduction. I know from experience that the fishing in a stream can change for the better (or worse) overnight. When the change is for the better, it is often a case of virtually no fish at all one day, then a river that teems with them the next. When this happens, I prefer to believe that the fish simply weren't there at first, then moved in suddenly when conditions changed to their liking.

At any rate, I fish landlocked salmon streams for fish which I visualize as on the move as well as for those which may behave like trout. In other words, I work the "trouty" spots and also any places where I think salmon might pause to rest before moving on — and the practice has a habit of paying off.

Salmon usually move into a stream from below. They are likely to continue on upstream through several separated stretches of fast water before dropping back into the lake when conditions become unattractive. It is during the upstream movement that they are on the feed and furnish good fishing. This, at least, is what I believe to be true.

Accordingly, I picture them as likely to pause before passing through any spot in which they risk exposure. Any long, shallow stretch presents this risk, and deeper water immediately downstream may hold resting salmon, even though it lacks "character" in terms of trout fishing. Other such possibilities suggest themselves, with the result that when salmon are on the move it is possible to intercept occasional fish in spots which, by trout fishing standards, seem to hold little promise.

I have already mentioned what in Maine is called the "top of the pitch" — the slick sheet of accelerating water just above the lip of a rapids. Its significance in fishing rivers for landlocks is so great that it warrants elaboration. The stream usually narrows at this point, the depth decreases and the product is a relatively thin layer of quickening, but unbroken, water through which the bottom of scoured rubble can be seen clearly. Unless fish are breaking, none will be visible, and because the bottom stands so clearly revealed this prompts the conclusion that no fish are present. But if there are salmon anywhere along the entire stretch, it is an odds-on bet that the greatest concentration will be in this accelerating flow.

Regardless of the lure employed — dry fly, wet fly, streamer or spoon — the best presentation is achieved by casting from a position sufficiently upstream so that the lure will cut across the lower end of the slick when retrieved. Cast across stream, and start the retrieve after the current has put a belly in the line. This maneuver will draw the lure through an arc crossing the lip of the rapids. It is at this limit of the swing that strikes are most likely to occur. It is fishing of the most thrilling sort, for fish seem to materialize from nowhere to strike with electrifying speed and suddenness.

Not that the top of the pitch is the only spot worth fishing. Landlocks are likely to lie almost anywhere throughout the length of any stretch of fast water. But the "top" is usually the hottest spot of all, and I stress that fact here because a fisherman lacking experience might never suspect this to be the case.

One of the things which lends additional spice to fishing for landlocked salmon is their willingness to take, at one time or another, just about every type of lure that can be cast with a fly rod. They will rise to mayflies during a hatch and at such times will come well to dry flies fished exactly as one would fish them for feeding trout. Salmon rivers are usually fast and bouncy, so flies smaller than No. 10 and No. 12 are seldom needed. This isn't always the case, however. In low, clear water salmon can be as critical as the most sophisticated trout, a fact of life which I first learned while fishing the West Outlet of Moosehead Lake in Maine.

The flow coming from the lake is controlled by a dam, and at the time the gates were closed. The stream was reduced to a series of clear and glassy pools, concentrating the salmon in obvious locations but making them anything but easy to take. They would have absolutely nothing to do with anything as large as a No. 12, and it wasn't until I dropped down to a No. 18 and a 6X tippet that I finally raised (and lost) a few fish.

In spite of the fact that dry flies of conventional size hold a strange fascination for landlocks when skittered over the surface, I have tried the same stunt with king-size dry flies and hair bugs with disappointing results. Because of the frequency with which they will chase after a No. 10 or No. 12 of any standard pattern, one would be inclined to believe that a big Wolff, Muddler or Cooper Bug would be even more provocative when skittered in the same way. That this doesn't seem to be the case is puzzling to me, and the puzzle is compounded by the fact that I have had considerable success with landlocks by floating the same big flies over them with a dead drift.

I have written of a particular day when streamers were all but useless, but any such day is an exception. Streamers are probably more generally effective on landlocked salmon than on any other freshwater species and are rightfully classified as standard salmon lures. No. 6 is probably a better size for stream fishing than the No. 4's that are usually used for lake trolling, and a No. 8 will sometimes take fish when larger sizes fail to produce.

Wet flies will account for their share of landlocks, although I prefer those I tie specifically for salmon to those of more conventional construction. The differences are not great: bulkier bodies, longer-than-usual wings and tail and a few extra winds of hackle. I tie these flies on No. 8 and No. 6 hooks without wasting time. If they are a bit scraggly, their appearance of bulk and substance is increased. As with streamers, I have no favorite patterns and doubt that differences of pattern are of any great concern to the salmon.

I feel certain that properly presented artificial nymphs would take landlocks, but I have never been tempted to try them. One of the big thrills of landlocked salmon fishing is that of seeing them strike at the surface. I like to see them break when they go for a fly and don't want to cheat myself of this thrill by fishing a sunken lure.

This is one reason why I am reluctant to use spinning tackle on landlocks, despite the fact that they are very responsive to small spoons and wobblers. Mine is a prejudiced viewpoint, of course, and it goes almost without saying that land-locked salmon will dish out plenty of thrills to the spin fisher-man. Actually, spinning for salmon is more sporting than fly fishing, if the term is used to denote the extent of a hooked fish's chance of escape. I say this because I estimate that nearly half of the landlocks I have hooked on spinning lures have thrown the spoon or wobbler on the first jump.

This has been equally true of any trout that have leaped when hooked, and the ability of trout and salmon to throw a metal lure has long intrigued me. Bass get credit for being specially skilled at ridding themselves of lures by jumping, and there is no question but that they try their darndest to do so. When they leap they often shake their heads so hard that their gills clatter, and it is true that they sometimes toss the lure. But if I were to hazard a guess, it would be that no more than one or two bass in ten succeed in throwing the lure, while approximately half of all leaping trout and salmon are able to do so with a single jump.

The point seems all the more remarkable, for trout and salmon, unlike bass, do not appear to be trying deliberately to shake the hook when they leap. They seem intent only on climbing as high into the air as possible, yet it is almost an even bet that if they have been hung on hardware the lure will go flying off to one side, which has led me to believe that leaping trout and salmon actually "shake" much more power-fully than do bass. Perhaps the effort is compressed into a single flirt that is too rapid for the eye to follow, and which takes maximum advantage of the inertia of the metal lure. In any event, the issue is usually decided during the first leap; if the lure stays stuck, the chances are high that additional leaping will not dislodge it.

Because flies are of such slight weight, leaping salmon have much less success at trying to shake them loose. Many fly fishermen play fish with the conviction that to allow slack to develop in the line would be a fatal mistake, and they do their darndest to avoid what they believe would result in calamity. If a fisherman can find the courage to experiment, he will discover that he can deliberately give slack to a fly-hooked fish without increasing its chances of escape.

It took me a long time to accept this contradiction of popular belief as fact. Having at last accepted it, I have found that it can be used to good advantage. The fly fisherman is usually holding coils of slack line in his left hand at the time of a strike, and these coils are a potential source of trouble whenever the hooked fish is a large one. The quicker the fish can be played directly from the reel, the better.

In order to bring this about as swiftly as possible, I "forget" about the fish until I have reeled in all the slack. This means that the fish is under no tension until brought against the reel, a circumstance which supposedly should result in his prompt escape, and which most fishermen try desperately to avoid. In practice, the fish is no more likely to come off than when held on a tight line, and the actual job of playing him can be safely postponed until the potentially troublesome slack has been wound on the reel. Naturally, one does not relinquish control of a fish at the risk of having him wrap the leader around known obstructions, but it is perfectly safe to do so wherever this danger is not a factor.

While the danger of allowing slack to a fly-hooked fish is largely imaginary, the large fish that leaps against a tight line is a real threat to fall on the leader and snap it, or pop it with a sudden yank against a bit too much drag. In theory, it is wise to reduce line tension by lowering the tip of the rod when a heavy fish leaps, but I rather suspect that this is beyond the ability of most fishermen. It is in my case, at least. A salmon is up, and back down, before I can do anything about it other than hope he won't bust loose.

I once read a yarn in which the author advanced the theory that salmon leaped only because they felt the leader against their tails. By way of proof, he stated that the tails of landed salmon often showed one or more slits which allegedly were due to contact with the taut leader. Had the fellow done much salmon fishing, his theory would have been refuted by one of the sport's most disconcerting experiences: to break off a fly in a salmon's jaw, and then watch helplessly as the furious fish tailwalks all over the pool in a frantic effort to rid himself of the *leaderless* fly.

A hooked landlocked salmon is usually in the air long before the leader has had a chance to make contact with his tail, and it is largely because of their spectacular leaps that landlocked salmon enjoy their reputation and high status. To the fisherman, the threat of escape seems implicit in every soaring leap, but the threat is substantially real only when the fish has been hung on hardware. The fly-caught fish is a good bet to stay stuck; if he manages to escape it is usually because the fisherman has forced him too hard, and not because he has "given him slack."

240

So far I have dealt mainly with stream fishing for land-locks, but only because it happens to be my preference. Unfortunately, at least for those who concur, opportunities for stream fishing are limited, and most landlocked salmon fishing is done on lakes.

Lake fishing is essentially an early season proposition, consisting of trolling streamers at or near the surface during the relatively short period that salmon are to be found near the top. As soon as a warm layer of water develops at the surface they retire to the cooler temperatures of deep water.

The turnover of water which follows ice-out, and the eventual stratification, is an interesting phenomenon. Water reaches its greatest density at about 40°. During the winter, the upper level is only slightly above the freezing point and therefore is not at its greatest density. As soon as the ice goes out the water at the surface grows warmer, its density increases and it sinks. It is replaced by colder water which goes through the same process. This continues until the lake stands at around 40° from top to bottom. From then on, the surface water becomes more buoyant as it grows warmer and remains at the top. As soon as salmon find it intolerably warm, usually before the middle of June, they move into the depths. Discounting unusual circumstances, the surface fishing is over until fall when cooler surface water may bring them up briefly.

It can be seen that timing is of great importance in planning a trip for landlocks. Good fishing is reputed to start as soon as the ice goes out, but I've been skunked too many times the day after ice-out to take this at its face value. I'd rather wait a week or so, for it has been my experience that the fishing is then likely to be considerably better. It can be expected to hold up throughout May, and to taper off, usually to nothing, during the first two weeks of June.

Opinions concerning the technique of salmon trolling tend to vary and it is difficult to either prove or disprove their validity. I have already voiced my personal opinion with respect to the matter of pattern choice: in spite of the fact that wherever one fishes a certain pattern is invariably regarded as the most deadly, there seems to be little reason to believe that other patterns won't do as well if one has the courage to try them.

Other strong convictions are equally suspect. Some guides insist on trolling at a particularly fast clip, and when their parties make good catches their success is attributed to this persuasion. In the meantime, canoes moving at more moderate speed may account for as many fish, or more, and it is impossible to arrive at any conclusion other than that salmon will hit a fly that is fairly zipping through the water, but will also hit one that's moving at a much more moderate pace.

One thing to remember, however, is that salmon are fast, dynamic fish that are best challenged by a relatively fast-moving lure and that streamers should be trolled at a faster pace than that associated with trolling for other species. I have never subscribed to the theory that excessive speed works any particular magic, but I do know that a streamer should move considerably faster than should lures trolled for bass, walleyes and pike.

Another moot question is whether anything is to be gained by working or twitching a trolled streamer. Common sense seems to indicate that a streamer which alternately spurts ahead and falls back should come in for the most attention, and I always feel bound to act accordingly. Yet I rather doubt that it really amounts to anything.

I once asked Grand Lake guide Kenny Wheaton how he felt about the need to "work" a trolled streamer.

"It *seems* as though it should help," he said, after due deliberation. "But the fellow who is half asleep, and paying no attention to his rod, is often the one who gets the strike."

There are some salmon fishermen who recommend propping the rod over a thwart and keeping hands off until after a fish strikes. The theory is that more fish will be hooked this way, and I'm rather inclined to agree. A surprisingly large number of striking salmon escape unhooked, and it is possible that the fisherman's attempt to set the hook does more to maintain this high incidence of failure than to prevent it. Much of the force of the yank is absorbed by the limber fly rod, and very little imparted to the fly — just enough, perhaps to deter fish in the act of striking, fish that otherwise would strike more solidly and hook themselves with no help from the fisherman.

At any rate, failure to hook striking landlocks is a common complaint and is usually attributed to the fact that the fish are "striking short." I remember one day when Pete and I came off Grand Lake after missing an unusually high number of strikes and had the answer to our trouble pointed out by Bev Weatherby.

One fisherman had come in at noon, he said, and complained that the fish were striking short. After lunch he consulted one of the fishing books in the lounge library and discovered that it recommended the use of streamers tied on tandem hooks as a remedy for this particular difficulty. He bought some streamers of this type at a shop just across the street and had already come in from the afternoon's fishing with the report that, just as the book promised, he had hooked nearly every fish that struck. Then, with great delight, Bev added that the book which had provided this gem of advice was my own *Tricks That Take Fish*.

Well, I'm ever suspicious of the cure-alls found in fishing books. I'm not even sure that tandem hooks will necessarily prevent "short" strikes — even though I once wrote in good faith that they would and thereby solved a problem for at least one fisherman. Maybe I have become too cynical for my own good; perhaps I could benefit from reviewing my own book and then practicing that which I was once brash enough to preach.

Disagreement crops up again in determining what length of line should be trolled. Some fishermen advocate a short line on the theory that salmon are attracted by the flash and sound of the propeller. Others recommend a long line for precisely the opposite reason: it will give fish time to recover from the startling effect of the canoe's passage. My convictions are not that positive. I don't think it matters how long or short a line one trolls — as long as it is within a foot or two of sixty feet!

I do greatly prefer to troll with a sinking line, for a floating fly line that is pressed into service for this purpose is always a considerable nuisance. The same line may have a perverse tendency to sink when used as a dry fly line, but you can bet it will float beautifully behind a canoe when one wants it to sink. It creates a noticeable disturbance, annoys the fisherman and may arouse suspicion in the fish.

Were it not for the fact that I like to stand ready to cast, my choice of line for streamer trolling would be monofilament of about ten-pound test. Such a line would approach maximum refinement, and I think it would give the fisherman a bit of an advantage. It is next to impossible to cast a fly with monofilament, of course, and this decides me against it.

The need to cast arises when fish are spotted breaking the surface. Whenever possible, it is better to work to within casting range than to put the canoe over them at the almost certain risk of putting them down. It is also possible to pick up salmon by casting while one's partner is playing a fish near the canoe. The struggles of a hooked fish often attract and excite other salmon, and sometimes they will even try to snatch the streamer from the jaws of a hooked fish. When aroused to this point they will nail a cast streamer instantly, and a few casts near a hooked fish may quickly result in a second. Needless to say, this should be attempted only after prior agreement. Two fish on at the same time can lead to a tangle — and to much hard feeling if it comes about unexpectedly.

A floating line belongs on any trip for landlocks, for there are often chances to take them on dry flies, even though these favorable moments are usually overlooked. Such opportunities generally arise when evening hatches of mayflies develop along shorelines, usually when the water is smooth and calm.

Rising fish can be seen for long distances, and stalking to within casting range by canoe is an intriguing business. A rise to a carefully placed fly after such a stalk is one of the most gratifying experiences in freshwater fishing, and a landlock's explosive reaction to the unexpected sting of the hook is something to behold.

Unfortunately, the fishing day ends at most camps with the return to headquarters for dinner. But if a guide can be persuaded to return to the lake, and cruise in search of rising fish during the dusk, it can result in the finest salmon fishing to be had.

During the early season, when salmon are near the surface, they are likely to show almost anywhere. They cruise about freely, and there is no real reason for them to be in any particular place unless it is one in which bait fish congregate. Guides keep any such spots well in mind, but if one fishes without the services of a guide he should be attuned to the clues by which these locations can be recognized. Rocky shoals which are surrounded by deep water are favored by salmon, and their presence is often indicated by jutting points which extend well into the lake and end in a dotting of partially submerged boulders. A reef is formed by the underwater projection of such a point and should be given special attention.

It is wise to swing through a series of loops in these specially likely spots. If a strike results, the location should alternately be rested and revisited. The same holds true for any area that provides action. Tiny islands and boulder outcroppings are usually surrounded by rocky shoals. It is a good policy to make several circles of successively greater diameter around such spots and to repeat any course which produces a strike. It is surprising how often additional strikes will occur in almost precisely the same spots on successive runs.

These are but generalities and in no way binding. The lessons learned by fishing a particular lake are not necessarily valuable when the attempt is made to apply them to another. In the first body of water, the hotspots can be anticipated in much the manner I have described. In another, the fish may roam over much greater areas, in which case it may be better to forget about shoreline clues and simply troll open water while trusting in percentages.

According to an old salmon fishing adage, the rougher the weather the better the fishing There is undoubtedly truth in this theory, for landlocks tend to hit best in a moderate to heavy chop, and sometimes when waves and wind make fishing very difficult. But there are exceptions to all rules. Some of the best lake fishing for landlocks that I have ever enjoyed took place when, by all usual standards, it shouldn't have happened at all.

In the first place, it began on the Fourth of July, when salmon usually have long since left the surface. Pete and I had driven to Grand Lake Stream with the idea of bugging for smallmouths. If we thought of salmon at all, it was only with regret that we were on the scene too late in the season to have any real hope of taking any.

On the first morning, guide Kenny Wheaton ran us up through Grand Lake to Junior Lake, in which there are few if any salmon, but lots of smallmouths. But when a morning of fishing produced only a few small bass, we allowed that we'd rather have poor salmon fishing than poor bass fishing, and we elected to troll streamers in Grand Lake. Greatly to the surprise of all, we took four good landlocks, several short fish and missed the usual number of strikes. This wasn't exactly spectacular fishing, but it clearly indicated that salmon were working the surface and that further investigation certainly was in order.

Kenny was the local postmaster and had been able to guide us that first day only because it was a Sunday. The next day we were scheduled to go out with George MacArthur and Eddie Brown. Both were guides of long experience, and we learned that both preferred salmon fishing to bass fishing.

It was therefore easy to persuade them to try for salmon, even though though they were plainly skeptical of our report of the previous day's fishing. Both insisted on going home for deep trolling rigs, declaring that in spite of our luck the day before our only real hope of taking salmon lay in getting down near the bottom.

Both guides, acting on this conviction, took us to deep water far offshore, and there we began operations. George and Eddie dredged bottom with their metal lines, while Pete and I trolled streamers along the surface. It was almost a case of each half of the party trying to prove the other half wrong.

It didn't look too good for our side when Eddie picked up a small lake trout on his rig and George followed with a good salmon, for neither Pete nor I had had a touch in the meantime. But we had been chugging over a course almost in the middle of the broad lake, and I finally hinted that it would be no more than fair to work closer to shore to where we had taken salmon on streamers the day before.

We did so, and very little time elapsed before Pete and I each landed a salmon. George and Eddie lost no time cranking up their wire lines, and we went to fishing exactly as though it were May and surfacing fish to be taken for granted.

Fish were indeed at the surface. Wretched weather blew up, forcing us ashore several times. Thunder storms delivered downpours which left our canoes filled inches deep with water. But between squalls and storms the salmon hit like crazy. George and Eddie were incredulous and declared over and over that in all their experience they had never known salmon to hit at the surface like that so late in the season.

You can bet that there was no mention of bass fishing when we regrouped the next morning. Neither were there any expressions of doubt about finding salmon at the surface. At our suggestion, both guides had come equipped with fly rods; if the fishing continued to hold up there would be plenty of salmon for everybody.

The dirty weather continued — and the salmon went on hitting. One thunderstorm followed another, but we welcomed them. Lacking any other evidence, we could only attribute the unprecedented fishing to the violent weather.

On the third day Eddie was signed up to guide for another party, so Pete and I both fished from George's canoe. The rough weather had finally blown itself out. The sky was cloudless, and there wasn't a hint of a breeze. The day promised to be hot, and it seemed a sure bet that the salmon had left the surface. Convinced that it would be foolish to try to stretch our luck, we decided to have another go at the Junior Lake smallmouths.

Results were as disappointing as before. After lunch, George voiced what Pete and I were thinking.

"You don't suppose those salmon are still on top?" he wondered aloud.

There was only one way to find out, but when we reached the salmon grounds I wouldn't have given much for our chances. The sun beat down on water that showed not the slightest ripple, save for the wake created by the canoe. The scene was one of great beauty — but because of conditions that reputedly spell failure for the salmon fisherman.

Yet we had hardly begun trolling when Pete hooked a salmon in that glassy water. I started to reel in my line, but my streamer was only partway to the canoe when another landlock socked it. Despite seemingly prohibitive conditions, Pete and I were fast to wildly leaping fish only moments after letting out our lines.

This moved George MacArthur to wild oratory, accompanied by extravagant gestures. Never in his memory, he declared, had any such thing happened. Here it was a hot day in July, and in a flat calm, mind you — and salmon hitting at the surface in pairs! His amazement grew as we continued to take fish, and he was still voicing it as we approached the landing that evening.

"Nobody is going to believe this," he declared. "Even when we show them our fish."

He wasn't far from wrong. I wrote an article about the unusual experience which appeared in one of the outdoor magazines. George told me the following year that people around Grand Lake Stream asked him if the yarn was as big a lie as they thought it had to be.

"I told them that I had seen it all with my own eyes, and that every word in that story was true," George said.

I suspect that this may have been a bit of an exaggeration. But as they say in the TV commercials, all the *facts* are true.

Although we brought in large catches of salmon for three straight days, the curious quality of human nature is illustrated by the fact that the sight of our fish failed to inspire other fishermen to fish for salmon. The conviction that salmon wouldn't hit in July was so deeply ingrained that it could not be shaken, even by openly displayed strings of fish. As a result, we caught landlocks left and right for three days with no competition from anyone.

I have tried to account for the appearance of salmon at the surface at such an unlikely time, but without much success. Rough weather could have been responsible the first two days, but certainly not on the third when the fishing was the fastest of all.

I did learn that the gates of the dam at the outlet of Grand Lake had been opened just prior to our arrival, and consequently the level of the lake had dropped by several feet. Possibly a layer of relatively warm surface water had been drained off and made the surface attractive to the salmon. If so, perhaps late-season surface fishing could be induced in salmon lakes where water levels could be regulated.

If this is a possibility, it is anything but a probability. I suspect that Pete and I were simply lucky enough to happen along when inscrutable factors combined to bring about the unexpected. This happens just often enough so that no fisherman should ever take anything for granted — and rarely enough to make each such event unforgettable.

I have ventured the opinion that the landlocked salmon rates second only to the Atlantic salmon as a trophy, and perhaps one reason is that the landlock, even more than the brook trout, is to be associated with canoes, campfires and wilderness waters. Like the brookie, the landlock is extremely sensitive to both tangible and intangible factors which are the products of civilization, and any concentration of human presence seems to result in his decline and retreat.

This trait is evidenced by his apparent inability to grow to maturity in waters which supported populations of sizable salmon only a few decades ago. The waters of a lake may remain pure insofar as one can determine, and ostensibly unchanged in all other respects. Yet as the number of cottages increase, and human traffic does likewise, the heaviest stocking of small landlocked salmon may fail to result in any appreciable number of fish of keeper size.

Lake Dunmore, only a few miles from Pittsford, is a good example. Twenty years ago this small lake was churned by dozens of outboard motors on opening day, but in spite of heavy fishing pressure, most parties left with good catches of sizable salmon. The water in the lake seems as pure, clear and cool now as it did then, and it certainly is as deep. It is stocked with young salmon regularly, or was the last I knew. Yet it has become a virtual impossibility to take a legal salmon from the lake. On opening day one is likely to see schools of young salmon surfacing for midges. These fish, stocked the previous year, live to reach a length of about a foot, then mysteriously disappear.

Fishing pressure has thus dwindled to practically nothing, and it would seem that the unmolested salmon, with plenty of smelt to feed on, would grow to interesting size. But the lake is churned to a froth daily by powerful motors, hundreds of swimmers flock to the beaches and cottages encircle the lake like tightly strung beads. Unfortunately, it is not the landlocked salmon's nature to tolerate the close proximity of so much sheer humanity.

Much the same has happened wherever similar conditions exist, and in most instances efforts to maintain significant landlocked salmon fisheries have been futile. In some cases the legal length of salmon has been reduced in order to maintain what is little more than a pathetic pretense of actual salmon fishing. Immature salmon are slender and smeltlike, with none of the splendid characteristics that come only with maturity. To classify these undeveloped fish as keepers seems almost vulgar.

Fortunately, although nobody knows for how long, there are still lakes and streams in Maine which are bordered by unbroken forests and which so far have escaped wholesale encroachment. Landlocked salmon still may be taken in these waters and continue to provide one of the top thrills in fresh water angling. Their days are undoubtedly numbered, however, and the fisherman who yearns to come to grips with this splendid game fish had best be about it while the chance remains.

II

An Apology to Bass

Over the past few years, many Vermont trout streams have become heavily populated with fallfish. For those who may not be familiar with the species, fallfish are members of the minnow tribe which often grow to be a foot long, and sometimes considerably longer. They are protected by large scales of a silvery color and are sufficiently graceful of line to present a reasonably pleasing appearance when viewed objectively.

Fallfish subsist largely on insect life and respond to a hatch of mayflies as do trout. Like trout, they will rise to a dry fly when they are surface-minded. Furthermore, since they are capable of respectable speed and power, fallfish hooked on dry flies are frequently mistaken for trout until finally brought close enough for visual identification.

An Apology to Bass

This moment of recognition invariably triggers a flow of choice cusswords from the fisherman, which in some ways is rather surprising. Since the fisherman often cannot tell a fallfish from a trout by either the rise or the initial struggle, his delayed invective seems to be more a confession of prejudice than a justifiable denunciation. The fact that he mistakes the fallfish for a trout until the final moment seems to indicate that the big minnow is every bit the trout's equal in those things for which the trout is held in an esteem which amounts almost to reverence.

I am no exception in this case, for the aforementioned moment of disenchantment invariably drives me to the use of strong language. Yet I am always keenly aware of the irony of cussing a fish that behaves so much like a trout that I must get a good look at it in order to tell the difference.

Such unjustifiable angling dislikes would stand out as anomalies were it not for the fact that most human standards of acceptability are as much the products of prejudice and hypocrisy as of reason. In view of this general circumstance, it is not strange that fishermen are often guilty of bigotry.

Fortunately, the angler's prejudice is harmless, for it would be absurd to cite the grievances of fish as examples of the massive evil inherent in prejudicial persecution. But if a fish were to be used as an example, the bass would be a likely candidate. This would be true, at least, in regions where all game fish are judged by the light of a century-old reverence for trout and salmon.

"Inch for inch and pound for pound, the gamest fish that swims . . ." Seemingly, the fish which inspired this glowing and oft-quoted tribute would need only to demonstrate the qualities which it suggests to win a status of nobility. But bass do not find the path to acceptance that direct. They can leap, tailwalk and fight to the last gasp, which indeed they do, only to find themselves relegated to a position of comparative inferiority on the arbitrary grounds that they are neither trout nor salmon.

It would be dishonest of me if I failed to admit that I am guilty of this injustice, at least to a degree. Reason and experience tell me that bass, particularly smallmouths, have few if any superiors among freshwater game fish. But while I am always happy if I can raise ten-inch trout to a fly, I would scorn the opportunity to fish for bass of this size. The fact that the bass fight as hard, or harder, doesn't seem to cut any ice. My warmest affection is reserved for trout, and there doesn't seem to be anything I can do about it.

Perhaps my prejudice is due in part to the fact that I have never understood bass as I think I understand trout. My empathy leads me to believe that I know what to expect from trout. When they defeat me, I can usually put my finger on what I believe to have been the reason. Bass deny me this satisfaction. I just can't figure them out.

This isn't to say that I can't catch bass when they happen to be in a hitting mood. At such times, anybody who can get a bug or plug into the water can take them.

Last year, early in June, I spent a fishing weekend with H. G. Tapply at his home in Alton, New Hampshire. The first morning Tap took me to a small pond which he said held largemouths. Tap had moved from Massachusetts not long before. This was my first fishing in his new territory, and he was eager to show me as much of it as possible.

We spent the morning fishing the pond, and each of us took several nice largemouths on popping bugs, to say nothing of numerous pickerel. It struck me as mighty fine fishing, and I said so.

But according to Tap, this had been just a warmup to get the kinks out of our casting arms. The main event was scheduled to take place that afternoon on nearby Lake Wentworth. There we should take at least fifty smallmouths, Tap declared, provided I held up my end of the deal.

We caught slightly over forty bass, a poor showing, according to Tap, and one which prompted him to apologize for fishing which he insisted was far below par. Indeed, shortly after returning home, I received a letter saying that he had just returned from fishing Lake Wentworth where the fishing had returned to normal, bass coming twice as fast and twice as big as when I was there.

The fact that a catch of over forty bass in a single afternoon can actually indicate poorer-than-usual fishing pretty well substantiates my contention that bass can be almost ridiculously easy to take under the most favorable conditions.

These conditions exist, with respect to smallmouths, during May and early June when the fish are in the process of spawning along the shorelines. Eggs are deposited in scooped-out depressions or "beds," and the male is alleged to guard the eggs during the incubation period and to seize and remove any small objects which intrude upon the immediate vicinity of the nest.

257

I cannot vouch for this from personal observation, nor can I refute it. My tendency toward skepticism leads me to suspect that bass are not as fanatically dedicated to these protective duties as they are alleged to be. In view of the inclination toward irresponsibility which tends to distinguish the males of all species, I find it easier to believe that Mr. Bass would be prone to step out for a quick frog just when his services were most needed.

Nevertheless, the belief persists that the sometimes incredibly fast fishing of May and early June is due to this guardianship, and no particular point is served by questioning its soundness. The spring fishing in heavily populated smallmouth lakes is often spectacular, and of a sort which appeals to the fly fisherman for it is then that bug fishing is at its best.

An area which has become justly famous for such exceptional smallmouth fishing is Maine's Grand Lake region. It consists largely of wilderness in which lie chains of large lakes which once held only trout and salmon, but in which smallmouths eventually were stocked. My knowledge of the history of this step consists only of hearsay, to the effect that the present widespread distribution of bass throughout virtually all of the region's lakes and waterways is the result of the introduction of bass to but a single lake. This may, or may not, be an exaggeration. In any event, the vast numbers of bass now present indicate conditions sufficiently favorable for such a thing to happen.

As was to be expected, bass were greeted with hatred and scorn in an area where only trout and salmon were looked on as worth fishing for. But the die was cast, and there was no stopping the smallmouths as they multiplied and spread from lake to lake. Eventually, less prejudiced fishermen from the other regions were attracted by bass fishing such as they had never experienced, and they came in increasing numbers from greater and greater distances. This did not necessarily inspire any local affection for the smallmouth as a game fish, but it brought about economic benefits which could neither be denied nor ignored. As a result, bass have been accepted as a bread-and-butter resource, even if not as a game fish to be mentioned in the same breath with trout and salmon.

I have fished over much of the region, and I must confess that I am nagged by the feeling that it is somehow improper to fish for bass in waters which so strongly suggest trout. Spruce forests overhang shorelines which are free of cottages and of all other signs of human congestion. The water is deep and clear, and the bottoms of the lakes are free from weeds and strewn with glacial boulders. Long association of trout and salmon with similar wilderness waters makes it difficult for me to accept the presence of bass as anything but anomalous.

Several years ago, Pete, guide Cret MacArthur, who is George's nephew, and I spent an afternoon casting bugs on Junior Stream, the connection between Junior Lake and Grand Lake. Although designated as a stream, it is marked by only a slight current, and leading off from it are shallow bays and coves which are liberally dotted by stumps and tangles of driftwood. Bass could hardly find habitat more to their liking, and on this particular afternoon they were in a hitting mood. Cret eased our big canoe among and around the many obstructions, and Pete and I took bass after bass along the edges of cover that spread in all directions. Most were fish of two pounds or more and they were crammed with energy. One jab of the hook and they took to the air, fairly bristling with belligerence, and when they went down they put a strain on a rod that was often alarming.

We kept at it until dusk and gave up then only because we had a long run to make. More important, at the end of the run we would have to ascend a narrow, rocky stream, and we needed at least a little daylight to help us thread our way among the rocks. We were not far from the mouth of the stream when Cret suddenly turned the canoe toward shore and slowed the motor.

His reason immediately became apparent. The water just off the mouth of a tiny brook fairly boiled with rising fish. Cret eased the canoe closer to the rising fish, and soon we could make out the bright orange of their sleek flanks. Those feeding fish were brookies that would weigh up to a couple of pounds!

And there we were, with our rods taken down and not daring to linger because of the rapidly fading light. The cruel irony of the situation was almost unbearable.

You may be sure that we were back at the same spot the next evening — and equally sure that the trout were not. Chances like that seldom come twice in a row.

I am still tortured by the knowledge that while Pete and I fished for bass that afternoon, those trout were feeding furiously only a few miles away. The fact that we were completely busy with larger and harder fighting fish is of absolutely no consolation. For the life of me, I cannot give bass their due and equate them with trout.

I come closest to full appreciation whenever I can take bass on a fly rod, and I think there is good reason to prefer fly fishing for bass above all other methods. Explosive surface strikes add greatly to the thrills, and bass hooked on bugs or flies can give much better accounts of themselves than those punished and encumbered by the multiple hooks of plugs and spoons. This difference is best appreciated by fishermen who use tackle no heavier than the job actually requires.

Unfortunately, many fishermen are under the impression that bass bugging requires a very stiff and powerful rod. It is indeed true that such a rod is needed in order to cast bulky lures which meet with great air resistance. It is equally true, however, that it is not necessary to use bugs so bulky that they are difficult to cast, and this is particularly true if the bass are smallmouths.

I believe this consideration to be important, for prolonged casting with a stiff and heavy rod becomes arm-tiring work. Such unpleasantness is easily avoided by using streamlined bugs which can be handled on a lighter rod with only mild effort. I am well aware of the difference which streamlined bugs can make, for I often use huge hair bugs when fishing for northern pike. I can heave these out with my stiffest rod, but it makes work out of what otherwise would be play. The small bugs I use for bass enable me to cast with a 7½-foot rod of pleasant action, which makes bass bugging much more attractive as far as I'm concerned.

Bulky bass bugs, with air-catching legs, wings and other projections, do seem more lifelike and provocative to the fisherman, but there is little evidence that bass see them in the same light. In my experience, at least, bass will attack a bug or popper which consists only of a streamlined body and a tail as readily as one with appendages.

I learned this truth years ago by fishing with H. G. Tapply. Tap is a strong supporter of the theory that bass bugging need be scarcely more tiring and unpleasant than dry fly fishing. His bug box contained none of the big powderpuff jobs which can be thrown only with a brute of a rod. Instead, it was stuffed with relatively small and compact bugs of clipped deer hair which could be tossed easily with a light, flexible rod. Tap demonstrated immediately that these easy-to-cast poppers would most certainly take bass — largemouths as well as smallmouths.

Tap ties his own bugs, and they are works of art. He has mastered the art of crowding a maximum amount of body hair on the hook, which is the big secret of bug tying. When he clips the tightly packed hair to shape, the result is a body which seems sculptured from solid material but which is extremely light and buoyant. Appropriately enough, body hair from a deer is used for the body, and bucktail for the tail. With no projections to create friction, these bugs cut through the air easily. On the water they can be made to dance and pop to create all the disturbance required to draw strikes from bass.

I also tie my own bugs, which fall considerably short of the perfection Tap attains. But they are equally easy to cast, and the bass don't seem to take exception to the flaws in their construction. For this reason, I do not hesitate to encourage fishermen of no great fly-tying skill to turn out their own bass bugs.

Among the commercially available bass bugs, none combines easy casting and fish appeal more successfully than the "Yates Deacon." This bug features a rounded head of clipped deer hair, which provides the "popping" effect, while the rest is constructed much as the conventional "bucktail" — bucktail wings, tapered body and a tail consisting of a pair of hackle feathers. The result is a lure that is no harder to cast than a large streamer, but which is a proven killer on bass. One source of these uniquely efficient bugs is the Netcraft Company, 3101 Sylvania, Toledo, Ohio.

Sometimes smallmouths are in the mood to hit surface lures that are smaller than the streamlined bugs; in that case I often have good luck by tying on a No. 8 Cooper Bug or a Muddler Minnow of the same size. These will bring enthusiastic strikes for as long as they remain sufficiently buoyant to ride above the surface, but lose effectiveness when they become soggy. It is therefore wise to change these flies frequently, even though it might be something of a nuisance.

In the chapter on landlocked salmon I dwelt at some length on the fascination a skittered dry fly has for landlocks. Because bass are so readily excited by action which suggests attempted escape, it has always seemed to me that they should be pushovers for a big dry fly that is twitched enticingly over the surface. I have tried to interest bass in a twitched dry fly many times, never with any marked success.

This disdain for items which lack substance seems to be a bass characteristic. Most bass lures are too large to be tolerated by trout, and many trout lures are too small to arouse the interest of bass. I have done a considerable amount of fishing in streams inhabited by smallmouths, and this difference has often been noticeable — particularly when hatches of mayflies quickly bring trout to the surface, but receive no attention from the bass which share the same water.

But while the bass are likely to show no interest in most hatches, every once in a while, for some unknown reason, they will feed steadily on hatching mayflies. When they do, if my experience is a valid criterion, they are usually devilishly hard to take.

I can remember a number of such experiences, strung over the years, and all have conformed to the same pattern: soaring expectations, frustration and finally, disappointment. The high expectations arise when I first see the feeding fish and gullibly mistake them for trout. With "trout" rising all around me, I rejoice at my good fortune. Then comes the frustration. My fly comes over feeding fish with what seems flawless innocence, yet absolutely nothing happens. I watch float after float with breathless anticipation, but each time my fly is ignored. In the meantime, fish pick off naturals all around the drifting fly with a show of discrimination that does anything but bear tribute to my skill as a fly fisherman. Disappointment sets in when finally a fish does take and a chunky bronze body shoots into the air and I realize at last that I have been bamboozled. It is to my shame that I feel so let down. I have just fooled a fish more discriminating than a trout, but am not fair-minded enough to admit it.

Perhaps it is because bass are fish of so many behavioral contrasts and contradictions that I have difficulty in trying to understand and outfigure them. At times they can be almost ridiculously easy to take, and at others almost impossible. And *absolutely* impossible, as far as that goes.

This behavioral range is greater among smallmouths, it seems to me, and of the two the largemouth is the lesser enigma. At least, no largemouths to date have made a monkey of me by impersonating and outdoing trout, and their habits are sufficiently consistent so that one can approach them with some degree of assurance. I have a fair idea of where to look for them, or think I have, and some confidence in their response to standard offerings.

Largemouths are somewhat like pike and pickerel in that they prefer spots that are rather easy to recognize. They tend to shift about in response to changes of light and temperature to a much greater extent than pike, and this point must be taken into consideration. But since their shifting is inspired by fairly obvious factors, their whereabouts at a given time can be predicted with considerable accuracy.

It is fairly safe to lead off with the assumption that the largemouth likes to lie close to shore wherever he can do so in safety. To offset the risk inherent in choosing a position in shallow water, he invariably seeks out some sort of cover which will help to conceal his presence. Like most wild creatures, a bass requires a surprisingly small amount of cover to make him virtually invisible, and an important attribute in shoreline fishing for largemouths is a sensitive eye for the slight irregularities which are all that a bass needs to achieve concealment.

Some hiding places, of course, are quite obvious: fallen trees, sunken brush, lily pads, weed patches. But outnumbering these by far are the many small pockets of shade and shadow which exist in endless variety along most shorelines. To the inexperienced eye these may seem to be spots in which a bass weighing several pounds could not possibly hide. But one need log no more than a modest number of bass fishing hours to discover the error in such a conclusion, and to appreciate the uncanny ability of bass to camouflage their considerable bulk with the help of only a hint of cover. Once this is realized, the configuration of the shoreline is seen in its true importance, and pockets formerly dismissed as unlikely become meaningful targets for bug or plug.

One also learns not to count on finding bass along shorelines which lie in bright sunlight. This does not mean that they are never to be found close to shore when such conditions prevail, but in general, they tend to shun the shallows when the sun beats down on them. Popular opinion has it that they move into deeper water to seek relief from the higher temperatures which supposedly develop along the shore, but I'm inclined to doubt that the temperature has much to do with it.

In the first place, shoreline temperatures are not driven upward substantially by a few hours of sunlight. Secondly, largemouths have no great aversion to warm water anyway. It seems much more likely to me that they tend to move away from the shoreline becasue the direct sunlight destroys the shadows upon which they depend for concealment. This seems to be borne out by the fact that bass will remain close to shore on the hottest days, wherever the desired shade exists.

Furthermore, they will return at dusk to a shoreline that has been directly exposed to the afternoon sun, long before the supposedly heated water has had time to cool appreciably.

Only a couple of Sundays ago, Pete and I bugged for largemouths in an impoundment which is several miles long but scarcely fifty yards wide where we fished. It was a hot, bright afternoon, and it came as no great surprise when no bass rose to our bugs along shorelines which, for the most part, were utterly devoid of shade. On a hunch, we paddled to the single short stretch of shore that was bordered by trees, and from a shaded area which extended no more than a couple of hundred yards we took half a dozen nice bass. Later, after the sun had gone down, we ran our total take up to thirty fish, most of which came from the shorelines that were barren of bass while the sun was high. The returning bass certainly had not waited for the water to cool; they returned as soon as the light began to dwindle.

So I believe I can usually find largemouths along the shorelines wherever there is shade, but if I can't find them there I won't shed any tears if I can't find them at all. If I did find them, probably somewhere in relatively deep water, I would have every confidence of catching at least a few by lowering live minnows to where the bass could see them. That's more than I could say if the fish in question were smallmouths.

Although the smallmouth is an easy mark during the spring, when he is close to shore, he becomes something else again as the fishing season advances. You may find him using the same close-to-shore spots frequented by largemouths, but more likely you won't. He may be in the locations he is alleged to favor: rocky reefs, the edges of sharp dropoffs and at the base of cliffs where the bottom is a jumble of fallen rocks. He may, indeed, be in any or all of these places, but then again he may not. You may even find him and not know it. Smallmouths are just ornery enough to refuse today what they went for the day before, and you can drag yesterday's bass killer through a boodle of them and never suspect the truth.

Just such experiences caused me to observe that while I would have considerable confidence in live minnows as bait for largemouths, I would have much less confidence in any minnows I used as bait for smallmouths. This is because there is no such thing as constantly reliable smallmouth bait. Perhaps the minnow is the closest thing to it, but the smallmouth fisherman who fishes exclusively with minnows, or with any other single bait, is doomed to put in some long, dull days when his particular choice is in disfavor.

Partly because of its effectiveness, but perhaps more because of the difficulty with which it is obtained, the hellgrammite is thought of by many fishermen as the one bait which smallmouths cannot resist. But although smallmouths will snap up these big, ugly nymphs eagerly on certain days, they will have nothing to do with them on others. The same is true in the case of night crawlers, crayfish, frogs, crickets and grasshoppers. All are excellent baits at one time or another, but each can be quickly rendered ineffective by the smallmouth's ever-changing taste. Success in bait fishing for smallmouths depends to a great extent on the degree to which the fisherman honors this caprice. The fishermen who take smallmouths on bait with anything approaching regularity are invariably those who habitually carry with them the widest possible variety of bait.

As far as I'm concerned, bait fishing is by far the most effective way of taking bass when they are in deep water. I have read a great deal to the contrary — advice which virtually assured the reader that he could take bass from the deepest holes if only he would give his plug or other lure time to sink to the bottom and then retrieve it at a very slow crawl. The claim is made so compellingly that for a long time I believed it. That it never seemed to pan out for me I accepted as evidence that I was doing something wrong.

But what? The directions always contained stern warning against reeling too fast, and failure was declared to be evidence of this cardinal sin. I have reeled in sunken plugs so slowly that I have almost fallen asleep in the process — and might as well have done so for all the fish I caught. Maybe the technique works elsewhere than on paper; maybe there's a knack to it that I just can't get the hang of. Actually, I don't very much care. It's a mighty dull way to fish, and I have long since relinquished all rights of practice to those experts who so pedantically endorse it.

At any rate, and this applies to both largemouths and smallmouths, no known combination of lures, baits, techniques and human skills comes even close to threatening the extermination of bass in even the smallest and hardest-fished bodies of water. Heavy fishing can result in poor fishing, but not because it decimates the bass population. Bass are far too cagey to commit mass suicide, and they wise up to the fisherman long before he constitutes a serious threat to their existence. The draining and reclaiming of "fished-out" ponds seldom confirms the suspected absence of bass. Usually, to the embarrassment of all concerned, such measures usually reveal a substantial number of bass that no fisherman was smart enough to catch.

Unlike trout and salmon, bass are not driven into decline, and eventual extinction, by the mere circumstance of excessive human presence. They soon learn to cope with any amount of fishing pressure, and the swimming, boating, water skiing and general aquatic hubbub common to most lakes nowadays seems not to bother them at all. They calmly doze in the shade of rafts from which people dive, hide under docks and moored boats and, in general, tolerate the most massive human encroachment with enviable equanimity. This I can no more understand than I can understand other oddities of bass nature. Were I a fish, in a lake that was continually whipped to a froth by the frantic antics of human recreation, I'm sure I would go into a state of nervous prostration and quietly give up the ghost along with the salmon and trout.

Although bass are not seriously affected by the daily turmoil, they tend not to manifest their presence while it is in full sway. Consequently, the daytime fisherman who braves the risk of being run down by speedboats often comes off a lake with little to show for his courage. With what seems to be blameless logic he may conclude that bass cannot exist amid the turmoil to which he has been witness and that they have passed from the scene. This is seldom the case, and the fisherman can usually continue to take bass if he does as the bass do and becomes nocturnal.

An Apology to Bass

It is a curious fact, and one which perhaps holds implications of interest to students of human nature, that very few fishermen care to fish at night — in spite of the fact that it is rather common knowledge that the rewards of night fishing for both bass and trout tend to run high. It would be going too far to conclude that most fishermen are actually afraid of the dark, yet it is a fact that few care to take advantage of the opportunity it offers.

Those who can bring themselves to try it discover that night fishing has a unique quality. Not only is it likely to result in larger than usual fish, but one often encounters fish where they are least expected. Nighttime bass are quick to take advantage of the fact that their need for cover no longer exists. Consequently, nothing more is required of the night fisherman than that he cruise along slowly and cast toward shore methodically. Strikes are as likely to come in spots that are devoid of cover as in those that are more protected.

Years ago I did a good bit of night fishing in a lake which, at one end, consisted of an expansive shallows over a bottom of clean sand. During the daytime this natural beach was usually crowded with swimmers, and I'm sure no bass ventured within hundreds of yards of the place during daylight. In the course of much fishing, I finally discovered that they often moved into these shallows at night. Indeed, their numbers indicated that it was a favorite spot, possibly because bait fish made the mistake of trying to seek safety in the shallow water. After I finally learned the truth, I took many a hefty bass from water which no fisherman would have dreamed of fishing by daylight.

Writers often delight in advising the use of dark, even black, lures for night fishing, and I have probably done so myself. It is sound enough advice, as far as it goes, for bass will indeed strike a black plug, bug or streamer on the darkest night. But I know from experience that they will also hit counterparts of the same lures which may be white, yellow, red, green or any other color. The theory that one should use a jet-black lure for night fishing probably persists because it contains the element of surprise. It is surprising, indeed, that bass and other fish have no difficulty in distinguishing it in almost total darkness. But the belief that black lures are superior for night fishing is open to serious question, and it is entertained, I believe, largely because it has the characteristics of a fishing "secret."

A companion theory holds that the darkest nights are the best for fishing, and experience leads me to agree. The darker the night the greater the safety of the cruising fish, so it is not surprising that they move about more extensively, and observe less caution, on a pitch-black night than on one when moon and stars grant predators more visibility.

How well bass actually see at night would be difficult to determine, but like most wild creatures they probably see with what seems to us to be remarkable clarity. On the other hand, they are specially responsive at night to surface disturbance, and the night fisherman should keep this in mind. It is wise to fish with surface lures, and to give them more action than is needed during daylight.

Humans do not see well at night, of course, but most of us can see better than we think if we allow time for our eyes to adjust to the darkness. For this reason it is best to use a flash-light or lantern as little as possible. The shoreline will gradu-ally become discernible and the fisherman can keep his boat or canoe the proper distance from shore. All that remains is to cast into the grab bag of utter darkness which lies between the boat and the faintly visible shore.

There is little uniformity among individual tastes, but I al-ways get a special kick from night fishing. All that happens does so unexpectedly, for there can be no visible warning. Strikes come as sudden, electrifying jolts, and one is always tortured by suspense while playing a large fish that fights powerfully but remains invisible.

Most bass are caught by methods in which little delicacy of terminal tackle is required. In bug fishing, for example, it is more important to use a leader that is short and stiff enough to facilitate casting than to use long, fine leaders in the hope that they will help win more strikes. The long leader won't have the desired effect on the bass, but it is likely to foul up one's casting by falling in a heap short of the target. By the same token, nothing is gained by using light lines while either spin-ning or bait casting. Bass that are excited by a spoon or a plug are never critical of the line to which either is attached. Actu-ally, it is a mistake to use light lines in most bass waters, which usually abound in weeds and snags toward which hooked bass inevitably head. Landing them often depends on the ability to turn them before they can reach these retreats, and this requires a stout line that will stand up under hard snubbing.

In bait fishing, terminal tackle is of much greater importance. Bass, like trout, are very critical of any bait's behavior and appearance. Light leaders and small hooks are big helps in achieving a convincing presentation and should be employed to the greatest degree that is in keeping with the situation. Most bait fishing for bass is done in fairly deep water which is relatively free of weeds and snags. In most instances, therefore, the bait fisherman can safely take full advantage of the benefits which result from the use of light terminal tackle.

Judging from what I have read recently, plastic worms and other sinking lures of soft plastic are real bass killers. I must admit that I haven't experimented with them, for I can't whip up much interest in bass that lie in deep water. But even though I could put in my two cents' worth concerning lures of this type, it would hardly be needed. Lately, or so it seems, I never pick up an outdoor magazine which does not contain an article devoted to new lures and new tricks which are alleged to make bass fishing easy and almost foolproof.

Maybe so. But my experiences with bass cover more than forty years, and I'm betting on them to cope with whatever strategical innovations fishermen can contrive. Bass can be conned, up to a point. But when they are leaned on too hard they retire behind defenses that no fisherman can penetrate. Maybe that is why I can't seem to feel about bass as I do about trout.

12

Walleyes

A SIX-POUND WALLEYE is considered to be a big one in
Vermont, and I once made an observation to that effect in a
magazine article about walleye fishing. My statement drew a
letter from a fellow somewhere in the midwest who stated
that fifteen-pound walleyes were common where he lived, and
that out there saugers grew to be bigger than the puny walleyes of the east. He also went on to declare that if I couldn't
write about bigger walleyes than those mentioned in the article, I should refrain from writing about them at all.

I would be very happy, indeed, if the walleyes of my acquaintance regularly attained a weight of fifteen pounds. On
the other hand, I count myself lucky to live where there are
any walleyes at all. Lake Champlain, to which I have easy
access, provides a hundred-mile-long walleye fishery. It is one

of the very few walleye fisheries in New England, and is by far the largest.

I am doubly appreciative of my good fortune, for the walleye furnishes year-round sport wherever fishing regulations permit. Walleyes are willing biters under the ice, and they continue to provide sport from ice-out to freeze-up. They may be difficult to locate at times, but they will cooperate with fishermen who succeed in making contact with them during each of the twelve months of the year.

Although often referred to as the "walleyed pike," the walleye is not a pike at all and exhibits neither the appearance nor traits which so clearly mark all members of the pike tribe. Instead, the walleye is a member of the perch family, a relationship which makes the name "pike perch" somewhat more accurately descriptive, save for the unwarranted inclusion of the term "pike."

Although the walleye may have strong family ties with the perch, these result in little similarity of behavior save for the fact that walleyes and yellow perch tend to move about in schools. The walleye's only near counterpart is the sauger, another member of the perch clan which grows to be only a fraction of the walleye's size, but which resembles the walleye so closely in appearance that those unfamiliar with the two species seldom can tell them apart.

One of the outstanding traits peculiar to walleyes, at least among those with which I have had experience, is a slow mass movement which covers considerable distance and area and follows an established pattern. Lake Champlain seems to have several distinct populations of walleyes which do not intermingle. The lake is so large, however, that the respective clans have many square miles in which to roam.

Beginning in April, walleyes run up some of the lake's largest tributaries to spawn. The Missisquoi, the Lamoille and Otter Creek are the rivers in which the major spawning runs take place. It is my unsupported belief that the fish which ascend these streams exist as separate entities and occupy respective sections of the lake.

By the middle of May, after spawning, they are all back in the lake and hungry, and their predictable arrival is eagerly awaited at points many miles distant from the streams in which they spawn. Later, their movements to offshore reefs are taken into account by summertime fishermen. By freeze-up they are back where they were during the spring and furnish sport for hundreds of ice fishermen. Late in January they depart and move slowly toward the mouths of the rivers in which they will spawn.

A hooked walleye doesn't jump or take off on long runs, but he puts up a good strong battle and I have never heard complaints from any fisherman while in the act of bringing a good one toward the net. At one time or another they will take almost every kind of bait and artificial lure. Depending on time and conditions, they will hit in very deep water, in the middle depths and sometimes at the very surface. On the table they have few equals among freshwater fish; their flesh is white, flaky and very sweet in flavor.

Although I fish for walleyes in winter, spring and summer, I find them somewhat like bass in that I have never felt that I have them properly doped out. One of the mysteries which I am at a loss to understand is what appears to be the rigid necessity of changing baits and lures as the fish change locations. In other words, specific baits and lures which produce best year after year in a particular spot become ineffective when used on the same fish after they have moved on to another place.

Some of the most productive fishing of the year takes place during April and early May when the fish move into the rivers to spawn. The most popular spot is in the Missisquoi River, in the village of Swanton, downstream from a dam which blocks further upstream progress and results in a high concentration of fish. When the run is on, the river is crowded with anchored boats and the shore tightly packed with parked cars from many different states.

In spite of the heavy competition, most boats trail heavily laden stringers whenever conditions are right to bring fish up from the lake. The last week in April is the time most highly favored, but the peak of the run cannot be predicted with absolute certainty. If the water level is lower than usual, the fish will await a rise of water; if the river is too high to suit them, they will lie off the mouth until it drops.

Heavy catches are the rule, once the run is on in earnest, and it is interesting to note that practically all the fish are caught by a single method. This consists of hooking a live minnow through both lips and fishing it only a few inches above the bottom. Since the water directly downstream from the dam is only a few feet deep, and the current only moderate, the proper depth can be maintained easily. A couple of buckshot pinched on a monofilament line will take the minnow down where it belongs, a requirement that is easily checked by dropping the rod tip and noting if the shot promptly strike bottom.

Once the fish move back into the lake they will be taken in large numbers by fishermen who troll night crawlers, spoons, spinners and plugs — almost everything other than minnows. It would be logical to conclude that these assorted offerings would also take fish in the river, but this isn't the case. I have tried them all, only to have them ignored while minnows were accounting for fish all around me. To make the puzzle more baffling, minnows become so ineffective when the time for trolling in the lake arrives that few, if any, fishermen use them.

The mystery deepens when one encounters the walleyes which dwell in Lake Memphremagog. Their annual spawning run takes place in the Clyde River, which enters the lake at Newport, Vermont, and although fishing for them during the run is now prohibited by law, it was allowed until recently. And here, when fishing during the run was permitted, night crawlers were the most effective bait and minnows went begging.

More cause for wonder arises when the fish move back into the lake, for then they disappear as completely as though removed from the face of the earth. While gathering data for an article about these particular fish, I sought out wardens, both active and retired, whose combined service covered the past half century. They told me that to the best of their knowledge not as much as a single walleye had been caught in the lake itself during all that time, this in spite of the fact that the lake is fished hard for other species, both winter and summer. Many walleyes show up in the Clyde River each spring, but incredible as it may seem, I have it on excellent authority that nobody has ever discovered where they spend the time between spawning runs.

The lower half of that section of the Connecticut River which separates Vermont and New Hampshire also holds walleyes, but I have had but little experience with Connecticut River walleyes since the days of my youth. I feel sure, however, that renewed intimacy would bring to light more enigmas which seem to be a characteristic of the species.

As I have already indicated, one of their oddities seems to be a wide range of preference which shifts with the season and their location, and which the fisherman is forced to indulge. Aware of their strong liking for night crawlers when they have returned to the lake after spawning, I was once inspired to believe that I could do a rushing business by baiting my ice fishing lines with the big earthworms. Acting on this hunch, I went to the trouble of laying in a supply of 'crawlers one fall, and tended them carefully until the lake froze. It was with smug expectation that I draped them on my hooks and lowered them to within inches of the bottom; surely they would stand out as an unexpected and welcome treat among the minnow-baited lines of my many competitors, and I would be richly rewarded for my shrewdness.

Unfortunately, the walleyes and I were miles apart in our ideas of what constituted a special treat. My tenderly nurtured night crawlers accounted for a couple of runty perch and were scorned completely by the walleyes.

This incident happened back in the days when I persisted in conducting a one-man campaign designed to make walleyes relinquish their idiosyncrasies and behave more as they should. But I finally gave it up, in the wake of a long string of defeats, and accepted the fact that walleyes can best be caught by catering to their seemingly illogical whims.

Each year I trailer my boat to Swanton during the spring run. I dangle minnows, as does everybody else, and if I hit the river at the right time I have no trouble filling my stringer. I still have the instinctive conviction that a slowly retrieved spoon or plug would work as well, but I know better. I have learned the futility of trying to catch walleyes by acting on my ostensibly logical, but misplaced, convictions.

A few weeks later, walleyes make their appearance in the southern end of Lake Champlain, an area from which they have been absent since the previous January. Here they are fished for by fishermen who troll the bays and shorelines, and who number into the hundreds when the fishing is in full swing.

The favorite trolling rig consists of a spinner-sinker-worm combination attached to a three-way swivel. A dipsey sinker bounces along the bottom, while the spinner and worm trails after and barely clears. To achieve this arrangement, the rigs are made up according to a specific formula: "an eight-inch drop and a thirty-inch lead." The "drop" refers to the short length of monofilament on which the sinker is suspended and the "lead" to the strand to which the spinner and hooks are tied.

Almost any small spinner will suffice, but the hook, or

gang of hooks, should follow close behind the spinner blade. The most popular combination is one which is made up and sold locally and which is named, with a bold flourish, the "Green Mountain Grabber." Rather disappointingly, in view of the aggressive qualities suggested by its name, the Grabber is nothing more than a small brass spinner with a trailing gang of three hooks. A night crawler strung on the gang shows off to somewhat better advantage than one hung from a single hook, and the triple hooks enhance the chances of hooking fish that strike.

It is virtually impossible to troll a worm-and-spinner combination too slowly, but very easy to troll it too fast. As one learns in ice fishing, walleyes tend to be very bottom conscious, and when their attention is focused on the bottom they seem to have eyes for no other levels. The trolled worm must, therefore, barely skim the bottom, and it is possible to keep it at this level only if the boat moves very slowly. Also, this very slow pace is in keeping with walleye temperament; walleyes are attracted by movement, but only if it is slight to moderate.

Strikes tend to be gentle and deliberate, and they often follow a pattern which enables the fisherman to employ a trick which results in surer hooking. Quite frequently the real strike is preceded by one or two tentative nips, and when these are felt the rod tip is lowered, and the rod thrust backward, to create momentary slack in the line. This action halts the forward movement of the bait for an instant and is a development in which walleyes seem to see reason for assurance. Almost always, if the pause follows a cautious nip, they will scoop up the night crawler during its brief halt. They are almost as inevitably hooked if the rod is given a jerk the instant the line draws tight again.

While the majority of fishermen troll spinners and worms, others depend on artificial lures. Their success tends to equal that of the worm trollers, for it is during this particular period that the walleyes come closest to exhibiting democratic tastes. A spinner and bucktail combination is used with good results. Nearly all who use this combination insist on a yellow bucktail, but whether with good reason I cannot say. Reason tells me that one of any other color should do as well, but I have already confessed that walleyes have a habit of refuting my logic.

I do know from experience that virtually all spinning lures will draw strikes if they can be held close to the bottom. One of the best is an F6 "Flatfish." One or two buckshot will take it down sufficiently (the depth is usually less than eight feet), for this lure dives of its own accord when drawn through the water. It has the added virtue of throbbing vigorously, even when trolled very slowly, and the two characteristics combine to make it an ideal lure for this particular purpose.

Small plugs are effective, but only if they are held close to the bottom. I have caught many walleyes on the sinking River Runt, and in recent years on the slender Rebel. To hold these lures down I troll them on the weighted rig used with the spinner-and-worm combination.

The late May and June migrations follow the shorelines, so trolling is done quite close to shore. It is a good policy to begin only a short distance from shore and then gradually work outward until fish are encountered. When a fish is landed, it is wise to rework the location immediately. Quite often another strike will result, and it is not unusual to pinpoint a spot which will continue to produce one or more fish with almost every pass for a considerable period of time.

When I find what appears to be a hotspot, I usually drop anchor and comb the surrounding water by casting. If there proves to be a concentration of fish present, I can cash in on it more effectively by casting among them than by trying to drag through them repeatedly.

Pete, Mike and I once drew up alongside two fishermen who were casting from an anchored boat, and who had a heavily laden stringer of walleyes which they raised for our envious inspection. They always anchored and cast, they told us, on the theory that walleyes would come their way eventually. Also, considerably to my surprise, they said they used nothing but Dardevle "Spinnies." Although I have caught walleyes on Dardevles from time to time, and in spite of my great respect for the Dardevle's general effectiveness, I had never thought of the Dardevle as a particularly good walleye lure. The obvious success of those two fishermen showed clearly that my feelings were not based on fact. It also pointed up the truism that the confidence with which a lure is fished has a great deal to do with how well it produces.

Walleyes remain in the southern end of Lake Champlain until about the middle of June and are fished for heavily throughout that period. As July approaches they migrate northward and disperse in what is known as the "broad lake." The southern end of the lake is relatively shallow, and the northward movement quite probably is in search of deeper and cooler water.

Once the fish scatter in the broader and deeper section, the problem of locating them becomes much more difficult. During the day they may be as much as fifty feet beneath the surface, but this doesn't mean that there will be walleyes wherever the water is fifty feet deep. Instead, they tend to gather along the edges of dropoffs which plunge sharply from moderate levels to much greater depths, and over sunken reefs which rise up from areas of deep water.

Serious midsummer fishermen come to know some of these locations and are very closemouthed when it comes to guarding their secrets. Unfortunately, from their standpoint, they cannot take advantage of these secrets without giving them away. It's a simple matter to keep an eye out for boats that hang to particular offshore spots and equally simple to deduce that the only reason they could have for remaining there is that they are over a walleye reef.

I feel certain that the known walleye hangouts are only a part of all that exist. I have had no experience with electronic sounding devices, but it seems to me that they would be of great value in prospecting for walleyes after they have gone into deep water. I have explored by using a sounding weight, but it is a process so slow and tedious that I lack the patience to stick at it for any appreciable length of time. But when I have been lucky enough to find a sharp dropoff, sometimes a matter of miles from shore, walleyes have been waiting in the depths to grab the minnows and night crawlers I have lowered to within their reach. From what I have heard and read, these spots are easily located with the electronic devices, and each new discovery should result in some good fishing.

When a concentration of walleyes is found in deep water, the discovery can hold a surprise for the fisherman who stays on into the evening. During the daytime he may have to fish from forty to sixty feet below the surface for a catch, but at dusk he is likely to find himself in the midst of surfacing fish. Until one learns better, he is likely to conclude that the breaking fish must be bass, that the walleyes are most certainly down near bottom where they have been right along. But if he hooks one of the rising fish, he discovers to his amazement that it is indeed a walleye. This tendency to come up from deep water and feed on the surface during the evening, and on into the night, is a common walleye characteristic.

Needless to say, fishing for surfacing walleyes is walleye fishing at its best. While they are at the top they not only give the spin fisherman and bait caster the chance to take them with surface lures, but they are then fair game for the fly fisherman who uses sizable streamers and bucktails.

I have seen large areas suddenly break out in a rash of surfacing walleyes and the first few times this happened I jumped to the conclusion that I could soon fill my limit by trolling a surface lure among all the rising fish. Unfortunately, as so often happens, results failed to live up to these optimistic expectations. Judging from my experience, surfacing walleyes are very sensitive to the disturbance made by a boat's passage, and once the boat puts them down they are in no mood to strike a lure which comes over them only seconds later.

After much fruitless trolling among breaking fish, I finally wised up enough to kill the motor and content myself with casting to fish which showed within range. This panned out much better. The temptation to chase after the fish persisted, even though all attempts to do so had proven abortive. But by resisting the impulse, and patiently waiting for fish to show within reach, I enjoyed some very interesting fishing. Actually, in this situation, remaining in one position is not the compromise it seems to be. The surfacing walleyes cruise about constantly, seldom rise twice in the same place and approach close to the waiting fisherman more frequently than if he unwisely elected to pursue them.

The bulk of my experience with walleyes has been gained while ice fishing (about which more later), fishing for them during their spawning runs and trolling for them during May and June. I have fished and explored for them late in the summer, but never with serious dedication.

My knowledge of walleyes and their ways is limited further because my experience with them has been confined to a narrow front. But although I neither know them as well as I would like, nor as well as I should, I know them well enough to appreciate them as fish surrounded by many mysteries, and as a rich source of fascination for all who devote themselves seriously to their pursuit throughout the year.

I am sure that this respect would deepen with experience of greater geographical scope. My limited observations have led me to conclude that walleyes are strangely inclined to develop and adopt quite different habits in different locations, and I suspect that the sum total of these regional differences would cover a surprisingly wide range of behavior.

Many books, and countless magazine articles, have been devoted to trout, salmon, bass, pike, muskies and even panfish, but comparatively little has been written about walleyes. Perhaps this is because their variability discourages generalization and is lacking in the common denominators by which other game fish are to be identified. This comparative lack of information bears testimony to the strange and subtle ways of walleyes, and to their deserved recognition as a unique and challenging game fish.

13

Northern Pike

TO THE BEST of my knowledge, the only northern pike fishing of any consequence in New England is confined to western Vermont, which is to say to Lake Champlain and to waters in and adjacent to the Champlain valley. Throughout this section, in virtually all waters suitable for warm water species, northern pike are common while chain pickerel are rare. Elsewhere in New England, the reverse holds true. Pickerel are usually plentiful, while pike are not present. Because I'm fortunate enough to have good northern pike fishing within a mile or two of my home, I have played host to a number of fishermen who have had no previous experience with northerns. In spite of the scorn which some trout and salmon fishermen profess to feel toward the ugly critters, I have yet to meet the fisherman who failed to get a kick from his first encounter with the species.

Quite a few years ago, my wife and I had the pleasure of entertaining Ed Zern for the better part of a week, and I had the added pleasure of fishing with him each day. Ed's company is as delightful as the piquantly humorous prose which he writes, and I still relish the memory of the few days we spent together.

Ed is a dedicated trout fisherman, so I took him to a stretch of Otter Creek which, at that time, was well populated with sizable rainbows. No fish were showing when we arrived, and I knew from experience that we were not likely to get any action until sundown. Since this was several hours away, I suggested that we move upstream to a large pool where northerns hung out in a slowly circling backwater.

We had brought along spinning gear with this possibility in mind, and a pike very obligingly grabbed Ed's lure on the very first cast. As I recall, each of his next four casts brought a strike, resulting in an introduction to pike fishing somewhat in excess of the norm. Other northerns took whacks at my spoon in the meantime, and there were few moments when one or the other of us wasn't busy with a pike.

We fished for a spell, and while I was thankful for the pikes' lavish cooperation, I was keenly conscious of the fact that they weren't the trout we had come for. Fearing that Ed would look on pike as a poor substitute for trout, I finally suggested that we move downstream to see if the rainbows had started to move.

They hadn't, and it wasn't until dusk that they began showing. But then they came on with a rush which I hoped Ed would regard as adequate compensation for the prolonged wait.

It was late when we arrived home, but before we retired I asked Ed if he had any preference as to where we should fish the next day.

"As far as I'm concerned," he said, "I'd like to go back to where we fished today." Then he added quizzically, "You know, I was having a good time with those pike until you dragged me away."

Ed Zern's reaction to pike fishing was typical, and I have learned since that I can usually offer the prospect of fishing for northerns without apology. In theory they do not enjoy a very favorable reputation. But when a pike that either appears to be, or actually is, a yard long hits a fisherman's lure, his response tends to be anything but one of contempt.

To evaluate the northern as a game fish one must weigh virtues against shortcomings, for the pike is an odd mixture of both. Sometimes, but by no means always, the northern puts up a very disappointing fight. Yet he makes up for this by dishing out a variety of surprises. One way is by suddenly exploding from nowhere with such speed and violence that the fisherman is nearly startled out of his wits.

I remember one such incident on an afternoon when Pete and I were fishing Otter Creek by canoe. I was casting to shoreline pockets while Pete paddled. Since it is rather rare to get strikes elsewhere than close to shore, I was fishing out only the first part of each cast and then reeling in as rapidly as possible.

I have the habit of keeping the tip of the rod low when retrieving a spoon, and it was either in the water or just above it when I zipped a Dardevle through the last few yards of a retrieve. The water was clear, the bottom plainly visible and I would have been willing to bet that there wasn't a pike within many yards of my lure. But as the spoon came to within inches of the tip of the rod a big pike made his charge, engulfing not only the lure but the extremity of the rod itself. The big fish came at me straight on, and my midsection took the full force of his attack as the rod butt jabbed me just above my belt buckle. Needless to say, I was too shaken to make any response until after the pike was gone. But I submit that a fish that swallows lure and rod while in the act of striking is a fish that cannot be taken lightly.

I remember another eyeball-to-eyeball encounter which almost capsized us. Pete was doing the fishing at the time, and he was letting his spoon dap along the surface, close to the canoe, as I cut across what seemed to be a barren section of water and headed for a more likely looking spot. An exploding stick of dynamite would have caused hardly more commotion than did the monster pike who chose that unlikely time to go for the dangling spoon. Pete took a bucket of water squarely in the face and promptly tumbled backward off the bow seat. No more prepared than he, I did less than nothing to trim the unbalanced canoe, and it was only by good fortune that we remained afloat. The pike, of course, got off free after all but sinking us.

In addition to being a master of the surprise attack, the northern is capable of unleashing tremendous power whenever it suits his fancy. Unless the fisherman has had experience with pike, these bust-all surges are likely to come just when they are least expected. It is typical of pike to allow themselves to be reeled in without any determined show of resistance, and then, when the fisherman is net-minded and confident, streak away with such speed and power that they break any ordinary tackle that is held firmly against them.

I introduced my friend Tap to pike fishing, and the first pike that nailed his spinning lure was a real buster. The fish hit with a mighty swirl, but then permitted Tap to lead him close to the canoe like a tired old hound on a leash. With all but a few feet of the monofilament on the reel, Tap stopped reeling. The big pike lay motionless, just under the surface and almost within sight of the net.

"Look at the size of him!" Tap exclaimed, and with good reason. At that close range the brute seemed too big to fit in the net.

We studied the pike, and in the meantime he apparently studied us and disliked what he saw. One second he was lying there like a log; the next he was a living torpedo going away. Unfortunately, line refused to pay off the reel; Tap had set the drag a few notches too tight. The tip of his rod plunged into the water, the line became as taut as a banjo string and then snapped with that dull plunk which is the most sickening sound a fisherman can hear.

Tap and I have done quite a bit of pike fishing together since that ill-fated beginning, and although I introduced Tap to the sport, he showed me the way to make the most of it. Tap is an inveterate bug flinger, and after a few trips he voiced the opinion that the use of fly rod popping bugs would almost double the excitement of pike fishing — if the northerns could be persuaded to come to the bugs.

I agreed, but never got around to doing anything about it. But Tap, on his next visit, came prepared to experiment with some big hair bugs he had tied especially for the purpose. On our first trip down the creek he shunned all hardware and went to work with the big bugs immediately. And the pike fairly murdered them!

It isn't stretching things greatly to use the word "murder" in this case, for this is exactly what pike seem to have in mind when they attack a surface bug. They come on with a rush that carries them partway, or completely, out of the water, then turn with a lightning-fast swirl that has the effect of a detonation. If the strike is from a ten-pounder or better, the result is one of the top thrills to be experienced in freshwater angling.

Thanks to Tap's pioneering, I have since taken a good many pike on hair bugs, and in so doing have learned several interesting facts about northerns. One is that while skinny little pike, sometimes no more than a foot long, will not hesitate to tackle a big Dardevle, very few small pike come to the big popping bugs, perhaps because the risk of exposure is pronounced and only the larger pike have the devil-may-care courage to ignore it. The larger fish's tendency may also account for the spectacular strikes; they may be conscious of their imprudence and strike with lightning speed to compress the risk to as little time as possible.

Pete and I have also found that it is not always easy, or even possible, to set the bug's hook in the jaw of a big pike. I remember one afternoon when we raised five lunkers, almost without moving the canoe, and failed to get a hook into a single one of the five. The rod would come against solid resistance, giving the impression that the striking fish had been hooked, but in a moment or two the line would go slack and the bug would rise to the surface.

I am certain that this was because each pike seized the bug with such crushing power that it was virtually immovable, making it impossible to set the hook. Northerns have a strength of jaw that is unappreciated until, as has happened to me, one deliberately bites down on a thumb or finger. It is fortunate for fishermen that pike seldom do this, for when they do the pressure is incredible and the effect much like that of having one's finger caught in a steel trap.

Because of this, bug fishermen should expect pike to grab a bug in a viselike grip and should whack back with the rod accordingly. Unfortunately, it is possible to haul back only so hard with a fly rod, and more than a few striking pike will go free simply because it is impossible to move the bug with the rod when they have the bug tightly clamped between their jaws.

Handling a big pike on a fly rod is not difficult — if the fisherman stands ready to give line any time the pike demands it. The time for the greatest caution arrives when the pike seems to be played out. Usually this first show of exhaustion is misleading, the pike retaining sufficient energy for a dash that can splinter a fly rod if the fisherman freezes instead of instantly providing free line.

Although it would be naive to conclude that pike deliberately scheme to catch fishermen off balance, their actions often seem to the fisherman to be inspired by this intent. The fisherman reasons that if a big hook was suddenly yanked into *his* jaw, he would fight to escape until every last bit of strength had been used up. Other game fish do exactly that, and when they finally cease to struggle it is a sure sign that they are exhausted and the battle is all but over.

The sting of the hook, which triggers other fish into a frenzy, does not tend to have this violent effect on northern pike. Neither do they seem to be greatly alarmed when they are reeled in. Quite often they come in so easily that they seem to take no serious objection to the process. If they do make a serious effort to escape during the initial part of the fray, their actions seldom reflect the great power and speed of which they are capable. If the fisherman makes the mistake of attributing this sluggish behavior to a lack of energy, he is in for a surprise, if not disaster, when he reaches for the net, or makes some other move, when the pike is lying close alongside. Due to the pike's peculiar temperament, he is likely to interpret this sudden movement as his first real cause for alarm. Then, for the first time, he takes off under full steam — and there isn't any stopping him.

The northern is so little affected by a lure's hooks that he appears to forget about them completely when all pressure from the rod is relinquished. Since fishermen are seldom so disposed, this incredible indifference is rarely observed.

I first witnessed it when the level wind mechanism of my reel jammed just after I had hooked a large northern. The fish had made a short, halfhearted run and then had stopped; when I tried to gain back line I found that my reel was locked up tight. I took the reel apart, corrected the difficulty and put the parts back together — and all the time the line hung limply from the tip of my propped-up rod. I supposed, of course, that the fish had come off, but when I went to retrieve my lure I discovered to my amazement that it was still firmly attached to the pike. Apparently the northern had regarded the dangling spoon as an inconvenience too slight to get worked up about and promptly forgot about it as soon as it ceased to exert pressure on his jaw.

Variations of the same theme have been enacted since. Many pike have obligingly remained motionless and unruffled while Pete and I worked to free our snagged lines. The most bizarre incident took place one day while we were bug fishing.

A thick tangle of driftwood and general debris had collected in the branches of a tree which had fallen into the creek, and the mass provided the sort of cover northerns like. A small patch of open water lay in the center of the tangle, and I couldn't resist the temptation to spat down a bug on this target. A ten-pound pike promptly assailed the lure and dove back under the tangle. I couldn't bring him out, and my efforts only inspired the pike to bull his way through the sunken branches of the fallen tree and on into the open water which lay upstream.

"Now what are you going to do?" Pete asked.

It was a good question, for any attempt to bring the pike back through the tangled branches would have been both futile and ridiculous. We were free to study the problem at our leisure, however, for the pike had apparently lapsed into a coma from which I had no intention of arousing him until a course of action had been devised.

"He won't go anywhere until I prod him," I told Pete. "Paddle out around the tree and I'll strip line as we go."

Thanks to plenty of backing, I was able to pay out the necessary slack while Pete circled the fallen trees and its catch of driftwood. Once we got upstream from the tree, we began searching for the forward section of the line and Pete finally located it. It led straight upstream, and, we hoped, to a pike that still was securely hooked. Pete reached down with the gaff and gently raised the line until he could grasp it.

This accomplished, I stripped the rest of the backing from the reel, cut it free and then hauled the loose line and backing through the tangle. Then I threaded the backing down through the guides, retied it to the reel and wound up the many yards of slack. It seemed too much to hope that the pike would still be on after all that rigmarole, but this was indeed the case. Some five or ten minutes later Pete scooped him up in the net and boosted his threshing bulk into the canoe.

Some angling authorities declare that the fly rod is a poor tool for pike fishing because it is so limber that the fisherman cannot put enough pressure on big pike to spur them to their best efforts. This may be true to a certain extent, but it has been my experience that pike do most of their serious fighting close to the boat or canoe, regardless of what sort of tackle is used against them. Whether I use a fly rod or a stiff casting rod doesn't seem to make any difference in this respect, for any extra pressure only gets them close alongside that much quicker.

Pete, Mike and I make the most of big pike in a different and rather unorthodox way. The man in the stern of the canoe jabs the pike with the paddle whenever the fish comes within range. This results in some incredibly fast and powerful runs, but the practice is not to be recommended for those who are seriously concerned with landing all the fish they hook.

With respect to landing and dispatching pike, I might add that the fisherman who deposits a freshly caught pike in a canoe or boat without first conking the fish over the head with a substantial "priest" seldom repeats the mistake. A big pike can make a shambles of the craft's contents in a matter of seconds, and if the lure on which he was hooked is still in his snout, he is quite capable of returning the compliment with vengeance.

The dubious prospect of sharing one or more hooks with ten or more pounds of wildly flopping pike has always made me chary of hand-landing northerns. They can be landed by grasping their eye sockets between thumb and finger, and with little danger if the lure is rigged with but a single hook. But whenever treble hooks are involved, an attempt to land a pike by hand can lead to some very nasty complications.

Returning to the case for the fly rod in pike fishing, the spectacular strikes at surface bugs, which can only be cast with a fly rod, more than make up for any deficiences it may have as a tool for playing hooked pike. Once hooked, the pike distinguishes himself more by perversity and eccentricity than by conforming to the standards by which the fighting qualities of game fish are usually judged. But when he rockets up for a big hair bug he is in a class by himself, and I know of no other freshwater fish that can so nearly create the effect of a bursting bombshell.

One of the secrets of interesting pike in surface bugs is to use jumbo-size lures — as big as can be cast with a fly rod. Sufficiently large ones are not generally available, and the fisherman must either tie them himself or have them tied to his specifications. I tie mine on the biggest long-shanked hooks I can find and jam all the deer hair on the body I can manage. I tie in a half-dozen long saddle hackles for a tail, then clip the body to shape: rounded on top, flat on the bottom and tapered toward the bend of the hook.

Casting the big bugs would be extremely difficult if a long or fine leader was necessary, but this isn't the case. I use a five-foot strand of thirty-pound test monofilament, and this short, stiff leader makes the big bugs much easier to cast than would be true otherwise. As for the lack of delicacy, this is of no apparent concern to the pike. They are fish which sometimes rise up to gobble ducklings and young muskrats and are not to be put off by a mere strand of nylon.

In any event, lures must be joined to leader or line by either a wire trace or one of heavy nylon out of respect for sharp teeth which shear off lines and leaders of ordinary weights. I use a short wire cable when bait casting or spinning for pike, but the thirty-pound test nylon doesn't seem to require one. At least, I have never had a bug chopped off when tied directly to nylon of this weight.

Float fishing a winding creek is one of the most interesting ways of fishing for northerns, but success depends a great deal on the ability to recognize the spots which pike favor. Most of the fish tend to lie very close to shore and almost always behind some obstruction which breaks the current and provides a pocket of quiet water.

Trout depend to a large extent upon insects for food, and it is probably for this reason that they are so often found in and around strong currents which bring nymphs and surface insects to within reach. Pike have almost no interest in insects, so for them these currents hold no appeal. Since they feed almost exclusively on vertebrates, their favorite spots are those which allow them to lie in wait for minnows and frogs, and which spare them the effort of resisting the current while they hold their positions.

I suspect that it is because of this difference that trout and pike can share the same stream with less disastrous effect upon the trout than one would be inclined to expect. This doesn't hold true in small streams, but in larger streams, which offer a choice of both fast and sluggish water, the trout and the pike will keep pretty much to themselves. The pike show little inclination to seek out trout in the stretches of fast water, and the trout avoid the backwaters where the pike lie in wait. I have caught many pike in trout streams and have always killed them with the self-righteous feeling that I was befriending the trout. Yet I must confess that I have caught very, very few pike that have had trout in their stomachs.

In spite of the fact that northerns can be taken with a fly rod, most fishermen associate pike fishing only with the use of plugs and hardware. The vast majority of pike that are caught are taken by bait casting, spinning and trolling.

There is good reason for this circumstance, for while pike sometimes provide spectacular fly rod fishing, they do so only when they happen to be in the mood for it. My experience has been that they can be counted on to respond to spoons and plugs with more regularity than to popping bugs. There are days, of course, when they won't hit hardware, but generally they tend to react to a flashing lure with even more excitement than that manifested by other game fish.

Because of the peculiar fascination which the Eppinger Dardevle holds for northerns, many fishermen come to think of pike fishing in terms of the exclusive use of this proven lure. To be honest, I tend to think along just such narrow lines myself. I have caught so many pike on the Dardevle, and have come to have such faith in it, that I usually snap on one of these lures as a matter of course and make no change thereafter.

I'm convinced that the Dardevle has no equal as a pike lure over the long haul, but I suspect that I sometimes cheat myself by stubbornly refusing to change lures when prolonged use of the red-and-white spoon results in no strikes. No lure is an absolute specific. The Dardevle is undoubtedly the closest thing to it with respect to pike, but concluding that nothing else will turn the trick when this old reliable fails is a mistake of which I am often guilty, and for which I'm sure I pay a penalty.

All fish are temperamental creatures, pike in particular. Generalization concerning their likes and dislikes is valid only up to a point. They display preferences which predominate most of the time, but they have the fickle habit of temporarily showing disinterest in the very lures which normally attract their sharpest attention. During these departures from the norm there is no telling what may strike their fancy. Even if the fisherman is lucky enough to hit upon it, there is no assurance that it will ever again be the answer.

Several years ago I received some samples of a lure called the "Vivif." For those not familiar with it, the Vivif is a rubber imitation of a bait fish, with a flexible tail designed to wag rapidly throughout the retrieve. The smaller models were displayed in tackle shops, where they were drawn around circular tanks by a motor-driven device to demonstrate their unique action.

Among those I received was a huge, two-ounce model designed for saltwater fishing. I put it in my box of pike tackle and forgot about it.

Then came an afternoon when, as we were setting out to fish Otter Creek, Pete discovered that he had forgotten some vital item of equipment. To kill time while Pete drove back for the missing article, I began casting from shore. I had no hope of hooking a pike, for our launching spot furnished nothing by way of cover. Consequently, when I happened to notice the big Vivif, curiosity prompted me to snap it on. Finding out what its action was like would supply at least some purpose for my casting.

My casting rod felt as though it had a brick suspended from its tip, and when I heaved out the big lure it landed with almost as big a splash as a falling brick would have made. I had retrieved it nearly to shore, its tail wagging vigorously as advertised, when a big pike came streaking after it and smashed it savagely, almost at my feet. Unfortunately, the lure was rigged with massive double hooks, and although I tried to yank them home my rod lacked the necessary stiffness.

Pete came back at that time, and I continued to experiment with the offbeat lure as we made our way down the creek. And so help me, the pike couldn't seem to leave it alone. It was too ponderous to cast with accuracy on a bait casting rod, and each time it landed it made a horrible commotion. But in spite of all this, pike after pike hit it viciously, and others with less courage trailed it all the way to the canoe. I saw more pike that afternoon than I had ever seen before in any comparable period of time.

To my disappointment, I was able to hook only a small fraction of the many that struck, and most of these were fish that took the lure so deeply that the big double hooks snagged in their gill rakers. This did not disturb me greatly, however. I had apparently, and at long last, discovered the one lure that northerns couldn't resist; I could alter the hooks easily enough.

After returning home I did so by cutting off one of the hooks and filing down the other until easy penetration was implicit. When the job was finished to my satisfaction, I smugly concluded that I was then in a position to catch every pike in Otter Creek if I felt so inclined.

Unfortunately, I made the common mistake of counting chickens in embryo. The lure which had stirred up unprecedented action only a few days before was almost totally ignored when I next tried it. Although I persist in trying it from time to time, it has never aroused more than casual interest since that single afternoon when it seemed to be virtually irresistible.

The experience increased my respect for lures such as the Dardevle which will take pike almost day in and day out and are only seldom in disfavor. On the other hand, it opened my eyes to the fact that lures of little general reliability may enjoy fleeting moments of superiority, and that stubborn faith in a single lure can be carried too far for one's own good. Unfortunately, I lack the willpower to break myself of most bad habits, so I usually go right on fishing a Dardevle when I know that just the right experimental change might break the bank.

The Dardevle certainly deserves recommendation as the pike lure most likely to succeed. Yet, at any given time, virtually no lure can be ruled out without a test. The least trusted one in the tackle box can suddenly rise to distinction and outfish all others over the space of a day.

Although hardware and plugs seem to hold special appeal for northerns, it is my belief that pike usually attack only those lures which come very close to their hiding places. This conviction may seem to be refuted by those pike which trail lures to within sight of the boat, but I choose to believe that the lure first had to come close to the fish in order to arouse the urge to trail after it.

It is often recommended that when a pike trails the lure right up to the boat the fisherman draw his reeled-up lure through a figure "8" with the submerged tip of his rod. A smashing strike is predicted, but this trick has never worked well for me. The pike usually lies close to the surface, only a few feet away, and almost invariably spooks at my first motion. Better, in my opinion, is simply to release the line and let the lure flutter toward bottom. If the pike hasn't become alarmed he usually will follow after the sinking lure, and he may take a belt at it before it reaches bottom. If not, a few jigs with the rod may bring a strike.

Returning to the matter of casting close to lurking fish, the importance of so doing cannot be overemphasized. Wherever pike tend to lie close to shore, lures should plunk down within inches of the shoreline for best results. It might seem that to splash down a big spoon in the immediate vicinity of a pike would be likely to startle the fish out of its wits, but the commotion seems to have exactly the opposite effect. Pike often react with such speed that that they give the impression of having caught the lure on the fly.

The same need applies where pike lie hidden in weeds. The lure should skim the tops of the weeds as closely as possible in order to satisfy the pikes' disposition to attack only those objects which come within easy reach. Where weeds provide the cover, one of the best places to fish for pike is along the edges of the weed beds, but here again proximity is of great importance. Lurking pike may very well *see* lures which pass no closer than several yards from their cover, but they are likely to remain indifferent to all but those which come within only a few feet of the edge.

Both the bait caster and the trolling fisherman should be very depth-conscious when fishing over sunken weeds for pike. The caster should give his lure time to sink to just above the tops of the weeds, then retrieve at a speed which will keep the lure at that depth as it comes in. Doing this is not too difficult, and when the hooks pick up tendrils of weeds, as they are bound to do, the damage extends only to that particular cast. The pike fisherman who trolls doesn't have it that easy. It is always very difficult to maintain the lure at the proper level, and almost impossible to troll at that exact depth for any appreciable length of time without picking up an accumulation of weeds. Trolled lures require constant checking, a nuisance which detracts from the pleasure of fishing, and there is always the strong possibility that a cleaned lure will pick up more weeds shortly after it is returned to the water.

I suppose there are waters where pike can be taken over a clean bottom, and in such places trolling is undoubtedly very effective. My lake fishing for northern pike has always been accompanied by the weed problem, and for that reason I take a rather dim view of trolling for northerns. I like to cast while the boat drifts over the weeds, or alternate with my fishing partner in rowing and casting along the edges of the beds.

Although I prefer to take pike on popping bugs whenever possible and lean toward either bait casting or spinning as a second choice, there are certain unique thrills which derive from fishing for northerns with live bait. For one thing, the bait can be as big, or even bigger, than the trout which fishermen often bring home in their creels, and the use of huge bait tends to generate keen anticipation of tangling with monster fish. The fact that pike weighing no more than two or three pounds will gobble a ten-inch chub or sucker does not stand in the way of an instinctive feeling that any pike which grabs a king-size bait fish is bound to be a lunker.

Otter Creek has a large population of fallfish, and Mike and I sometimes use them for bait. It seldom takes us more than a few minutes to catch a half dozen between six and eight inches long, and then we pull into the nearest eddy and drop anchor. We tie on big hooks, pinch a couple of buckshot to our spinning lines and then attach bobbers three or four feet above the hooks. We secure our bait by running the point of the hook under the skin, just ahead of the dorsal fin. Then we turn the lively fallfish loose and let them carry our lines where they will.

They are strong enough to tow the bobbers around easily, and we pay out line, and watch expectantly, as the bobbers are drawn here and there. The plastic balls dance constantly, and sudden spurts by the fallfish result in movements of our bobbers which are normally associated with bites. But we know that this is not the real thing; when a pike finally grabs one of the roving fallfish, the bobber is jerked under with an audible *plop* and begins to move off steadily. Now there is no more dipping and bobbing — just a steady and inexorable march which continues until the bobber finally disappears from view. From here on it is a matter of feel. We wait for the fish to stop, then wait some more while he swallows the bait.

Finally, he moves off again. We wait for the line to tighten, then sock the hook home. What follows may not live up to the emotional buildup which preceded it. But even though the pike may turn out to be of no more than ordinary size, this cannot erase the long moments of anticipation already experienced. And just often enough to keep us ever hopeful, we whack into a pike that is every bit as big as we expected him to be.

As already pointed out, northern pike are active throughout the entire year. In all probability, however, the rod and reel fisherman stands the best chance of taking really big pike late in the fall — when most fishermen have stowed their tackle away for the winter. I seldom take advantage of the fall fishing, for my thoughts turn to grouse and woodcock as soon as the leaves turn color. But I can vouch from experience that big northerns are likely to be in a hitting mood only a few days before freeze-up.

One day, late in November, a friend and I set out down Otter Creek on a duck-hunting trip. It was a cold, grim day with the threat of approaching winter unpleasantly evident. The trees along the creek had long since lost their leaves, and their gnarled trunks and naked branches were ominously skeletal against the gray November sky. The dead vegetation along the creek's high banks rattled and rasped in the cold wind, and the water around our canoe looked black as ink, so hostile in appearance that it suggested the enforced hibernation of whatever living things it might contain.

Consequently, when my friend placed a spinning rod in the canoe, nothing could have seemed more out of place. Appearances to the contrary, the pike apparently gloried in the seemingly unfavorable conditions. It was so cold that our hands became numb each time we fished, but whenever we forgot about ducks long enough to try a likely spot, there usually was a big pike ready and eager to pounce on a lure.

Unfortunately, my friend's spinning line was too light for

serious pike fishing, and he had brought only a half-dozen lures. Those six lures had either been broken or bitten off by big pike before our trip was half finished, and we had lost count of the fish we had caught and released by the time one finally swam off with our last spoon.

We could not have hoped for action from other species under those conditions, and this is in keeping with the character of northern pike. Quite probably the northern's failure to win full acceptance as a game fish is due in no small part to his habit of breaking all the rules by which other fish abide. He tends to lie where one least expects to find him. He submits passively when other fish fight madly for their lives. Then, when by all protocol he should await the net in a state of exhaustion, he suddenly explodes a burst of hoarded energy that can reduce expensive rods to splinters.

Like him or not, the northern is full of surprises. It is for this reason that I hold the ugly cuss in considerable esteem. And as I said at the outset, I have yet to meet the fisherman whose contempt for northern pike lasts after a big northern has walloped his lure.

14

In Defense of Ice Fishing

I N MANY CIRCLES anybody who fishes through the ice has to be crazy. Usually the aversion to ice fishing is attributed to the tortures one must suffer in order to participate, but actually modern insulated boots and clothing assure reasonable comfort on even the coldest days, and a snug fishing shanty makes prolonged exposure to cold unnecessary. Actually, I'm sure I have suffered greater agony from cold in canoes and boats, during early spring fishing, than I have ever endured on ice-covered lakes.

The usual protests might ring true if it were human nature to let unpleasant consequences deter the pursuit of strong desires. But since the truth lies in precisely the opposite direction, I think it can be more accurately assumed that those who take a dim view of ice fishing do so because the prospect of fishing through the ice does not awaken those urges which are aroused by the contemplation of open water fishing. Lacking this enthusiasm, it is easy to downgrade ice fishing on a wide variety of counts: it permits little exercise of finesse and delicacy, it is but a poor test of angling skill, it involves little more than dangling baited hooks and hauling in fish hand over hand.

All these charges are essentially true, but rod and reel fishing and ice fishing are as different as grouse hunting and coon hunting. To condemn ice fishing for this difference is much like shooting a good tree hound for his failure to point birds.

The techniques of ice fishing are unavoidably crude which tends to dissuade those who fail to look beyond this single consideration. Actually, the ice fisherman is intrigued by a change in relationship between man and fish which, to him, makes fishing at even the most basic level an enterprise of deep fascination. This change occurs suddenly and dramatically as soon as lakes freeze over sufficiently for safe fishing. Now a man can walk at will over a surface that previously denied him that privilege. The surface is barren, devoid of all life, and by its sterility suggests an absence of life in the hermetically sealed water below. The fisherman is instintively moved to accept this illusion at its face value — to concede that all aquatic life has been immobilized by sheer environmental austerity.

But while he is pleased to entertain this notion emotionally, he is objectively aware that a living world exists beneath his feet, its tempo no more than moderately affected by that which has the appearance of overwhelming adversity. It is this ostensible paradox which is the source of ice fishing's fascination. The fisherman is challenged to resolve the contradiction of appearance and reality by making contact with life in the dark and sealed-off waters and thereby confirm the surprising truth of its existence. It is because all concern is focused on making this contact that it matters but little if no great amount of refinement is employed in effecting its achievement.

It is a typical December day on Lake Champlain, which is to say that the thermometer stands between zero and twenty above, and a stiff wind blows steadily from the north. Snow lies deep on shore, but the wind has swept the surface of the lake clean, save for thin, crusty patches of white which accentuate the dull, gray somberness of the bare ice. Our tilts are set in lines which extend spokelike from the tiny fishing shanty. Inside, the little kerosene heater radiates welcome warmth, and Pete, Mike and I are hunkered down on benches along the walls of the shanty.

The shanty was designed to provide no more than minimum comfort, but we are not conscious of this circumstance. Instead, we are tense, watchful and expectant. Each has his eye glued to one of the shanty's tiny windows, hoping for a tilt to flip.

The tilts stand starkly outlined against their neutral background, their rigid immobility depressing and unanimous evidence of continued inactivity. Their stubborn refusal to budge seems to attest to the futility of our efforts, but we reject this implication. Instead, with an optimism that is often misplaced, we prefer to reason that each unproductive minute brings the hoped-for action that much closer.

Suddenly, and of course without warning, one of the

wooden arms is yanked off balance and upends. It stands out as a delightful anomaly among all its undisturbed neighbors, a signal of contact with life of an alien world which we greet with excitement that is quite out of proportion to its true significance. We all but tear the door from its hinges in our rush to get outside.

The first to get to the sprung tilt notes that the trigger loop has been drawn from sight, indicating a purposeful bite. He grasps the line gently between thumb and forefinger and raises it cautiously. The line tightens, and he feels a throbbing which tells him the fish has the bait. A quick, deft yank sets the hook, and in only a few seconds he has a three-pound walleye flopping on the ice.

It is a good fish in all respects, and one of the best when it comes to texture and flavor. But its capture was accomplished in the almost complete absence of all which characterizes the usual concept of sport fishing, and the food value of a dozen fish of the same kind and size would be but poor pay for the prodigious effort that went into the setting of the many tilts. What, then, supplied the incentive?

It can only be defined in terms of the subjectivity which served as its sounding board — which perhaps is no definition at all. At any rate, the source of fascination was neither the fish nor its capture, but the setting in which the latter took place, a setting which seemed to position the prospect of success behind a barrier of almost hopeless odds.

Nothing could have held less promise than the grim, wind-swept surface of the frozen lake, and this aspect of futility was compounded by the motionless string of tilts. Crude devices at best, they radiated little by way of promise. If anything, they seemed to have been rendered ineffectual by their very inertia. We stared from the shanty with hopes that were mocked by reality. Suddenly, amid the ingredients of despair, a tripped tilt gloriously affirmed that human resolution is more than a match for the longest odds. All that followed was anticlimatic.

That there are those who see drama in so trivial an event is proof that man is indeed a strange creature. Among his peculiarities is an abhorrence of the impossible, due, I suspect, to the fact that the aspect of impossibility is a sharp and distasteful reminder of his fallibility. Pride, another behavioral oddity, drives him to refute the impossible, wherever it exists. Those of marked talent address formidable challenges commensurate with their genius. The rest of us must content ourselves with the minor challenges which we are capable of meeting, but the basic urge to assert our omnipotence is no less pronounced. Some seek to gratify this urge by building model ships in bottles, some by breaking par (or a hundred) on the golf course, and I submit that some do so by going ice fishing.

This conclusion may be utter nonsense. Perhaps ice fishermen fish only to carry home fish. But if this is the case, then they are indeed idiots. No fish, by themselves, are worth the work it takes to catch them when lakes are covered by twenty inches of ice — or by merely six inches of ice, for that matter.

The fisherman whose love of fishing is a congenital passion is keenly conscious of his limited ability to understand the fish he fishes for, and he welcomes any fresh opportunity to peer into their affairs. Ice fishing provides a chance to establish contact with fish in a context that is markedly different from that in which they are encountered during spring and summer, and the effect of ice fishing is to increase one's angling enlightenment.

At first glance, this opportunity would seem to arise because of the environmental changes brought about by winter. In reality, however, this holds true only with respect to those species which are significantly affected by the low temperatures. Bass, for instance, seem to feed very little during the winter in the northern states and furnish little chance of sport for ice fishermen. This is somewhat less true of trout, but ice fishing for trout is usually a slow business. In recent years, certain Vermont trout lakes have been thrown open to ice fishing. Although the prospect of taking trout through the ice attracted many fishermen, surveys showed that results fell far below expectations.

On the other hand, certain other species seem to go on feeding in winter, much as in summer, and it is by fishing for these relatively unaffected species that the ice fisherman gains added insight. Those species which remain active include walleyes, saugers, northern pike, pickerel, yellow perch and smelt.

The ice fisherman can draw inferences from the responses of these species which have general application. But his fresh vantage point is supplied more by the employment of uniform angling methods on a broad front than by environmental changes. In ice fishing, the manner of presentation is much less varied, and this provides the opportunity to observe mass fish reaction to uniform inducement.

In Defense of Ice Fishing

A favorite Lake Champlain spot for winter walleye fishing is White's Bay, in the town of Orwell. As soon as the ice is safe (and sometimes even sooner), dozens of fishing shanties are hauled into position and thirty or forty tilts are set in around each shanty. Lines are wound up at the end of the day, but the tilts are left in position throughout the season.

A part of these layouts will be in use on any day of the week, but on weekends virtually every line is baited and no shanty unoccupied. Thousands of live minnows dangle close to the bottom of the bay, and to all intents and purposes they are of the same kind and size. On poor days, nobody catches anything to speak of. On good days, flags flip all over the bay, and there is hardly a time when fishermen, in one place or another, are not running to tend bites.

It is an accepted fact that walleyes are school fish, and the springtime troller who runs into a streak of fast action usually attributes this to the fortunate discovery of a school of fish. He may be correct, of course. Yet there is also the possibility that he may have been over fish all along, and that the flurry of strikes may have resulted from a change of mood on the part of the walleyes.

The change-of-mood possibility does not receive serious consideration from the open water fisherman, but ice fishing observations seem to indicate that it is often the reason for success. As an example, noticeable currents come and go in Lake Champlain, and their sudden appearance usually has a marked effect upon the fishing. With typical lack of agreement, some fishermen insist that the arrival of a current means an end of the fishing, while others declare that it puts fish on the feed. There is reason for each belief, for when a current sets in during a period of good fishing it often kills the action. On the other hand, a current which springs to life during a dull spell can set the fish to feeding with dramatic suddenness. I have seen it work both ways.

Whenever it has a favorable effect, and the walleyes suddenly come to life, it is interesting to keep tabs on the many fishermen scattered over an area of nearly a square mile. When our flags begin to flip, the tilts of all the fishermen on the bay invariably keep pace. Bites keep us running to tend them, but by glancing north and south between bites it is apparent that all the other fishermen are as happily engaged. In view of the large area so suddenly affected, it is obvious that the breakout of action is much too widespread to be attributed to the sudden arrival of a school, or schools, of walleyes.

The lone fisherman might jump to this conclusion, just as the springtime troller usually does. Observed in isolation, a sudden rash of bites seems to indicate that fish have moved in on the fisherman, or that he has moved in on fish. Ice fishing provides an opportunity to observe this phenomenon in much greater latitude and reveals the fact that the truth often lies in quite another area: the fish were there all the time, but just wouldn't bite until suddenly overtaken by the mood to do so.

I remember one day so cold that all but a few of the shanties on the bay stood empty. Pete and I were among the handful of fishermen rash enough to set in lines on such a day, and all the others had the sense to pull up and leave when hardly a fish bit during the entire morning. By afternoon we had the bay completely to ourselves, but this seemed a dubious privilege when it came three o'clock and we hadn't yet caught a single fish. Then, as though by edict, tilts began tripping all up and down our spread. Fish ran us ragged for the next couple of hours, and we took our limit of twenty nice walleyes, plus fully as many yellow perch and saugers that joined in the biting spree. Under the circumstances, it would have been reasonable to conclude that all those fish had suddenly moved in on us, but I doubt very much that this was the case. Had the usual number of fishermen been present, I feel sure that all would have shared in the lively fishing. It is this belief, gained largely from ice fishing experience, which prompts me to suspect that fishing failure is due to a lack of fish considerably less frequently than is usually supposed.

A few miles from the village of Vergennes, Vermont, at a spot on Lake Champlain known as Ive's Landing, there is a smelt fishing ground which attracts ice fishermen by the hundreds. A deeply sunken reef extends for a mile or more. Depths over the reef average about sixty feet, but the adjacent water is a hundred or more feet deep. Astronomical numbers of smelt are attracted by the reef, and a small city of closely packed fishing shanties springs up over it as soon as the ice permits. On good days fishermen tote home the small, silvery fish by the pailful, but while the annual take is beyond estimate, it never seems to make a dent in the smelt population. This clearly indicates that the water under the ice fairly swarms with fish, and there is little reason to believe that this is anything but a constant circumstance.

Nevertheless, there are times when catches dwindle to near

the vanishing point in spite of this great abundance of fish. A morning of fast and furious biting may be followed by an extremely dull afternoon. On the following day the exact reverse may apply. There come strings of successive days when the smelt bite ravenously from daylight to dark, but there are periods of equal length when they bite scarcely at all.

These are phenomena of considerable interest to the fisherman who thrives on speculation. They are specially intriguing because they occur relatively free of those variables which often stand in the way of valid conclusions. In other words, the inquisitive fisherman can study fluctuations of fish response and behavior in a situation involving huge numbers of fish and a small army of fishermen using identical equipment, baits and methods. The widespread lack of success on poor days cannot reasonably be attributed to angling inefficiency, nor can the equally general success of good days be credited to any increase in expertise. Not only do the fluctuations come and go according to an unpredictable pattern, but they appear to assert themselves as waves of a mysterious influence to which virtually every fish is instantly responsive.

The standard (Lake Champlain) smelt fishing outfit consists of a jig stick with a hundred or more feet of monofilament wound on a handle designed to serve also as an elongated spool. A two-ounce sinker is used to ensure rapid descent of the bait, and since it is legal to use two hooks, one is suspended from the sinker and one tied to the line above it. The universal bait is a slab of skin and flesh cut from the tail section of a smelt. This rather odd bait combines appeal and toughness; smelt bite it eagerly when they are active, and a substantial number can be caught before the need to rebait arises.

Smelt have a peculiar manner of biting, which comes as a surprise to the beginner. For some unknown reason they tend to rise after grabbing the bait, and instead of feeling the expected tug, the fisherman experiences the odd sensation of having his heavily weighted line suddenly go slack. The effect is that of having the line suddenly *pushed* upward.

The experienced smelt fisherman pays little heed to bites, however. Instead, he jigs his line lightly for several seconds, then raises it quickly with a sudden snatch. This results in a much faster rate of hooking than can be achieved by yanking after a bite is felt. Smelt are extremely fast, and by the time the fisherman has reacted to a bite they usually have dropped the bait. The jig and snatch method works best simply because a substantial percentage of the arbitrary snatches will be made at the precise moment when a smelt is in the act of grabbing the bait.

Usually this action takes place at depths of fifty or sixty feet, and the fisherman can only guess what is going on. Sometimes, however, it is possible to lure the fish nearer and nearer to the surface by periodically winding in line, a few turns at a time. Now and then they can be tolled from the depths to within plain view, and their almost uncanny ability to avoid hooking can be observed directly. The bait may be surrounded by dozens of fish, all of which take turns at darting in and grabbing it. But although they are plainly visible, and the fisherman is free to act accordingly, smelt after smelt will seize the bait without being hooked. Actually, a yank while the bait seems free is more likely to hook a smelt, for it is usually only by blind chance that the fisherman can contrive to snatch at the precise moment when a bite first occurs.

When the biting is fast and furious, the baits of hundreds of fishermen are surrounded by swarms of fish, and the fact that this rapid tempo may suddenly dwindle to almost nothing is an angling mystery. Also, it is one which may reasonably be assumed to have general application.

Among the myriads of fish present it would be logical to expect each one to manifest its hunger as an individual, feeding as he felt the need and desisting whenever he succeeded in filling his stomach. But if this were the case there would be a significant number of hungry fish at all times, and there would be little fluctuation in the rate of biting. As many fish would be going on the feed as were coming off, and the tempo of fishing would remain essentially constant from hour to hour and from day to day.

As I have indicated, no such condition prevails. What may be millions of fish respond simultaneously to the same mysterious signal, and they either start or stop feeding for reasons which defy human detection.

It has long been believed that all species of fish are subject to this strange, cyclic influence, but the rod and reel fisherman must draw his conclusions from situations in which relatively few fish and fishermen are involved. He can never be certain that the effect is not due to coincidence, a fortuitous change of lures or some other circumstance which lays his theory open to question. But when what well may be millions of fish are observed to fluctuate temperamentally as an entity, it seems overwhelmingly apparent that some external force is indeed responsible for their irregularities of mass behavior.

Attempts to identify the nature of this influence have been made, and claims of success are not lacking. Changes in the combined gravitational effect of sun, moon and stars have been declared responsible. Since these changes can be predetermined, various charts and tables have been devised which purport to identify those periods most favorable for the fisherman. Each has won a certain amount of acceptance, and all have been intriguing additions to angling lore. But these tables seldom stand up under objective testing, and it seems quite probable that those who swear by them are ruled by much the same unreasoning emotions as are those who have faith in patent medicines.

This in no way refutes the existence of influences which have dramatic effect upon fish behavior. Observation leads me to believe that they are realities, so subtle that they have as yet escaped identification, but factors which probably play a more important role in determining angling success than does angling skill.

Because modern anglers take great pride in their skill, they tend to discount the importance of what was once accepted as a principal determinant of success — angler's luck. They are quick to point out that ninety percent of all fish caught are caught by only ten percent of all fishermen — this ten percent presumed to be those of the greatest skill. But in all probability this ten percent also includes the most avid anglers who fish at every possible opportunity and are thus *lucky* enough to be in the right places at the right times.

At any rate, skill cannot be counted as the sole determinant, for if it were, all highly skilled fishermen would be consistently successful. That this is far from the case is very apparent, for when fish "aren't biting" the expert takes his lumps along with everybody else, a fact borne out by guides who do not hesitate to tell even the most expert fisherman, "You should have been here last week." If skill alone were enough, the expert would never have to worry about arriving on the scene at a particular time, for his expertise would prevail at all times, and there would be neither good nor poor fishing days as far as he was concerned.

This statement seems further evidence of the impossibility of reducing angling to anything approaching an exact science. Where, as in smelt fishing, mass responses can be observed, it becomes apparent that the responsible stimulus not only asserts itself according to an unpredictable pattern, but also with varying degrees of intensity. The opposite extremes of this intensity result in those days when smelt can be hauled in by the hundreds and those when very few can be caught at all. In between lie many gradations which furnish material for more speculation.

Results seem to suggest that the tendency of fish to exercise caution varies inversely with the strength of the impulse which induces feeding. When this impulse is strongest smelt not only bite with unbroken regularity, but with what, for them, is reckless abandon. Consequently, a high percentage of snatches results in hooked fish, which of course makes it comparatively easy to catch a great number. There are other days, however, when smelt bite with only moderately reduced frequency, but when the incidence of hooking falls off much more sharply than can be accounted for by the reduction in the rate of biting. If the smelt continued to be as easy to hook as before, large catches could still be made on such days, but this is not the case. The smelt bite frequently enough, but not with their previous abandon. They are therefore much more difficult to hook, and catches tend to be small in spite of the comparative abundance of bites.

I believe this shading of response applies to all species of fish in general and has a lot to do in determining the size of a day's catch. I have had days on trout streams, for example, when almost every rise to my dry fly resulted in a solidly hooked fish. On these days I have little reason to cuss the slowness of my reflexes. Each rise is a full commitment, and I can be deliberate in setting the hook. In contrast, there are often other days when I can persuade a fair number of trout to rise, but have a devil of a job hooking them. They are inspired to feed, but only moderately so, and the inverse relationship between strength of motivation and the exercise of caution asserts itself.

Ice fishing for yellow perch, at least as it is commonly done in Vermont, is much akin to ice fishing for smelt. The same tools are used, and the chief difference is that a perch eye is used for bait. Like smelt fishermen, perch fishermen do not wait to feel a bite, but make blind snatches at regular intervals. When perch are biting readily, properly timed snatches will often account for a pair of fish, and it is possible to catch a large number of these tasty panfish during a day's fishing.

In winter, perch usually frequent water of considerable

depth, and most of the time the fisherman can only guess at what is going on around his hooks. Rapid bites are clear evidence of an abundance of fish, of course, but the fisherman who concludes that a lack of bites is a positive indication of the absence of fish is often badly mistaken.

This is impossible to prove under usual circumstances, but I have fished shallow ponds for perch where it has been possible to see what went on by lying flat on the ice and peering down through the fishing hole. I have done this when perch grabbed my eye-baited hooks almost as fast as I lowered them and again when fishing was at a complete standstill. What seemed of interest and significance to me was that my baits were surrounded by approximately the same number of perch at all times.

For as long as the biting mood prevailed, a jig or two of the line promptly resulted in bites and easily hooked fish. When the mood shifted to indifference, it was quite another story. Up to a dozen perch might eye my baited hooks, but no amount of jigging could persuade them to bite. Movement of the bait usually caused them to drift closer, but every last fish refused to bite as though by decree.

If a fisherman takes pride in his skill, such starkly visible evidence of his limitations can be rather humiliating. On the other hand, it is sustaining to the fisherman's pride to realize that failure and defeat are not necessarily due to his deficiencies, but to the fact that there are no known tricks that will make fish hit when they aren't in the mood to do so.

If I have dealt with ice fishing as though its chief attraction consists of the opportunity it provides to study fish in a different context, it is not because my interest in ice fishing is purely academic. When I fish through the ice my chief aim is to catch fish, every bit as much as this is my objective when fishing a trout stream.

As for the rigors of ice fishing, they are seldom as severe as imagined. Even when they are, they serve a subtle purpose.

In *Moby Dick,* Herman Melville observed that the blessing of warm bedcovers could be fully appreciated only if some small part of the body remained exposed to the cold. Any tortures endured while ice fishing supply the same element of contrast and thereby bring about fuller appreciation of the many comforts which we take for granted.

One bitterly cold afternoon the Lake Champlain walleyes bit so well that Pete and I continued to fish until nearly dark. We finally gave up only because the fishing holes froze over faster than we could skim them, and fish were stealing our minnows without springing our tilts. We completed the agonizing task of winding up our many lines with bare hands, turned off the heater in the shanty and locked the door. Stars were out when we had finished, twinkling with that exaggerated brilliance which intense cold effects. The expanding ice boomed and thundered, and the thermometer on the side of the shanty stood at thirteen below zero.

We had driven three miles up the lake from the nearest access point, and as we climbed into the car I looked forward to a succession of delights. The car's heater would soon drive the chill from our bones, and we had all the details of a fine day's fishing to hash over on the drive home. Then would come several slugs of bourbon, followed by large quantities of hot food. All would culminate in that mellow mood which makes the comfort of an open fire too exquisite for description.

These were the delightful visions I had in mind when I stepped on the starter and discovered that the battery was stone dead. I could dwell on the demoralizing effect of this dismal discovery and on the agony of the long hike for help in the merciless cold. Instead, I would like to point out that when we finally reached home the anticipated pleasures were delightful beyond all precedent. No whiskey ever achieved more blessed effect, no food ever tasted more delicious and no fire was ever more comforting.

15

Labrador-Ungava

THE FRONTIERS of fishing have been pushed back so rapidly in recent years that very few remain. It is futile to hope to find virgin fishing in regions which can be reached by automobile. Even beyond the last roads there are wide belts of territory which are relatively easy to reach by plane or boat, and whose waters see many fishermen. Only by flying hundreds of miles beyond the last overland approach can one find what every fisherman dreams of: unfished waters which teem with fish, exactly as they have for centuries. In spite of our rapidly mounting affluence and the wonders of modern transportation, very few fishermen have been fortunate enough to fish waters which fall into this category.

In this class I am including only those waters which truly lie beyond the beyond. If one has the necessary means, it is fairly simple to fish waters which fall just short of this category. But to reach waters which perhaps no civilized man has ever fished is quite another matter. To do so it is necessary to invade country so remote and hostile that it is shunned by all but the most daring and competent pilots.

Ever since I can remember I have dreamed of fishing such waters, and three years ago my dreams finally came true. At that time Norm Hathaway and his partner Smudge Grant were operating a recently opened fishing camp in western Labrador. They were looking for publicity in the form of magazine articles and invited me to sample their fishing in the hope that it would provide the necessary material. Since Pete and I had teamed up on similar, but less ambitious, projects, I sold them the idea of including Pete in on the deal. He would play his usual role of photographer and member of the party who generally catches the fish worth writing about and photographing.

With only the vaguest notion of what was in store for us, we drove to Bangor, Maine, from where we would fly with Norm and Smudge to the camp in Labrador. This, we learned, was a distance of approximately a thousand miles. A thousand-mile flight in a commercial plane is nothing to get excited about, but Pete and I were to learn that to fly a thousand miles in a tiny plane is another matter altogether.

Early the next morning we took off into a cloudless sky which seemed to guarantee ideal flying conditions. Pete flew with Smudge in a Piper "Apache" equipped with wheels; Norm and I took off from the Penobscot River in a Cessna rigged with pontoons.

We landed at Van Buren to clear customs, then headed for Seven Islands, Quebec, where we would take on gas. It had been smooth sailing up to then, but in crossing the St. Lawrence we ran into bumpy going. Our perfect day had turned into something quite different, and when we sat down at Seven Islands it was in weather that had become downright nasty.

We headed north from Seven Islands and began climbing to clear the Laurentide escarpment. The air was as full of holes as Swiss cheese, and we bounced and banged along in a steady series of tooth-jarring impacts. Rain hammered at the plane and visibility diminished.

We were in touch with Smudge and Pete by radio, and when the weather steadily grew worse Smudge announced that they were turning back toward Seven Islands. We continued on, and soon we were over the Labrador plateau, a region which, from the air, seemed to be made up of almost as much water as land. Norm assured me that a forced landing, which seemed a likely possibility, would be nothing more serious than an inconvenience. He could kill the motor anywhere and bring the plane down safely, he declared. So he elected to continue on.

The iron mining town of Schefferville, Quebec, is connected with the outside world only by a 350-mile railroad which ends at Seven Islands. We picked up the railroad after our climb and followed it as a guideline. By that time the weather had forced us down to an altitude of only a few hundred feet.

Our flight plan called for us to land at Schefferville, but the seaplane base was too socked-in for a safe landing. Norm canceled the plan by radio and declared his intention of heading directly for the fishing camp, sixty-five air miles east of Schefferville. There, he hoped, we'd have enough visibility for a landing.

We had been in the air over ten hours when Norm announced that we were only a few miles from the camp. But ahead of us lay a solid bank of fog and clouds, and he appended this welcome announcement with one which was not as encouraging. He didn't dare proceed, he said; the camp was guarded by low, but very substantial hills, and it would be foolhardy to risk an approach until the hills could be plainly seen.

Talk about frustration! It seemed that we had come a thousand miles, only to spend a cold and wretched night in the little plane only a few miles from our destination. But I resigned myself to this unpleasant development prematurely, and with too little respect for Norm's skill as a pilot.

He banked the plane and studied the situation carefully while we flew in a tight circle.

"We're in a pocket of visibility that seems to be drifting toward the camp," he said. "We'll keep circling, and if the pocket moves over the camp we'll duck in."

Sure enough, after we had flown several circles, the hills Norm feared suddenly came into view.

"We've got it made," Norm declared. "We'll be drinking coffee in the cook shack inside of ten minutes."

To my inexpressible relief, we were. By that time the weather had closed in completely again, and the rain came down in sheets. A delay of only a few minutes in our arrival, and we would have spent the night in the plane exactly as I had anticipated.

It was only late August, but the next day was so cold and wretched that fishing was out of the question. As the wind howled and rain beat on the roof, I rather envied Pete. He and Smudge were undoubtedly drowning their frustration in some snug bar in Seven Islands.

Early the next morning I was startled from a sound sleep by a plane which buzzed the camp at little more than treetop level. I crawled from my sleeping bag and stumbled outside the plywood cabin. Every cloud had been swept from the sky, and the plane gleamed in the rays of the rising sun as it made another pass over the camp. It was Smudge's Piper, and the buzzing was to serve notice that Smudge and Pete would soon be waiting in Schefferville for Norm to pick them up in the seaplane.

Less than two hours later they were eating breakfast in the cook shack and telling their story between bites. After returning to Seven Islands they had decided to make another try with the mistaken idea that the weather had cleared. It had done so only to the extent of decoying them beyond the point of no return. Then conditions became so hopeless that they had no choice but to attempt a forced landing.

They were following the railroad, and during its construction airstrips had been bulldozed here and there along its course. These had long been abandoned and neglected and were in sorry shape. But with luck, Smudge had managed to bring the plane down safely on one of the rough and rutted strips.

There they had spent two cold and miserable nights in the

ruins of what had been a tool shack. We had foolishly stowed gear in the two planes with no eye for such an emergency, and this compounded their plight. Fortunately, they had their sleeping bags with them and enough food to make out. But their heavy clothing and rain gear were in the Cessna with Norm and me. Launching the plane that morning had been a difficult and risky business, but their luck had held.

Now that we were regrouped, Norm and Smudge disclosed plans which they had kept secret. They had prospected for fishing over much of Labrador, and during one prospecting trip they had landed near an Eskimo village on the coast. There they were told of a spot so teeming with arctic char that the Eskimos called it the "Home of the Fish." Following directions that were anything but specific, they had found the place — and had discovered the fishing to be every bit as spectacular as described.

Later they flew a tent, supplies and extra gas to a deep fjord a considerable distance from the actual fishing spot. The outlet of the fjord was alive with arctic char, they said, and the chosen campsite would provide access to both places. Pete and I were to be the first guests to sample the fishing.

Our destination lay approximately 250 miles northeast of the permanent fishing camp, and where we would be beyond radio contact with Schefferville. I listened as Norm gave the approximate fix of the fishing spot and left instructions to notify the airbase at Schefferville if we weren't back within five days. The sobering implications of this precaution intruded on my visions of big fish, but only momentarily.

Although the task looked impossible, Norm soon had all our gear stowed in the little plane, with room for Pete and me to cram ourselves into the rear compartment. Very shortly thereafter the four of us were aloft and headed for the coast. It was the beginning of a never-to-be-forgotten experience.

Labrador is an immense plateau which tilts upward in the direction of the coast. The western part includes chains of lakes and rivers which stretch in all directions as far as the eye can see. The region is totally uninhabited and virtually impenetrable. Because of this, the waters, which make up approximately twenty percent of the total area, are largely unfished and await exploration. Since vast areas of virgin wilderness are foreign to common experience, such an expanse of unfished water is hard to imagine in the abstract. Only when one can look down upon it from a plane does it become a conceivable reality, and for a fisherman the sight is almost overwhelming. As I drank in the full implication, I was all but intoxicated by the realization that I was at last where I had always dreamed of being: in a region where fish lived and flourished beyond all human encroachment, with every mile taking us deeper into this exotic context.

The land below us was sparsely spiked with spruce trees. The ground was covered with deep moss in which a network of caribou trails was constantly visible. As we continued northeast the tree growth dwindled, the lakes became fewer and the brown carpet of moss gave way to outcroppings of naked rock. Rushing streams appeared as the land became more elevated and irregular, and patches of perennial snow lay on shaded slopes and in depressions. Finally, as we neared the coast, snowcapped mountains loomed ahead.

The coast of Labrador is a region of ominous grandeur, the sight of which inspires exotic emotions that are beyond description. Mountains of naked rock rise to heights of several thousand feet, lending abysmal perspective to the many fjords which thrust inland from the sea. The effect is so awesome that the Eskimos refer to the section as the "Home of the Spirits," and one is tempted to believe that the name derives from more than superstition alone. It is a land so openly hostile to human presence that guardianship by evil spirits seems a strong possibility.

Close to the coast, we flew over a fjord so deep that the bottom of the earth seemed to have fallen away. Norm guided the little plane down into this chasm, and we had the experience of flying between walls of rock which rose high above us on both sides. Moments later we could make out a tiny patch of green on a small shelf on the shore of the fjord. It was the tent in which we would spend the night. Satisfied that it was still standing, Norm pulled the plane out of the deep canyon and headed it for the river in which we were to fish for arctic char.

In making our approach we first flew out over the sea, crossing a bay in which floated icebergs of dazzling whiteness. Soon we came opposite the mouth of a rushing river, and Norm pointed the nose of the plane directly upstream. A few miles from the sea we reached the place where the river was born, the outlet of a large and beautiful lake which threaded its way inland among towering mountains. Norm eased the plane down on the calm surface of the lake, and as we stepped ashore a startled Canada goose led her flotilla of half-grown goslings toward the safety of the opposite shore.

As we drew on waders and set up rods, Pete and I experienced emotions that are denied all but the most fortunate fishermen. We had left our homes to travel over 1600 miles, many of these across a land utterly devoid of human habitation. We had watched the proof of the almost incredible remoteness of our destination flow beneath us, and we were appropriately attuned to the exotic nature of the package we were about to open. If our hands trembled as we fumbled our rods together, it was not without good reason.

Unlike the many dreams which fail to materialize, ours came true to the last detail. We hiked around the shore of the lake to where the river began, and there drank in a spectacle which had not been apparent from the air. Tons of white water came thundering out of the lake, spewing over a dike of solid granite in a great chute of leaping foam. Below, the escaping water spread to form an enormous pool of conflicting currents before flowing off to the sea.

Pete, Norm and Smudge cast big Dardevles into the pool almost simultaneously. With a devotion to duty beyond all normal call, I first dug into my pack for a camera. Before I could ready it, all three fishermen were fast to wildly fighting fish. Their spinning reels buzzed in unison, so loudly that I could hear them above the roar of the river, and three arctic char tore downriver as though they had no intention of stopping until they reached the sea. I snapped a picture of the trio braced against bucking rods, then hastened to heave out my own lure with feverish anticipation.

I let the spoon sink well down into the swirling current, then felt it smacked almost as soon as I started to retrieve it. My line streaked straight toward the tossing foam, and a glis-

337

tening body of gunmetal hue hurtled high above violent water in a magnificent leap. In another instant the frantic fish headed straight down the pool in a run that took nearly a hundred yards of line from my spinning reel. I had questioned Norm about the fighting qualities of arctic char, and he had told me that in his opinion they would outfight Atlantic salmon. Moments after hooking my first char I was ready to agree.

The great pool was alive with fish, and for the remainder of the afternoon there were few moments when one or more of us didn't have a fish on. Pete caught the biggest, a char of twelve pounds, but we all had fish break off which undoubtedly were larger. This was practically unavoidable, due to the nature of the pool and the great force of the current which each hooked fish immediately used to advantage. Many reacted to the sting of the hook by making a single, wild leap; all took off downriver at full speed, sometimes running an estimated hundred yards or more of line without stopping. They would then bulldog against the rod while they regained strength and take off in another downstream dash which often threatened to clean the reel. The pool spread back from the fast water in a backwater so enormous that it was impossible to follow a hooked fish; we had to stand pat, put on all the pressure we dared and hope for the best. When it became a case of either stopping a fish or letting him clean the reel, the line sometimes parted under the increased pressure.

My previous impressions of arctic char had been gained only from pictures of highly colored fish. As a result, I had expected fish which outdid the brook trout with respect to coloration and was surprised when the char we caught exhibited only neutral colors. They were a metallic blue-gray along their backs and sides and sparsely peppered with light gray spots. Their bellies were a gleaming white.

This lack of coloration, I learned, was due to the fact that the fish were fresh from the sea. As they moved inland to spawn they, the males in particular, would take on the vivid colors I had seen in pictures.

The char were so eager to hit a spoon that I jumped to the conclusion that they would certainly go for a big streamer. I set up a fly rod with high expectations, but my efforts with it came to naught. I suspected at the time that the trouble was inability to sink the streamer deeply enough. Later experience convinced me that arctic char are just hard to take on flies. In any event, it was very difficult, at least for me, to fish vainly with a fly for any significant period of time while those around me were hooking fish on spoons almost as fast as they could land them.

As is often the case, the heaviest and strongest fish were the least inclined to leap, and their first runs invariably took them so far downstream that we could only estimate their size from the savage power of the runs. We came away with no actual idea of the size of the fish which broke our lines, but some of them must have been truly tremendous. As an example, Pete had one on for a solid hour, and the fish seemed as strong as ever when Pete finally had to break him off.

He hooked the fish late in the afternoon, and during the hour-long battle never regained any of the line taken out in the first sizzling run. The sun sank behind the mountains, and at last Norm announced that our departure couldn't be postponed any longer. Pete would either have to bring in the fish or break him off.

Pete grimly tightened the drag of his reel and began cranking slowly. His line lifted from the water under the strain until it stood clear for many yards downstream. More reeling extracted the last bit of stretch from the great length of nylon. Pete ceased reeling, ounces short of the breaking point, but the big char refused to yield under the pressure. Reluctantly, Pete gave the reel handle a few more turns, and the tortured line finally parted. It was a heartbreaking experience, but not a total loss. For the rest of his days, Pete will cherish the conviction that for a thrill-packed hour he was fast to an arctic char that would have challenged all records.

We climbed above mountains whose tops reflected the rapidly waning daylight, but the deep fjords already were vast pools of shadow and darkness. I had lost all sense of direction and orientation, but Norm and Smudge held a running consultation in which they checked off what, to them, were recognizable landmarks. Just when it seemed that darkness would overtake us, Norm guided the plane down into the somber depths of the fjord in which our tent was pitched.

The hard nip of frost was already in the air as we built a fire and fried steaks. By the time we had finished eating, the wet waders which I had draped over the tail of the plane were frozen stiff. As I recall, it was the first day of September, but Norm told us that the ground was likely to be deep with snow before the month was half over.

Night came on with a rush, and as we yarned around the fire we were treated to a display of northern lights which I can still see vividly in retrospect, but for which I can find no adequate words of description. What seemed to be the beams of giant searchlights swept the skies above us, while vertical curtains of brilliant and ever-changing hues danced and undulated as though wafted about by angry storms. It was a spectacle of magnificent beauty, but also one of implied threat. It conveyed the disturbing feeling that human presence was frowned on, and that our intrusion might at any moment make us the unfortunate victims of cosmic wrath. Then, even more keenly than before, I shared the Eskimos' awe of that magnificent but ominous region.

Early the next morning we crowded into the plane and flew down the fjord, landing just above a rips below which the outlet became a tidal river. Norm and Smudge promised that here we would find even more char than existed in the big pool we had fished the previous day, but they added that they would not run as large.

It was a beautiful place to fish, posing none of the difficulties which had contributed to the loss of so many big fish the previous afternoon. A smooth, sandy bottom made wading easy, and the flow of the river was even and sedate. And talk about fish! Almost every cast brought a prompt strike from arctic char which ranged from those of two pounds in weight to six-pounders, and which fought like supercharged demons.

To my great delight, fish were breaking the surface within easy reach, so once more I rigged up a fly rod with great anticipation. In the meantime, Pete, Norm and Smudge were taking fish on medium-size Dardevles as fast as they could whip one char down and cast for another.

But although I floated a dry fly among dozens of rising fish, none paid it the slightest attention. Finally, unable to stand the torture of going fishless in the midst of plenty, I waded ashore to swap my fly rod for a spinning outfit.

Norm saw me making the change and shouted to ask if I had any wet flies. When I told him I had plenty, he asked if he might borrow a few, as well as my fly rod. I placed a box of wet flies beside the fly rod and told him to help himself.

Norm had the wisdom to guess that the char were taking something just under the surface. He began fishing a sunken wet fly among them, allowing it to come over them with a dead drift. After a prolonged period of casting he finally hooked and landed a char, and at the end of an equal interval he hooked another. In the meantime, I had caught at least a dozen fish on a spoon.

Norm proved that arctic char can be caught on flies. But it took considerable time and effort to take a pair of fish from a river that was fairly teeming with them. Before I could make a second try the fish suddenly stopped rising, and my hope of taking at least one arctic char on a fly went down the drain. But I had experimented enough to conclude that if all arctic char behaved as did those which we had encountered, they are a relatively poor bet for the fly fisherman.

We had caught so many of these fish that we had lost all sense of actual numbers, so that afternoon we decided to fly back to the base camp. Norm and Smudge had wanted us to take and photograph char (we had snapped dozens of pictures); now that that had been accomplished, they were equally eager for us to sample the fishing for big brook trout and ouananiche in their home waters.

On the flight to the coast we had flown over a particularly inviting lake which Norm declared to be fully as large as Moosehead Lake in Maine. Many lesser streams ran into the lake, but it was fed also by what obviously was a very large river. The lake was an unknown quantity to Norm and Smudge, and although such a thing is hard to imagine nowadays, it probably had never been fished by a sport fisherman. Just the thought of heaving out a lure at the mouth of that river was enough to make one's pulse quicken, and Norm had declared that we would try it on the way back if possible.

Pete and I looked forward to prospecting that unfished lake, which most certainly must have held some huge fish. Unfortunately, we didn't get to do so. It was late in the afternoon as we came over the lake, and we were still at least a hundred miles from our home base. Our reserve cushion of gas was minimal, Norm declared, and after carefully weighing the risks involved he decided against the stopover.

The temptation to fish that lake was tantalizing, and Pete and I often speculate about what results would have been had we gone down for a try. Maybe we will never know. On the other hand, maybe Norm has that remote lake in mind as an objective for another trip.

Not only is Labrador one of the few regions where unknown and unnamed lakes and rivers still exist, but the fish which exist in its waters are made up of the species most ardently sought by sport fishermen — and they all grow to trophy size.

Labrador is one of the few areas in the world where really large brook trout are abundant. Many of the lakes and streams which hold big brookies have populations of ouananiche which include fish up to ten pounds in weight. In both the streams and lakes, right along with the brook trout and salmon, are lake trout which reach enormous sizes. Moreover, the lakers will take flies and lures near the surface, for the water never grows so warm that it drives them into the depths.

The fishing season is relatively short, restricted to July, August and no more than the first half of September. Norm told us that during July and the first half of August, large hatches of mayflies resulted in dry fly fishing that had few, if any, equals. In the waters surrounding the base camp, the daily take with dry flies (per fisherman) was almost certain to include several brookies of more than four pounds, plus ouananiche of equal, or greater, size.

Unfortunately, freezing nights and chilly days had put an end to the hatches by the time we arrived. In fact, they seemed to have put an end to the fishing in general; we spent the first day after our return fishing proven spots with disappointing results.

That evening Norm voiced the opinion that perhaps the trout and salmon had moved into smaller streams preparatory to spawning, and that we might locate them by acting accordingly. Norm and Smudge had to fly to Schefferville the next day to arrange details concerning closing camp for the year, but a guide would take Pete and me to a small stream which Norm looked on as a good bet.

The stream was nothing more than a short connection between lakes, half a mile long and small enough for easy wading. Still hoping for surface fishing, we tied on dry flies and began working upstream. We had hardly started when Pete let out a whoop that brought me on the run with camera ready. I arrived in time to photograph him in the act of landing a brook trout of over four pounds, a male fish decked out in spawning colors of spectacular beauty.

Needless to say, we went at the stream in earnest with dry flies, but to our bitter disappointment we couldn't raise another fish. I fished carefully through a long, boulder-studded pool that had to hold trout if any were present anywhere. Failing to get a single strike, I finally decided it was time to give up the hope of bringing fish to a dry fly.

I changed leaders, tied on a big streamer and cast it across the current. It arced across the stream without results, and I twitched it upstream close to the shoreline. As it came abreast of a foam-covered pocket it was suddenly seized amid a mighty swirl and a flash of brilliant red and orange. I was fast to a brookie that was a near twin of the one Pete had taken. When I had landed the fish after a stubborn and powerful battle, a second cast brought a wallop from another lunker. I yelled to Pete to come and take *my* picture.

After photographing me with the second fish, Pete switched to a streamer, waded across the stream above the pool and then took up a position directly across from mine. For the next hour, and without moving, we had a taste of what paradise would be if fishermen could have their say.

Brook trout of all sizes came to our streamers in what was almost a regular pattern. A fish of three pounds or more would be followed by several smaller trout — brookies that would arouse envy if taken in close-to-home waters, but small by the standards which gave a dreamlike quality to our happy circumstance. Then, after several lesser trout had struck, there would come another rod-plunging belt from another whopper, and the cycle would be repeated.

When at last the trout in the pool ceased hitting, I asked Pete to estimate the number we had caught. He said that in his opinion we had taken at least a hundred. It had seemed that to me, but I had hesitated to voice an estimate for by that time I was too overwhelmed by the experience to trust my judgment.

I had only trout in mind when I moved downstream to refish water that had yielded nothing to dry flies. Consequently, I was quite unprepared for the enormous ouananiche which came to my streamer on the first cast. The big fish showed most of its length and bulk as it hit, and at the sight I yelled to Pete that I had hooked a salmon of at least ten pounds.

With all due allowance for my excitement, I doubt that I exaggerated by much, if at all. The reel wailed as the dynamic fish tore across the pool — then the line suddenly went slack. I had given the fish no pressure to work against save for the light drag of the reel, but the hook must have engaged only superficially. At any rate, it simply let go.

Numb with disappointment, I cast again and got another hard strike. This turned out to be from a ouananiche of over five pounds which ran and leaped like a fish gone mad before I finally netted it. But by following the huge ouananiche that had come off, this splendid fish seemed hardly more than a pygmy.

We kept only a few of the largest fish for photographing, but if it could have been done without injury to the fish, I would have liked to photograph our total take for the day. I'd like such a photograph if for no other reason than to prove that it hadn't all been a fantastic dream.

All good things come to an end, but with luck they can repeat themselves. Norm and Smudge were forced to give up their fishing camp the following year. Their lease was canceled by the Newfoundland government because of anticipated hydroelectric developments. Smudge entered into a partnership in developing a fishing camp on the George River in northern Quebec. In the meantime I had placed an article about the first trip, and the following year Smudge invited Pete and me to fish the George for Atlantic salmon with another article in mind.

The camp on the George, the George River Lodge, is located about fifty miles upriver from Ungava Bay. It is buried in the wild wasteland that is typical of the Labrador-Ungava region, but this time, thank goodness, our trip was uneventful.

We drove from Pittsford to Montreal, flew via Quebec Air to Schefferville and were flown from there to the George River in a twin-engine seaplane. Compared to our trip to the Labrador coast, this jaunt seemed almost indecently easy.

The George is one of the great rivers of northern Quebec, and one of the finest Atlantic salmon rivers in North America. It is huge and brawling, and anything but easy to fish. Difficulties arise not only because of the wild character of the river itself, but also because of subarctic winds and cold which make casting difficult and prolonged fishing a test of endurance.

347

We arrived during the last few days of August, but the next day a freezing sleet storm kept everybody in camp. The weather cleared that night, but not before blanketing the land with fully six inches of snow. I caught my first George River salmon, a fourteen-pound fish, against the wintry background commonly pictured on Christmas cards.

Not only does the George River have an annual run of large salmon, but it holds brook trout of trophy size, plus many lake trout. Lakers up to ten pounds rise to flies cast for salmon, and fish of several times that weight are there for any who choose to go after them with king-size hardware.

The salmon run begins around the middle of August and reaches its peak in September. The trout fishing, excellent earlier, falls off about the time the salmon begin showing, but with salmon in the river all attention focuses on this king of freshwater game fish. Splendid brook trout are landed with what amounts to indifference, and inadvertent hang-ups with lakers are looked on as a nuisance. The lakers are strong and heavy, but comparatively sluggish. Their refusal to burn themselves out in fast runs results in a dull and drawn-out battle that is to be deplored when one is eager to tie into a salmon.

The salmon which run the George average larger than those common to most North American salmon rivers. This is due in part to the fact that some weigh as much as thirty pounds, but more to the fact that grilses are virtually absent. These smaller salmon, which return to rivers to spawn after spending a comparatively short time in the sea, make up a large part of the take on many salmon streams. Smudge

Grant assured us that we would take few, if any, salmon weighing under ten pounds, and this proved to be true. We caught no salmon that were appreciably under the ten-pound mark, nor did we see any brought in by other fishermen.

We were new at the game, but I suspect that the George River poses problems for experienced salmon fishermen accustomed to smaller and tamer rivers. No holding pools exist on the George, for one thing, and there is no opportunity to fish for previously located fish. Most of the water lies completely beyond reach, too violent to be fished from canoe or boat and unapproachable by wading. The fisherman must endure the frustration of seeing salmon break, roll and leap in midriver while forced to confine his efforts to only the edges of the massive flow. This is not as prohibitive to his chances as it may sound, for at various points the salmon favor the easier shoreline current, and in such places plenty of fish pass within casting range.

Pete and I came well stocked with conventional salmon flies: standard patterns of wet flies in a variety of sizes, plus bushy dry flies which we hoped we could use to good effect. Contrary to our hopes, none of our flies produced the desired results. Apparently, something out of the ordinary was needed to attract the salmon's attention in the tossing currents of that mighty river.

This was proven when one of the fishermen began taking salmon on a fly which I have mentioned in a previous chapter, and which I had seen Norm Hathaway use with telling effect in Labrador. Its construction has already been described, and from the description it can be seen that it violates the artistic standards to which conventional salmon flies usually adhere.

We had seen bands of caribou every day, and along their trails we had seen hair which they apparently shed in thickly matted patches of fleece. Pete had tucked a patch in his fishing vest to take home to his oldest boy who is a budding naturalist, and it provided us with material for duplicating the crude and shaggy fly that had proven its effectiveness. I had a spool of rod-winding thread in my kit, and from the caribou hair I fashioned copies on hooks stripped of dressing that had proven to be ineffective.

The next morning, Pete made a noisy job of stomping into his waders as it was just turning light. Given back twenty years, I would have been quick to join him. But my older bones still ached from the previous day's fishing, and I only groaned and scrounged deeper into the comfort of my sleeping bag.

We were eating breakfast when Pete returned, bouncing with excitement. A huge salmon had walloped one of the caribou hair creations almost immediately, and during the remaining time Pete had been playing the big fish. He had had him almost within tailing distance several times, only to have the salmon make yet another long run. Finally, the fish apparently took a turn around a sunken rock and then snapped the leader.

We weren't long in getting to the river. As usual, a wind of nearly gale force made casting an arm-wearying job, but by timing the gusts, and beefing into each cast, it was possible to drop the hair flies on currents the salmon were using. For perhaps the tenth time I cast as far as I could manage, and then watched the buoyant hair fly leave a wake as it cut across the current on a tight line. It dipped under as waves and small whirlpools engulfed it, but always it bobbed to the surface again and resumed its course. I was thinking how much it resembled a mouse swimming valiantly for its life, when it suddenly disappeared in the center of a violent swirl. The line came taut against the rod, then it ripped upward as a dozen pounds of salmon climbed high above the water.

There followed one of the hardest days of fishing I have ever put in. A guide brought us our lunches at noon, and apart from the short time it took us to gobble sandwiches, and the time devoted to photography, we stood waist-deep in icy water, flailing with leaden arms against a wind that showed us no mercy. Despite insulated underwear and heavy woolen outer garments, we were chilled to the bone from almost the first minute. When we finally quit that evening I felt as though I had been frozen and then beaten with a length of rubber hose.

But we were as happy and fulfilled as we were cold and bone weary. During the day we had landed six salmon weighing from ten to seventeen pounds. We had hooked and lost others and had had strikes which we missed. Furthermore, we had found the answer to our needs in the rough hair flies, for they continued to produce throughout the remainder of our stay.

As a result of writing a couple of articles about the Labrador-Ungava region, I have been asked many questions by interested fishermen. This has been rather embarrassing, for one hardly becomes an authority on a region so vast and little known with the help of only two trips of short duration. Yet I am keenly aware of a fisherman's burning desire to fish where few others have fished, and I have tried to be as helpful as my very limited experience will permit.

In answering queries I have tried to point out both the good and the bad in order to help the fisherman decide if a Labrador-Ungava trip can fulfill a lifelong ambition. It did just that for Pete and me, but I'm sure that there are others for whom such a trip would be unpleasant and disappointing.

In the first place, if my experience is a valid criterion, the weather is likely to be hostile and even downright bitter. Both of our trips carried over into September, and that must be taken into account. But if one hopes to catch Atlantic salmon he has no choice but to go late in the season and should expect to encounter freezing weather.

The weather enters the picture from another angle, for the success of any trip depends absolutely on conditions which will permit flying. One can be grounded for days on end, and there is never any assurance that a trip will not be ruined because of the inability to fly. Pete and I were relatively lucky, but we listened to stories about parties who spent most of their allotted time waiting for the weather to clear.

Relatively few comforts can be offered by fishing camps in the far north. Distance and transportation difficulties preclude all but the most basic necessities. If trips are made to outlying waters, one must be prepared to put up with much less.

I'm sure that most people are quite unaware of the vastness of the uninhabited and impassable regions which exist in Labrador and northern Quebec. I can assure you that if you penetrate these regions deeply you will be beyond any prompt help from the outside in case of an emergency. The need for medical attention could arise when foul weather made flying impossible; plane damage or malfunction would result in a serious predicament. These risks are part of the deal and could offset the most spectacular fishing for those who could not accept them with equanimity.

The country is wild and rugged, and I have reached an age when I find the physical demands of such a trip to be exhausting. I have gladly paid the price of creaking joints and aching muscles for exotic fishing, but this could be a no-go factor for those who feel that no fishing is worth suffering for.

I have been asked many questions about tackle, mainly by those of the opinion that a considerable amount of specialized tackle would have to be bought. Pete and I chose our equipment from what we had at hand and found it to be entirely adequate. I feel sure that the rods and reels any other fisherman uses on his home waters would suffice for him equally well. Spare rods are a wise precaution and plenty of extra spinning line almost a must. Fly reels should be well filled with backing; hardware and flies should run to medium and large sizes. Waders are of vital importance.

The prospective Atlantic salmon fisherman may hesitate to tackle fish which may exceed twenty pounds in weight with a fly rod which has never stood up to anything larger than trout. But any rod which will deliver long casts is adequate if equipped with a reel which holds sufficient backing — a couple of hundred yards if one wants to be on the safe side.

353

I took two fly rods with me on the trip to the George River. One was an 8-foot Orvis which handles a No. 8 line, the other a 7½-foot Orvis which takes a No. 7 line. I found the 8-footer to be perfectly adequate, and when Pete stepped on the butt of his rod he used the 7½-foot rod and found it to be up to the job.

Actually, the greatest need for backbone in a salmon rod comes when making long casts, rather than while playing fish. Salmon wear themselves out by leaping and making long runs, and the reel, rather than the rod on which it is mounted, is the instrument which plays the chief part in their undoing.

Although the cost of a Labrador-Ungava trip need not include expenses for special tackle, it adds up to what, by my standards, is a sizable amount of money. Most outfitters take over at Schefferville, and furnish air transportation to fishing sites as part of their services. Round-trip plane fare from Montreal to Schefferville is about $150.00. A week at a fishing camp costs between $400.00 and $500.00 during the first part of the season. The charge for a week during the salmon run, or for a trip such as Pete and I took for arctic char, is about double that figure.

What do you get for your time, effort and money? If our two trips are valid measurements, you come away with the memory of a thrilling experience that will stay fresh in your mind for the rest of your days. You will have seen wild, primitive country and wildlife that has little fear of man. And you will have fished waters that teem with big fish, and which, as yet, have suffered no significant depletion at the hands of mankind.

Unfortunately, the fish of cold, subarctic waters grow and reproduce at a much slower rate than those of warmer regions, so the consequence of only moderate fishing pressure is rapid deterioration. For the present, Labrador-Ungava is a land of many unfished waters, but this circumstance cannot endure for long. The exotic, primitive quality of each unfished lake and stream will soon be destroyed by the inexorable expansion of civilization's frontiers.

The rate of this expansion is so rapid that it is sadly obvious that it can be only a few years before the few remaining regions that have been spared encroachment will be swallowed up and stripped of that grandeur and dignity which can exist nowhere but beyond the limits of human invasion.

We who are living today have the dubious distinction of being among the last ever to know the exquisite and deeply moving emotions which derive from setting foot on land that has defied all human influence. The more remote sections of Labrador-Ungava still fall in this category, and the fisherman who fishes in this still wild and untamed land will be among the last to savor one of the most exotic of all human experiences.

16

The Philosophical Fisherman

PEOPLE WHO CAN go about their business with never a
pause for introspection are to be envied. They enjoy a peace
of mind that is denied those whose thoughts tend to turn
inward, for to look upon oneself is to come face to face with
an appalling array of contradictions. What one seems to be is
refuted by that which lies just beneath the surface, and outward manifestations of character represent little more than
an uneasy truce between opposing forces of nearly equal
strength.

When I am trout fishing, my equipment, from expensive
bamboo rod to felt-soled waders, seems to reflect a dedication
to refinement. I prefer to fish with dry flies, and doing so enhances the effect. One might conclude that I am a fisherman

who restricts his fishing pleasure to the realm of angling sophistication.

The devil of it is that this statement is both true and false. Much of the time I observe the niceties of angling by choice. But within me lie the seeds of rebellion, and from these sprout feelings which sometimes triumph and hold sway. Then I have the urge to fish without the need for skill and concentration hanging over me like a cloud. I long to prop my rod in a forked stick and relinquish all further responsibility to luck. When I do exactly that, the feeling of release is so refreshing that I wonder if I haven't cheated myself of much pleasure by taking fishing seriously.

This side of my fishing nature becomes dominant and overpowering each spring. When the ice breaks up, and the first robin appears, I feel the need to go fishing. I don't want this early fishing to be complicated by more than the simple process of threading a worm on a hook.

As soon as the ground thaws, Mike and I pick up a supply of night crawlers. The following Saturday we head for Lake Champlain, some thirty miles away. We know a spot off a clay bank where fish of various species work close to shore in early spring, and to do our first fishing of the season there has become an annual ritual.

We rig up two spinning rods apiece, bait our hooks with squirming night crawlers and heave these gobs of bait as far from shore as we can cast. We rest each rod in a forked stick and leave the bail of each reel open; there are big fish in the lake, and a locked reel could mean a lost outfit.

Then we lie back and relax, soaking up the April sunshine

and all related springtime blessings. I can do this on the shore of Lake Champlain with greater appreciation than elsewhere. I fish the lake each winter, and the remembered bitterness of days so recently endured is a backdrop against which the comforts of spring stand out in bold relief.

In winter the windswept lake promises naught but torture for those rash enough to venture upon it. Gazing out across the open water, I marvel at the sudden reversal of character. All signs of threat and hostility have vanished. In the sunshine, the lake looks inviting and hospitable.

A pair of black ducks swerve from their northward course and set their wings for a landing. They splash down in a cove just south of us and begin an inspection of the shoreline. Their trudging pace is in sharp contrast to the bulletlike speed of their approach. They putter about, then one of the pair rises high in the water to fan its wings in a burst of sheer exuberance. It pleases me to believe that the black and I share common emotions, that the delights of this spring morning arouse identical feelings in the two of us.

Suddenly we hear the gabble of Canada geese. As usual, they are not where they sound to be. Although their loud clamor suggests that they are close upon us, we finally spot them so high in the sky that their wavering V is barely visible. The haunting quality of their chorus, and the magnificence of their march, inspire a strange sadness that is probably a reflection of my envy of their wild freedom.

Then I realize that for the time being I am as free as they. We share alike in the warmth of the sun, the purity of the air and the utter perfection of the day at hand. I call a halt to all further reflection and cast myself adrift on the gentle currents of a brand-new spring.

Mike brings me out of my pleasant trance by jumping up to tend one of his rods. His line has lifted and tightened, and the tip of his rod dances as monofilament spirals from his reel and flows through the rod guides. The manner of biting signifies a catfish. Once a catfish picks up bait it moves off steadily, with none of the erratic twitches and jerks which signal bites from lesser fish.

"Look at him go!" Mike exclaims delightedly. He loves to fish for catfish, and now he is exultant at the prospect of setting the hook in what he hopes is a really big one.

"You'd better take him," I say, even though I know this may be poor advice. "He may drop it."

"He won't drop it," Mike answers confidently, proving that he is a better catfish fisherman than I am.

"No? What's he done now?" I ask, as the line suddenly falls slack.

Mike gently tightens the line and again feels the fish.

"He's still on," he declares. "I'm going to let him get it down good."

The line shows no sign of motion for long moments that I find difficult to endure, but finally it begins to spin off the reel at a smarter clip than before. Mike lets the fish go until I can barely resist the urge to grab the rod and set the hook myself. Finally, he hauls back with a hard yank that bends his rod nearly double. The line draws wire tight and the rod throbs and plunges with the slow cadence that bespeaks the struggles of a big fish.

"He's a big one!" Mike shouts triumphantly. The reel buzzes as the catfish takes line against the drag. There follows a prolonged period of give and take, marked by alternate ponderous rushes and the slow regaining of line.

Finally, far out in the lake, a huge, blue-gray head breaks the surface and remains visible for a matter of seconds.

"Looka that!" Mike yells. "He'll go twenty pounds!"

"Phooey," I exclaim. "They always look bigger than they are."

"You wait and see," Mike answers, pumping away steadily now and gradually gaining line.

Finally he has the catfish close enough to shore for me to take up a position with the landing net. The water in that section of the lake is made opaque by clay in suspension, and this hampers my efforts. At last I get the big fish in the net with a blind but lucky stab, but I dare not try to raise the net by its long handle for fear it will break under the strain. I grasp opposite sides of the rim and struggle up the bank, fighting to keep my balance against the mighty flops of the imprisoned fish.

We take scales from the tackle box and proceed, not without difficulty, to weigh Mike's prize. Eighteen pounds, the pointer indicates — close enough to twenty to justify Mike's prediction. I apologize for accusing him of exaggeration.

We unhook the ugly critter and snap a few photographs. Then, because in spite of all we have heard to the contrary, we have found big catfish unpalatable and slide him back into the lake. No sooner has he disappeared in the opaque water than it seems impossible to believe that the lake holds any such ponderous and ugly creatures.

Mike is still rebaiting when the tip of one of my rods begins to bob. This is no twin to Mike's monster, but when I set the hook I feel solid and satisfying resistance. My fish turns out to be a bullhead of more than a pound in weight. I am pleased, for I favor bullheads over most other freshwater fish for eating. I holler for Mike to fetch the stringer from the tackle box while I unhook my prize.

The air steadily grows warmer and we shed outer garments that were needed against the chill of the early morning. A breeze springs up from the south, but it is a gentle flow of warm air which confirms winter's unconditional surrender.

We bask in the blessed warmth. We watch ducks speeding northward, hurrying not from choice but because nature has denied them the luxury of leisurely flight. In contrast, gulls soar slowly and effortlessly along the shoreline in search of food.

One gull virtually comes to a halt directly in front of us and hangs motionless on set wings in order to make minute inspection of whatever has attracted his interest. We watch his head turn this way and that as he cranes his neck for a better view. In the meantime his body remains stationary as though suspended by invisible strings. We marvel at this defiance of gravity. We speculate whether the gull is blest with the ability to glory in his mastery of the impossible.

We speculate idly about an assortment of things, for it seems a proper time and place for speculation and wonder. It is perhaps because we occupy ourselves so casually that the fish bite steadily and frequently.

We get to wrestle with two more big catfish before the day is over, although neither comes within several pounds of equaling Mike's whopper. Upward of a dozen more big bull-heads go on the stringer, with a like number of large yellow perch to keep them company. A lone calico bass comes as a surprise bonus and is a welcome addition to the stringer.

Other species cooperate, and although we don't fancy them as food, their patronage is not unappreciated. We catch and release a number of sheepsheads, all of which put up strong scraps. Mike ties into a fish which he calls a catfish, but which turns out to be a six-pound carp. We have several hectic hassels with eels and heap curses on the slimy critters with ostensible disgust. But secretly we tally each sticky encounter as an addition to the day's fun.

We linger until long after sundown, and take leave reluctantly only when darkness is close upon us. We are quiet and subdued as we pick up our gear and our fish, for there is good reason to mourn the passing of such a day.

We climb the high bank and pause for a final look at the lake. In the rapidly deepening dusk it is serene, majestic and hauntingly beautiful. Although its physical presence is close at hand, it is spiritually alien and remote. All sense of intimacy is erased by its aloofness, and in this moment of parting we feel rebuffed and disillusioned.

We trudge toward the car, humbled by our exclusion from the drama which grants roles only to those things which are ageless and selfless. We yearn instinctively to play a part in their inscrutable scheme, but it is by reason of our human yearning and mortality that we are disqualified.

We stow our gear in the car, and it is quite dark by the time we finish. I switch on the headlights, and our world is reduced to the area illuminated by the twin beams.

"Wasn't that some old catfish," Mike says after the car is under way.

We rehash the highlights of the day, reluctant to relinquish them to the category of events which have passed and exist only as memories. But we cannot alter the transitory quality of human experience, and the pleasures of the day are already beyond our grasp.

A red fox streaks across the road, his flowing brush an undulating summary of his graceful flight. His beauty is a part of us for a split second, and then is gone beyond recall. The glimpse of the fox seems symbolic of our inability to transcend that fleeting differential of time which constitutes the present, and explains, perhaps, why overtones of sadness tinge all human memories.

For a day I have fished in a manner which, by popular concept, does not yield the esthetic rewards which are alleged to accrue to angling methods of greater refinement. Yet it has been during this day that I have managed to achieve a panoramic view of the context within which the feeble spark of my existence is suffered to flicker. I have not resolved the enigma of reality, but I have sensed the awesome dimensions of its magnitude. In spite of all that can be said for trout fishing, it has never resulted in comparable insight.

When I fish for trout, I am intent on all the minute details of the job at hand, and I believe this to be true of all serious trout fishermen. Izaak Walton wrote of the poetic and romantic feelings which trout fishing supposedly inspires, but I seriously doubt the validity of his observations in this instance. The truth is that the trout fisherman is usually as tense as a coiled spring, his attention focused on his fly to the exclusion of all else. He is as little given to reflection as is a chess player who is deeply involved in an important game.

The respective rewards of serious and casual fishing are enormously different and mutually exclusive. A man fishes seriously with personal triumph as his goal and is nurtured by any success he attains. Furthermore, he is under self-imposed pressure to succeed, for his pride is at stake. Casual fishing brings freedom from this pressure and provides an atmosphere that is conducive to reflection and to keen appreciation of one's surroundings.

In the world of reality I can only measure my worth by yardsticks which tend to attest to the insignificance of my stature and attainments, and which do all too little to sustain my self-esteem. When I am trout fishing, these standards of measurement no longer apply. For the time being I need only to take a few trout to enjoy feelings of success and accomplishment which otherwise I am often denied.

But this illusion of success soon fades, leaving me with only the realization that I have resorted to fantasy as a palliative to relieve the painful reality of my limitations and fallibility. This realization, an open confession of weakness, yanks the rug from under my bolstered morale.

When I fish casually, I find that instead of trying to refute my insignificance I am disposed to accept it in good grace. For the time being I am not in competition with the general scheme of things and therefore am able to view the world with unusual objectivity. The futility of my struggle for identity no longer seems a tragic denial, but grounds for a comfortable truce. I throw down my arms in surrender, and a hostile world suddenly becomes friendly. Plainly, it is a world which rebuffs those who make demands upon it but one which lavishes benevolence upon those who ask for nothing.

It is this paradox which leads me to suspect that the esthetic derivatives of fishing are inversely proportional to the complexity and refinement of the angler's methodology. This, of course, is contrary to traditional concept, for the philosophical joys of fishing are supposedly most fully savored by those who employ the most elaborate techniques. Although this is generally accepted as a truism, there seems good reason to believe that it is a non sequitur, and that the truth is precisely the opposite.

Unfortunately, most of us shape our creed to conform to whatever level we may reach in our evolution as fishermen. The more discriminating our preferences, and the more convergent our interests, the more closely our piety approaches fanaticism. This is all well and good, for it is only when viewed from such a position that the act of taking a twelve-inch trout on a dry fly becomes a feat of marked significance.

The only sad part about it all is that it becomes increasingly difficult to back off once in a while in order to see things in truer perspective. A man can become so caught up in fishing that it actually becomes a grim business, and when this happens it is time to slow the tempo and take a breather. It is time to fish simply and without affectation, and time for the fisherman to shift his attention from the fish and focus it upon himself.

If a fellow can do this, if he can sit quietly for a day and do nothing more pretentious than keep half an eye on a bobber or the tip of his rod, he will see many things that he has been missing. If he becomes sufficiently passive and contemplative he will be treated to a clear view of himself, an experience that can hold many surprises.

If he attains the proper state of objectivity, he will see in himself all the ludicrous qualities which make him the human being he is. He will see himself in all his vanity, a trivial speck of matter pathetically attempting to defend the absurd conviction that somehow he is of cosmic importance and significance. When he sees himself this clearly, he will gain respect for his sheer audacity. He will know that he is not the man he pretends to be, but he will take pride in the courage it takes to effect the pretense.

After the day is over he'll go back to dry fly fishing and to kidding himself as usual that whenever he raises a trout to his fly he has done something noteworthy. At the same time he will know the truth: he is mortal, ephemeral and of little consequence unto all but himself. And, no matter how puny and contrived, he will not be ashamed of his efforts to make something of his nothingness.